British Rail Main Line Electric Locomotives

A pair of Class 73/0 electro-diesel locomotives, Nos 73002 and 73003 approach Redhill on 30th August 1984 with the then daily Cliffe – Salfords aggregate train.

Colin J. Marsden

British Rail Main Line Electric Locomotives

Colin J. Marsden & Graham B. Fenn

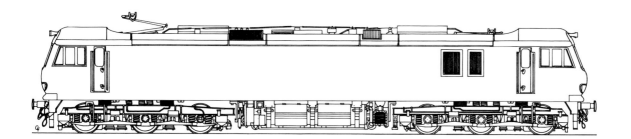

Oxford Publishing Co

First published 1993
Second (revised) edition 2001

ISBN 0 86093 559 0

© C. J. Marsden & G. B. Fenn 2001

Published by Oxford Publishing Co.

an imprint of Ian Allan Publishing Ltd, Hersham, Surrey KT12 4RG.
Printed by Ian Allan Printing Ltd, Hersham, Surrey KT12 4RG.

Code: 0109/A2

Posed outside Willesden electric depot, now operated by Alstom under a contract for Virgin Trains, Class 86/2
No. 86245, painted in Caledonian blue but in Virgin style, poses next to VT red-liveried Class 90/0 No. 90002. The
Caledonian blue Class 86 was repainted at Willesden in February 1998 to mark the 150th anniversary of the
Caledonian Railway.

Colin J. Marsden

Contents

Introduction

Following the update of content and reprint of the companion volume *British Rail Main Line Diesel Locomotives*, it was decided to do a similar revision on this title covering the UK electric locomotive classes.

Although it is only a few years since the first edition was published, a huge amount has happened in the electric locomotive field, the Class 92s having been introduced and technical refinements made to a number of classes. Some of the most significant changes have been to liveries, mainly following UK rail privatisation in the mid-1990s. This total alteration to our national rail system has also seen a significant change in deployment and has hastened the upgrading of some classes.

This revised edition has also been enlarged to include the most significant recent developments in UK electric-traction technology, namely the Eurotunnel Bo-Bo-Bo locomotives which ply between the UK and French terminals of the Channel Tunnel, and the development of French TGV technology for UK operation with the building of the Class 373 Eurostar sets which now operate passenger services from London to mainland Europe. Although these train sets are officially multiple-units, they are included in this volume as they have a complete power car or locomotive at each end, which *could* (if required) operate without the rest of the passenger formation.

The technical and text sections have been fully updated to reflect the recent changes, and where possible new illustrations have been included to demonstrate some of the new colours now seen on the UK rail network.

Drawings of each class have been specially prepared and are reproduced at the recognised 4mm:1ft scale – ideally suited for modellers. These are brought together for the first time in one title. For each type or class, roof, side and end elevations have been drawn by joint author Graham Fenn; for those classes where significant detail differences exist or sub-classes have been formed, separate drawings are included (where practical) for each variant.

The choice of photographic illustrations has been made carefully to show as many modifications and detail differences as possible, while still illustrating the locomotives in their working environment. At the beginning of each class or type section, a full data panel is included, this covering the major technical items such as dimensions, weights, and equipment types. In general, the railway supply industry, the staff of the former British Rail and now those of the private operators have been most helpful in supplying the required information and a special thankyou must be given to the numerous industrial and railway officials.

The authors would like to thank the many people who have provided information and illustrations for inclusion in this title. It is hoped that readers of this major reference work will benefit from its contents and derive pleasure from browsing through its pages.

Colin J. Marsden
Graham B. Fenn
August 2001

ES1

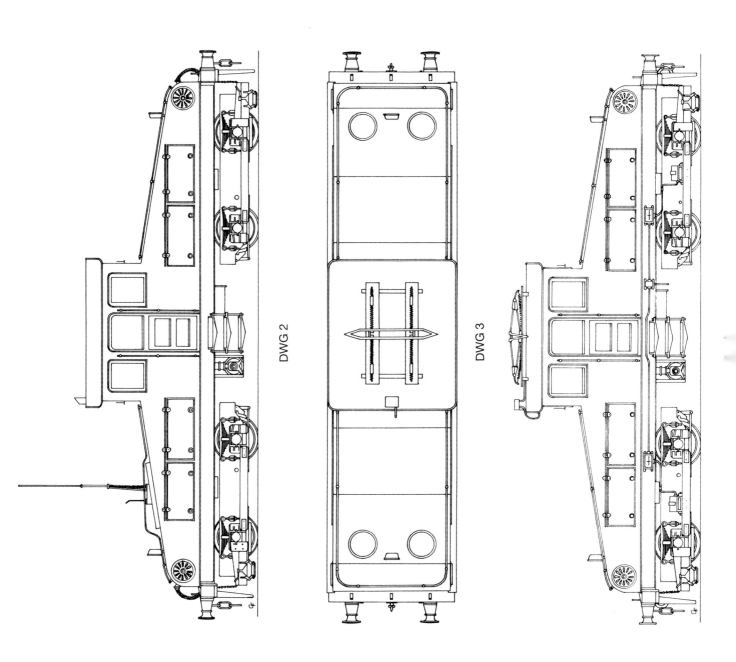

DWG 2

DWG 3

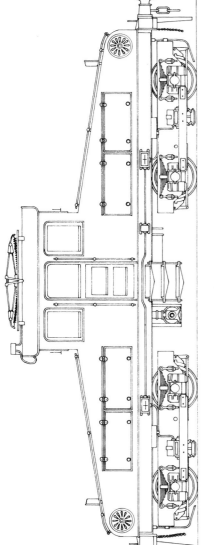

DWG 5

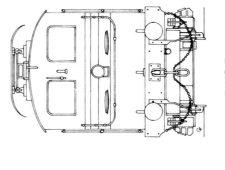

DWG 6

DWG 7

DWG 2
Class ES1 side elevation, showing original bonnet-mounted bow power collector.

DWG 3
Class ES1 roof layout, showing locomotive with roof-mounted power collector.

DWG 4
Class ES1 side elevation showing locomotive with roof-mounted power collector and third rail pick-up slippers on bogie frame corners.

DWG 5
Class ES1 side elevation showing locomotive with roof-mounted power collector and third rail pick-up shoes mounted towards the centre of the bogie frame.

DWG 6
Class ES1 front end elevation, showing bonnet-mounted bow power collector.

DWG 7
Class ES1 front end elevation, showing roof-mounted power collector.

7

Class	ES1	Bogie Pivot Centres	20ft 6in
BR Number Range	26500-26501	Wheel Diameter	3ft
Former LNER Numbers	6480-6481	Brake Type	Air
Original NER Numbers	1-2	Sanding Equipment	Pneumatic
Built by	Brush	Heating Type	Non fitted
Introduced	1905	Coupling Restriction	Not multiple fitted
Wheel Arrangement	Bo-Bo 0-4+4-0	Horsepower	640 hp
Weight operational	56 tons	Tractive Effort maximum	25,000lb
Height - pan down	12ft 11in	Number of Traction Motors	4
Width	8ft 9in	Traction Motor Type	BTH
Length	37ft 11in	Control System	DC Direct
Maximum Speed	25mph	Gear Ratio	3.28:1
Wheelbase	27ft 8in	Nominal Supply Voltage	600V dc overhead
Bogie Wheelbase	6ft 6in		and third rail

The North Eastern Railway electrification scheme of the North Tyneside lines in 1904 included the one mile long freight only branch from Trafalgar Yard at Manors to Quayside Yard. The Quayside yard was around 130ft lower than the main line, on the banks of the River Tyne, access was arduous with a gradient of 1:27 including steep cuttings, and had a curved, single bore tunnel. Steam operation over the route caused appalling conditions, so the decision was taken to electrify the branch. Overhead power collection was the most desirable, but due to very limited clearances in the tunnel section, third rail power collection had to be used. However to avoid the presence of dangerous live rails in the yard areas, overhead power pick-up equipment was erected at these locations, which gave rise to dual power collection locomotives.

The North Eastern Railway gave authorisation to build two locomotives for the line, allocated numbers 1 and 2. These were centre cab locomotives with a bonnet at each end, and when built, a bonnet-mounted bow power collector for the overhead was fitted. For third rail power collection four standard slipper shoes, mounted on the corners of

the bogies were fitted. Construction of the two locomotives was effected by Brush in 1905. Traction equipment was supplied by British Thomson-Houston (BTH).

At the Grouping, the NER was absorbed as part of the LNER, who renumbered these two electric locomotives as Nos 6480 and 6481. Under eventual BTC (BR) ownership in 1948 the locomotives were again renumbered to became Nos 26500 and 26501.

One noteworthy modification made to the locomotives was the replacement of the bow power collector by a cab roof-mounted cross-arm pantograph, which was done soon after entering service. At around the same time the bogie-mounted slipper pick-ups were moved from the ends to a more conventional mid-bogie position.

The two locomotives successfully operated the short line until 29th February 1964 when diesel traction was introduced, making these unique electric locomotives redundant. After their replacement the locomotives were stored at Gosforth and Heaton, being withdrawn the following September. Thankfully one of the pair, No. 26500, was saved from the breaker's yard and is now on display at the National Railway Museum, York.

Front ¾ view of No.1, later Class ES1 No. E26500, showing the as-built condition with bonnet-mounted bow power collector, and third rail collector shoes mounted on the ends of the bogie frame. Note the omission of the third rail shoe fuse from the shoe beam, which was originally carried under the bufferbeam on the front of the locomotive.

Author's Collection

A general view of Class ES1 locomotive No. 26500 showing its later guise, with cab roof-mounted power collector, and third rail collector shoes mounted in the centre of the shoe beam. The livery applied is green adorned with both the second style BR crest, and a North Eastern Railway coat of arms. This view shows the locomotive at Heaton in August 1961.

L. Price

Thankfully one of this unique pair of electric locomotives has been saved, enabling today's enthusiasts to observe a Class ES1 at first hand. Locomotive No. 1, the later 26500, is preserved at the NRM York, where it is seen in Autumn 1988 painted in North Eastern Railway livery.

Colin J. Marsden

EB1

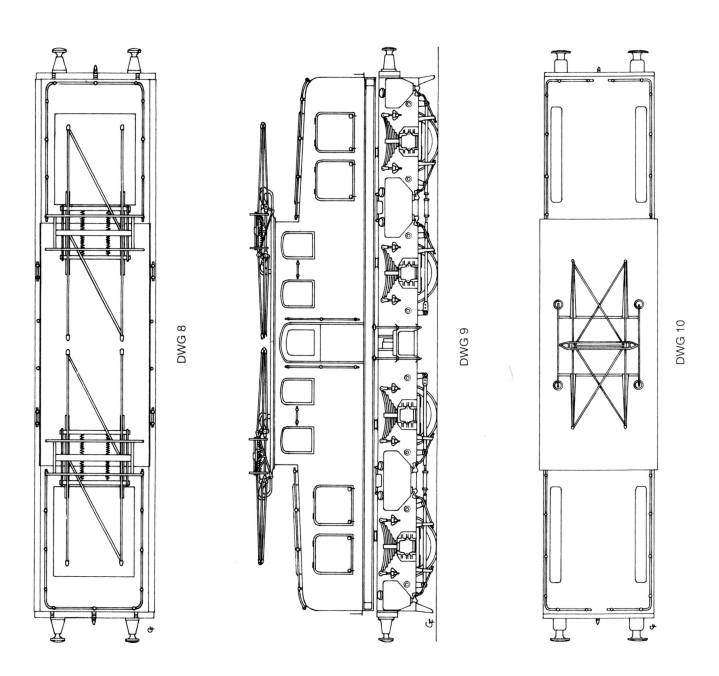

DWG 8

DWG 9

DWG 10

10

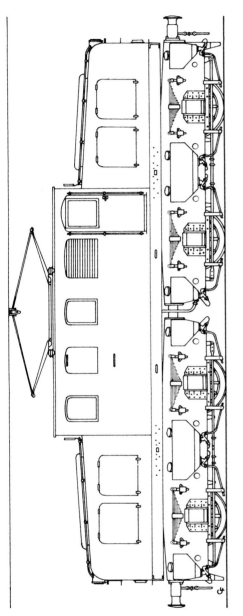

DWG 11

DWG 8
Class EB1 roof detail, showing original layout with two power collectors.

DWG 9
Class EB1 side elevation, showing original layout.

DWG 10
Roof detail of EB1 locomotive No. 11, modified for operation between Manchester and Sheffield.

DWG 11
Side elevation of EB1 locomotive No. 11, modified for operation between Manchester and Sheffield.

DWG 12
Class EB1 front end elevation.

DWG 13
Front end elevation of modified EB1 locomotive No. 11.

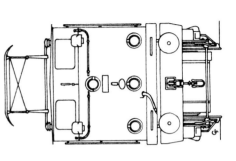

DWG 13

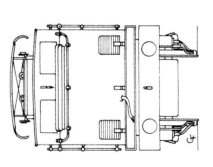

DWG 12

Class	EB1	Brake Type	Vacuum
BR Number Range	26502-26511	Sanding Equipment	Pneumatic
Former NER Number Range	3-12	Heating Type	Not fitted
Former LNER Number Range	6490-6499	Route Availability	Not issued
Built by	NER Darlington	Coupling Restriction	Not multiple fitted
Introduced	1914	Horsepower	1,100hp
Wheel Arrangement	Bo-Bo (0-4+4-0)	Tractive Effort (maximum)	28,000lb
Weight (operational)	75 tonnes	Number of Traction Motors	4
Height - pan down	13ft 1⁵/₁₆in	Traction Motor Type	Siemens
Width	8ft 4in	Gear Ratio	4.5:1
Length	39ft 4in	Pantograph Type	Siemens
Maximum Speed	45mph	Nominal Supply Voltage	1,500V dc overhead
Wheelbase	27ft		
Bogie Wheelbase	8ft 9in		
Bogie Pivot Centres	18ft 3in		
Wheel Diameter	4ft		

Locomotive No. 26510 was later rebuilt for the Manchester – Sheffield – Wath line, and subsequently taken into departmental stock as No 100.

The ten Bo-Bo Class EB1 locomotives were ordered by the NER in 1913 for use on the Newport – Shildon electrification scheme, authorised in the early months of the same year, in a vague attempt to save money by the use of electric traction. Under the NER the ten locomotives were allocated the numbers 3 - 12, while under subsequent LNER ownership the fleet became Nos 6490 - 6499, and eventually under the BR(BTC) banner Nos 26502 - 26511.

Construction of the locomotives was carried out at the NER Darlington workshops with Siemens Bros acting as chief sub-contractor supplying all electrical equipment. The building of the first eight locomotives was completed towards the end of 1914, but transfer to the electric system was not made until June 1915, when Nos 3-10 were sent to Shildon. Trial running commenced on 1st July 1915, and by early August an electrically operated freight service was introduced. The full compliment of locomotives was available for service from May 1920.

In daily operation the locomotives proved very reliable, but due to changing traffic flows, including the closure of Shildon marshalling yard, electric services ceased during January 1935, with the locomotives being transferred to Darlington for store. The fleet remained at Darlington until 1942, when No. 11 (LNER No. 6498) was moved to the LNER Doncaster Works for rebuilding as an experimental locomotive for use on the Manchester – Sheffield via Woodhead route, which was authorised for electrification in 1936. The rebuilding work carried out was considerable with the twin roof power collectors being replaced by a single pick-up, while body alterations included the

repositioning of the cab doors. The output of the rebuilt locomotive was also amended from 1,100hp to 1,256hp and the tractive effort figure raised from 28,000lb to 37,000lb. Completion of the rebuilding work was in October 1944.

By 1947 the remaining nine locomotives at Darlington were moved to South Gosforth for storage, and prior to departure were renumbered into the LNER series. After being at South Gosforth for about a year, the locomotives were again renumbered into the BR series. Due to World War II the completion of the Manchester – Sheffield electrified system was deferred and in mid-1947 No. 6498, the former NER No. 11, was transferred from Doncaster Works to South Gosforth to join her sisters in store. In mid-1948 the locomotive was renumbered 26510.

Further life was found for No. 26510 in August 1949 when the locomotive was reallocated to Ilford electric depot on the ER(GE) system for carriage shunting. For its new role the locomotive was renumbered Departmental No. 100.

The nine locomotives stored at South Gosforth were eventually withdrawn on 21st August 1950 as surplus to requirements, and, with the exception of No. 26504, were sold to Wanty of Rotherham for scrap. No. 26504 was later dismantled by BR at Darlington to provide spare parts for the departmental survivor. The end of the road for the departmental locomotive came in 1960 when the 1,500V dc system of the GE was replaced by the standard 25kV ac system. The locomotive was dismantled by BR Doncaster Works.

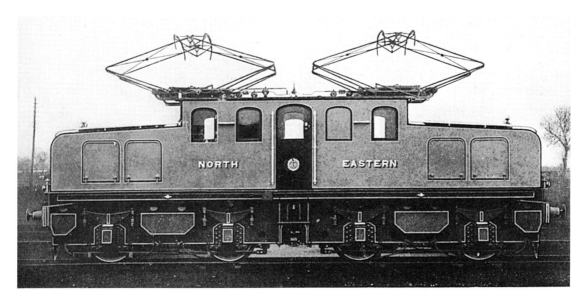

The first of the Newport – Shildon 1,500V dc electric locomotives, No. 3 is seen posed in the works yard at Darlington on 11th May 1914, painted in workshop grey livery for the official photographs. The pantographs are raised, but there was of course no catenary available!

Author's Collection

Still painted in its original grey livery, No. 3 is seen near Simpasture on 16th July 1914 during one of its many trial runs before being permitted to enter normal service.

Author's Collection

NER No. 11 was the subject of a major rebuilding programme in 1942, when it was modified for use experimentally on the Manchester – Sheffield – Wath system. The modifications included the installation of one single roof mounted pantograph, the fitting of additional sandboxes, and a revised position for the cab door. After conversion the locomotive saw little use, but was later sent to Ilford for departmental operation in the depot where it was renumbered 100. As such it is seen at Ilford on 11th June 1960.

Alan Jackson

EE1

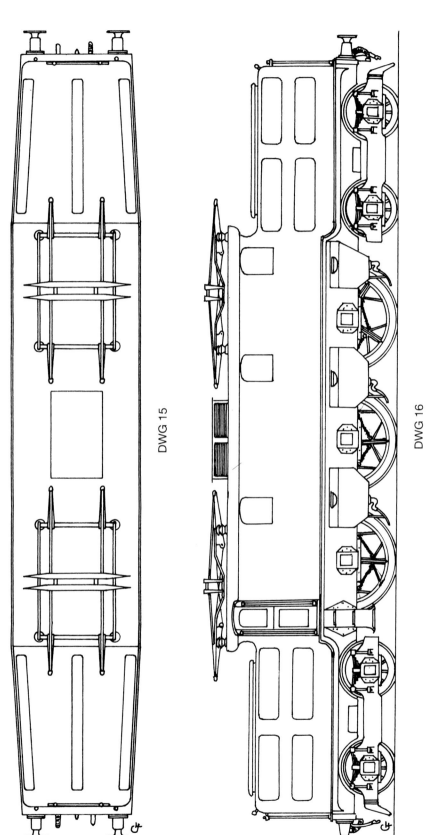

DWG 15

DWG 16

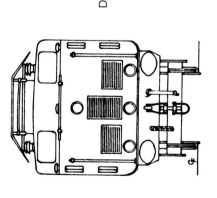

DWG 17

DWG 15
Class EE1 roof detail

DWG 16
Class EE1 side elevation.

DWG 17
Class EE1 front end elevation.

Class	EE1	Pivot Centres	37ft 2in
BR Number	26600	Wheel Diameter (Driving)	6ft 8in
Former BR Number	26699	Wheel Diameter (Pony)	3ft 7¼in
Former NER Number	13	Brake Type	Dual
Former LNER Number	6999	Sanding Equipment	Pneumatic
Built by	NER Darlington	Heating Type	Steam
Introduced	1922	Coupling Restriction	Not multiple fitted
Wheel Arrangement	2-Co-2	Horsepower	1,800hp
Weight (operational)	110 tons	Tractive Effort	28,000lb
Height - pan down	13ft 0⅛in	Number of Traction Motors	6
Width	8ft 10in	Traction Motor Type	MV
Length	53ft 6in	Gear Ratio	24:85
Maximum Speed	90mph	Pantograph Type	Siemens
Wheelbase	43ft 8in	Nominal Supply Voltage	1,500V dc overhead
Fixed Wheelbase	16ft	Boiler Water Capacity	570gal

During 1919 various memoranda and reports were prepared dealing with the projected electrification of the NER route between York and Darlington. After visits by NER engineering staff to the USA in 1920, to inspect their electric locomotives, the NER sought, and were granted, in March 1920, authorisation to construct a 'prototype' mainline electric locomotive, at a then projected cost of £20,000. Planning and design work was completed at the end of 1920 and a construction contract was placed with the NER works at Darlington in January 1921. Assembly of the locomotive progressed well and deliveries of the Metropolitan – Vickers power equipment arrived on time to permit delivery of the completed locomotive in March 1922. The NER class designation allocated was EE and the running number allocated was No. 13.

No. 13 was basically the same at both ends, with a lower bonnet section. However, the No. 1 end housed a train heating boiler. The central (slightly elevated) driving cab area accommodated two roof-mounted cross-arm power collectors. Driving positions were located on the right of the cab layout in either direction.

When built No.13 was outshopped from Darlington North Road Works in 'workshop grey'; it is unclear whether the locomotive ever acquired NER green livery, but by July 1925 No. 13 was painted in LNER green.

Following completion of the locomotive, the only section of line it could work over was between Newport and Shildon, where on 4th June 1922 No. 13 was the subject of extensive tests, hauling a rake of NER passenger stock. After these trials No. 13 was placed in store at Darlington, being exhibited at various rail events until 1935 from when it remained at Darlington Works until 1947. During 1947 No. 13 was renumbered to 6999 and transferred to South Gosforth, along with the Newport – Shildon locomotives. In 1948, after Nationalisation, No. 6999 was again renumbered to 26600.

It is, of course, sad to recall that electrification of the York – Newcastle section was not effected under this scheme and with no available or projected work foreseen the Raven designed prototype main line electric locomotive, No. 26600, was withdrawn in August 1950 and sold for scrap the following December to Wanty of Catcliffe, Rotherham.

Side elevation of No. 13, posed outside Darlington Works soon after completion in May 1922. The livery applied in this illustration is workshop grey, which was retained for the locomotive's original tests on the Newport – Shildon line.

GEC Traction

Class 70

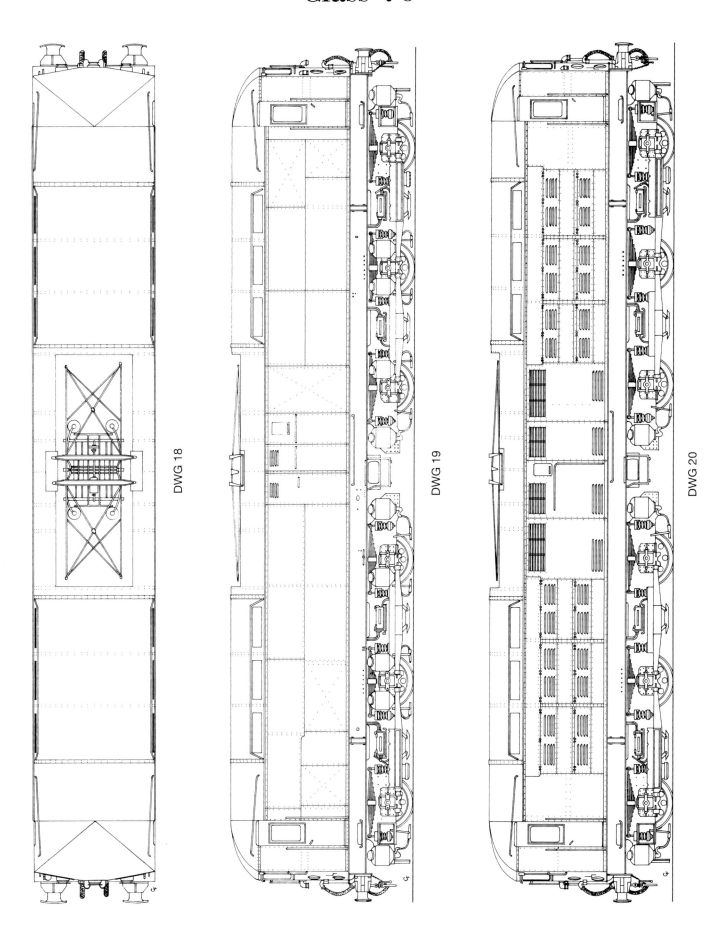

DWG 18

DWG 19

DWG 20

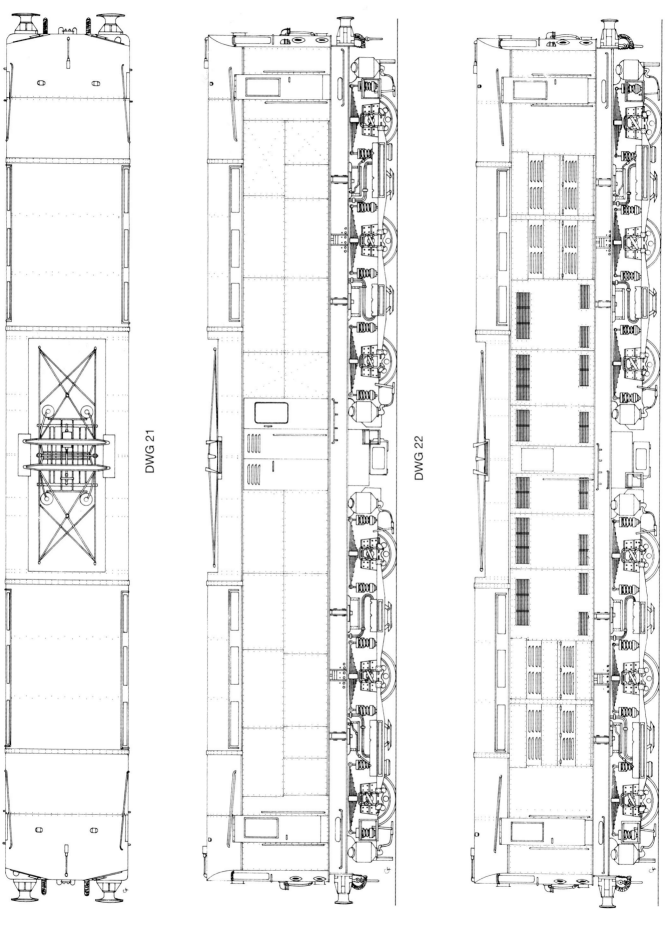

DWG 21

DWG 22

DWG 23

17

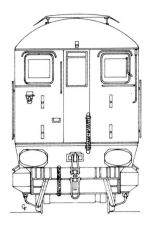

DWG 24

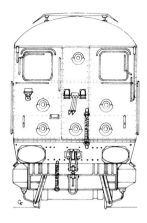

DWG 25

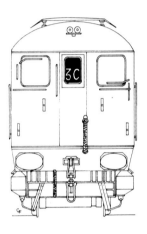

DWG 26

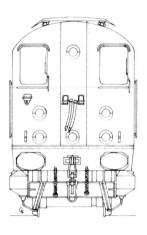

DWG 27

DWG 18
SR prototype electric locomotive roof detail, applicable to locomotives Nos CC1 and CC2 (20001 and 20002) in original condition.

DWG 19
SR prototype electric locomotive side 'A' elevation, as applicable to locomotives Nos CC1 and CC2 (20001 and 20002), showing original bogie style with five sand boxes per bogie.

DWG 20
SR prototype electric locomotive side 'B' elevation, as applicable to locomotives Nos CC1 and CC2 (20001 and 20002), showing modified bogie detail, ie with two sand boxes per bogie.

DWG 21
Roof detail of SR/BR electric locomotive No. 20003.

DWG 22
Side 'A' elevation of BR/SR electric locomotive No. 20003, showing as-built condition.

DWG 23
BR/SR electric locomotive No. 20003 side elevation of 'B' side, showing as-built condition.

DWG 24
Front end detail of SR prototype locomotives Nos CC1 and CC2 (20001 and 20002), showing original condition with stencil style headcode position.

DWG 25
Front end detail of SR prototype locomotives Nos CC1 and CC2 (20001 and 20002), showing the addition of multiple operation jumper equipment, waist height air connections and marker lights.

DWG 26
Front end detail of SR prototype locomotives Nos CC1 and CC2 (20001 and 20002), showing revised front end with two-character roller blind route indicator.

DWG 27
Front end detail of locomotive No. 20003, showing the original as-built style.

Class	70	70	70
Former SR Classification	CC	CC	
BR Number	20001	20002	20003
Southern Railway Number	CC1	CC2	Not Allocated
Built by	SR Ashford	SR Ashford	BR Brighton
Introduced	1941	1945	1948
Wheel Arrangement	Co-Co	Co-Co	Co-Co
Weight (operational)	100 tons	100 tons	105 tons
Height - pan down	12ft 6in	12ft 6in	12ft 8in
Width	8ft 7¼in	8ft 7¼in	8ft 7¼in
Length	56ft 9in	56ft 9in	58ft 6in
Min Curve negotiable	5½ chains	5½ chains	5½ chains
Maximum Speed	75mph	75mph	75mph
Wheelbase	43ft 6in	43ft 6in	44ft 6in
Bogie Wheelbase	16ft 0in	16ft 0in	16ft 0in
Bogie Pivot Centres	27ft 6in	27ft 6in	28ft 6in
Wheel Diameter	3ft 7in	3ft 7in	3ft 7in
Brake Type	Vacuum	Vacuum	Vacuum
Sanding Equipment	Pneumatic	Pneumatic	Pneumatic
Heating Type	Steam - Bastian & Allan	Steam - Bastian & Allan	Steam - Bastian & Allan
Boiler Water Capacity	320gal	320gal	320gal
Multi Coupling Restriction	Within type only	Within type only	Within type only
Brake Force	85 tons	85 tons	89 tons
Horsepower	1,470hp	1,470hp	1,470hp
Tractive Effort (maximum)	49,000lb	49,000lb	45,000lb
Number of Traction Motors	6	6	6
Traction Motor Type	EE 519A	EE 519A	EE 519-4D
Control System	DC Booster	DC Booster	DC Booster
Pantograph Type	EE Cross-arm	EE Cross-arm	EE Cross-arm
Nominal Supply Voltage	600-750V dc	600-750V dc	600-750V dc

Following the rapid extension of the third rail passenger network of the Southern Railway in the 1920s, it became apparent that the freight operation would benefit from electric propulsion. In the mid-1930s the Southern Railway Special Development Division at London Bridge produced plans for three prototype electric locomotives – these were originally intended to be of Bo-Bo design with an output of 1,500hp. The mechanical portion of the design became the responsibility of Southern Railway CME, R.E.L Maunsell, while the electrical equipment was designed by A. Raworth - Chief Electrical Engineer. By the time all designs and subsequent modifications had been put together the projected weight was around 84 tons, far too heavy for a Bo-Bo axle configuration, therefore a further re-design took place to produce a Co-Co locomotive design.

During the course of the Co-Co re-design, O.V.S Bulleid became the new Chief Mechanical Engineer of the SR, and took over the project. Construction of the first locomotive commencing at Ashford in 1940, and after completion it was taken to Brighton for technical fitting out. The second locomotive of the order followed, but was not completed until 1945. The third locomotive incorporating many technical and structural changes, did not appear on the main line until 1948.

During design work much attention was given to the bogies as the Co-Co configuration led to difficulty in providing a suitable bogie centre. The design adopted for this type had a large segmental bearing to improve ride quality. At an early stage it was intended to articulate the bogies and mount the drawgear on the end, however the final design was more conventional with the buffers and connections mounted on the body frame. When originally released to traffic the bogies were centrally attached, but the connector was later removed.

Power collection on this design was effected by two collector shoes on either side of each bogie, as well as a single cross-arm pantograph mounted centrally within the roof, the latter being used in yards where the presence of live rails would have been dangerous. In order to overcome the problem of 'gapping' due to the short shoebase a flywheel was installed which kept an electric 'booster set' running while short gaps were encountered.

The length of the locomotives was 56ft 9in for the original two and 58ft 6in for the third, while the width of all three was just over 8ft 7in, permitting use over the Hastings route, which was not electrified!

The first of the Co-Co locomotives, No. CC1, emerged in July 1941 and commenced trial running, mainly being deployed on freight traffic. primarily in its early days on wartime duties. No. CC2 emerged from Brighton Works in mid-1945 and was almost identical to No. CC1 except for technical modifications incorporated in the light of operating experience. The third locomotive of the design emerged after Nationalisation in 1948 and was numbered 20003 in the new BTC main line numeric sequence. This locomotive had a number of differences from its predecessors, it incorporated a larger flywheel, modified traction motors and modified body styling, with a more pleasing frontal design.

Although intended primarily for freight duties, by May 1949 all three were deployed on Victoria – Newhaven boat trains as well as Central Division freight services. The small fleet of three remained on the Central Division until 1968 when all were deemed as surplus to requirements and withdrawn.

When built Nos CC1 and CC2 were painted in SR green, while No. 20003 emerged in main line black/silver livery. In later years standard rail blue was applied to all three examples, and two-character headcodes replaced disc identification.

Southern electric locomotive No. CC1, the later 20001, is illustrated at the head of a freight train just prior to Nationalisation. Note that the former stencil route indicator position had been replaced by a marker light.

L. Price

Displaying its 'main line' black and silver livery, No. 20001 is seen inside Brighton Works during a major overhaul in the summer of 1960.

T. Wilson

During the mid-1950s the main line black and silver livery gave way to malachite green, offset by a white/red/white body stripe mid way up the body side. No. 20001 is seen passing Clapham Junction on 23rd September 1958 with the 9.30am Victoria – Newhaven Harbour boat train service.

John Faulkner

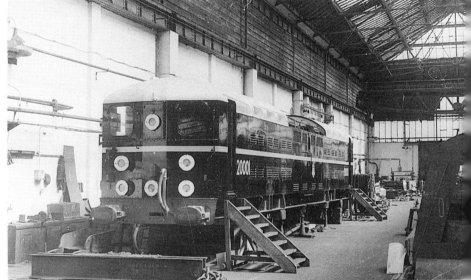

Sporting the 'British Railways' legend on its body side, the second of the SR electric locomotives, No. 20002 is illustrated painted in green livery in 1950.

T. Wilson

With the customary luggage vans coupled behind the locomotive, No. 20002 storms through Three Bridges on 12th April 1958 with an up Newhaven – Victoria boat train. The route diverging to the left by the locomotive was the line to East Grinstead.

John Faulkner

A route that became synonymous with the early SR electric locomotives was the Victoria – Newhaven line. Here, on 15th May 1949 the final member of the trio, No. 20003 is seen departing from Victoria with the first regular boat train service.

BR

It was rare to find the pantographs raised on the three SR, later Class 70, locomotives. However this illustration of No. 20003 with the pantograph raised, although devoid of an overhead supply, has been included to show the mechanical construction of the pick up assembly.

BR

Although ordered by the Southern Railway, the final locomotive of the class was delivered after Nationalisation, and thus assumed its BR number 20003 from new. Here we see No. 20003 brand new, painted in main line black and silver livery at Brighton.

BR

After only a relatively short period painted in main line black and silver livery, No. 20003 was repainted in a more suitable malachite green livery, offset by a white/red/white body side band. When painted in this livery the roof and sole bar were finished in grey.

J. Harris

In the later years the locomotives were modified to carry standard two-position headcode boxes fitted with roller blind units. No. 20003 painted in green livery shows this modification on 17th September 1966, while passing Tooting Bec with the 09.50 Victoria – Newhaven Harbour boat train.

John Scrace

Class 71

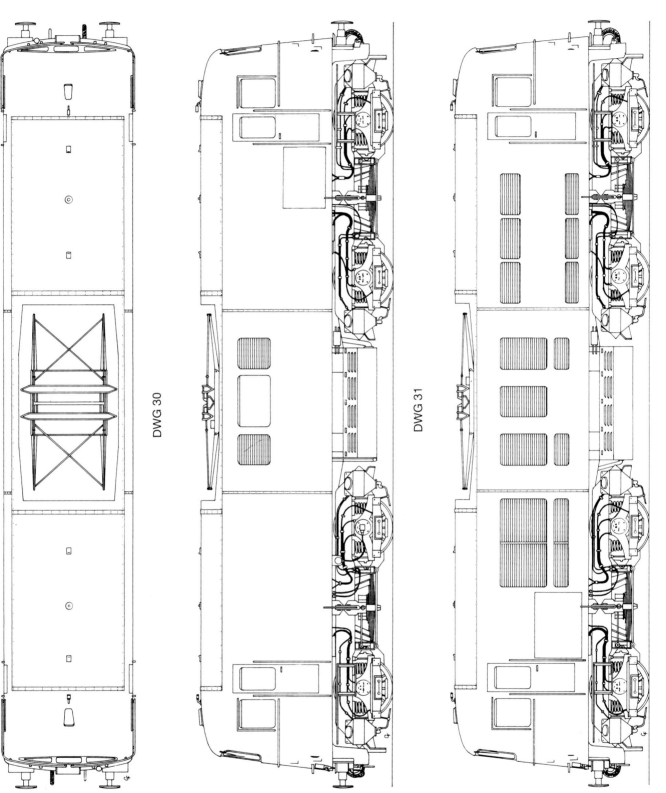

DWG 30

DWG 31

DWG 32

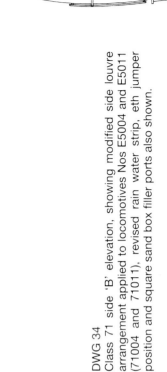

DWG 33

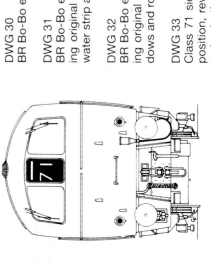

DWG 34

DWG 30
BR Bo-Bo electric (later Class 71) roof detail.

DWG 31
BR Bo-Bo electric (later Class 71) side 'A' elevation, showing original layout with body-mounted eth jumper, no rain
water strip above cab windows and round sand box fillers.

DWG 32
BR Bo-Bo electric (later Class 71) side 'B' elevation, showing original layout, without rain water strip above cab windows and round sand box fillers.

DWG 33
Class 71 side 'A' elevation, showing pantograph in raised
position, revised rain water strip above cab side windows,
revised eth jumper position and square hinged sand box
fillers.

DWG 34
Class 71 side 'B' elevation, showing modified side louvre
arrangement applied to locomotives Nos E5004 and E5011
(71004 and 71011), revised rain water strip, eth jumper
position and square sand box filler ports also shown.

DWG 35
BR Bo-Bo (later Class 71) front end layout, showing original
condition.

DWG 36
Class 71 front end layout, showing revised style.

DWG 35

DWG 36

Class	71	Route Availability	6
Number Range (TOPS)	71001-71014	Coupling Restriction	Not multiple fitted
Former Number Range	E5000-E5024 (Note: 1)	Brake Force	41 tonnes
Built by	BR Doncaster	Horsepower (continuous)	2,552hp
Introduced	1959-60	(maximum)	3,000hp
Wheel Arrangement	Bo-Bo	Tractive Effort (maximum)	43,000lb
Weight (operational)	77 tons	Number of Traction Motors	4
Height - pan down	13ft 1in	Traction Motor Type	EE 532A
Width	8ft 11in	Control System	DC Booster EE836
Length	50ft 7in	Auxiliary Generator	EE 910B
Min Curve negotiable	4 chains	Gear Ratio	76:22
Maximum Speed	90mph	Pantograph Type	Cross-Arm
Wheelbase	37ft 6in	Nominal Supply Voltage	660-750V dc
Bogie Wheelbase	10ft 6in		
Bogie Pivot Centres	27ft		
Wheel Diameter	4ft		
Brake Type	Dual		
Sanding Equipment	Pneumatic		
Heating Type	Electric		

Note: 1   A total of 24 locomotives were constructed, ten being converted to Class 74 electro-diesel locomotives in 1966-67. When built the first locomotive was numbered E5000, but was renumbered as E5024.

Much was learned from the building and operation of the three Southern Railway Co-Co locomotives, and when the Modernisation Scheme orders were placed in 1955 for 'next generation' electric traction a batch of 24 'booster' electric locomotives was ordered for use on the then newly electrified Kent Coast system. Their intended use was to be on main line passenger/freight services. The 'booster' electric locomotive order was placed with BR Workshops Doncaster, from where the first locomotive emerged in late 1958. The number range allocated was E5000-E5023, which under the BR TOPS renumbering system was amended to the 710xx series.

This fleet, unlike their prototypes, was mounted on a Bo-Bo bogie configuration, but retained the ability to collect power from both the third rail and overhead system, via a single roof-mounted pantograph, or bogie mounted shoes. Again, in common with their predecessors the locomotives incorporated a 'booster' system with a large flywheel to assist in power continuity over gaps in the live rail. A change from the prototype fleet was the use of fully spring-borne traction motors and a flexible drive system from traction motors to axles.

The delivery of the E5000 fleet was made initially to Ashford (Chart Leacon) where commissioning and testing was carried out. Driver training was effected throughout 1959-60 on the South Eastern Division main line, and only included drivers from the South Eastern Division depots. By the end of 1960 all 24 locomotives were available and had entered service. The livery applied was BR green with a grey roof; on the first locomotive a red mid height body band was applied between the cab doors. Over the ensuing years the fleet, always remaining allocated to the South Eastern section,

was deployed on main line freight services as well as the prestigious 'Night Ferry' and 'Golden Arrow' passenger duties.

In 1965-66 changing traffic flows led to ten members of the fleet being deemed as redundant. At the same time the SR was looking into the possibility of introducing 'high power' electro-diesel (dual-power) locomotives on the South Western Division's Waterloo-Bournemouth line. Therefore a major rebuilding scheme was authorised for ten members of the Class 71 fleet. The now-depleted Class 71s soldiered on until 1977 when the few diagrams that still existed were taken over by Class 33 and 73 locomotives. The entire fleet became extinct from December 1977. For many months after withdrawal members of the fleet could be found laying at a number of locations, including Ashford, Hither Green and Stewarts Lane. It was hoped at one time that further work might be found for them, but alas this was not to be, and all examples except No. 71001 were sold for scrap and broken up. No. 71001, the former No. E5001, was saved by the National Railway Museum at York and restored to as near as possible original condition by BREL Doncaster.

Until mid-1992, No. E5001 was a major exhibit at the NRM, making a number of trips to BR depots for display at open days. Following display at Ashford in mid-1992, the NRM gave authority for Chart Leacon to technically restore the locomotive to main line standards. Its return to BR running was on 12th September 1992 when it powered a private charter from Waterloo to Bournemouth. After this the locomotive operated a small number of special services over BR/Railtrack property. It is now stabled at Stewarts Lane and is likely to operate with the VSOE stock.

The second of the Doncaster-built SR electric locomotives, No. E5001 stands outside Stewarts Lane Electric Depot in February 1959, soon after arrival from the builder's works. Note the original position and style of the electric train heating jumper and the larger sized train reporting numbers.

Author's Collection

Apart from being deployed on the Victoria – Dover Continental boat train services, the SR electrics, classified 'HA' by the Southern, were used on various South Eastern section freight and van trains. No. E5001 is seen passing Shortlands Junction in 1960 with a vans train for Bricklayers Arms.

GEC Traction

To provide maintenance facilities for the new electric locomotives, a purpose-built inspection and repair shed was constructed at Stewarts Lane, Battersea. This view of the new building, taken on 2nd May 1959, shows three 'HA' electric locomotives receiving attention. In the foreground the depot's wheel lathe can be seen.

Jim Oatway

At the head of an engineers train, No. E5003 is seen near Sevenoaks during the autumn of 1961. The train consist is somewhat unusual as its contains passenger stock, a goods brake van, a coal wagon and engineers' department stock.

Author's Collection

For much of 1959 the SR Traction Training School was undertaking driver training courses on the 'HA' locomotives, these involving both classroom and practical tuition. In June 1959 No. E5003 is seen near St Mary Cray with an up training special bound for Stewarts Lane.

The late Derek Cross

The duties for which the 'HA', later Class 71s, will be best remembered must surely be the "Golden Arrow" and "Night Ferry" trains between London and the Continent, which the locomotives operated between Victoria and Dover. Bearing the "Golden Arrow" headboard No. E5007 passes Petts Wood Junction on 1st October 1968 with the down service.
John Cooper-Smith

On 3rd August 1971 No.E5009 traverses the coastway between Dover and Folkestone with an up Continental mail train. The first two vehicles of the formation are Royal Mail tender and sorting coaches.
John Cooper-Smith

After restoration to working condition, No. E5001 made its first public run, as the first preserved main line electric locomotive to operate on BR tracks on 12th September 1992, when it powered the 09.00 Waterloo – Bournemouth enthusiasts' special. The train is seen near Totton, with Class 73/1 No. 73132 coupled behind to provide a train supply.
Colin J. Marsden

Class 73

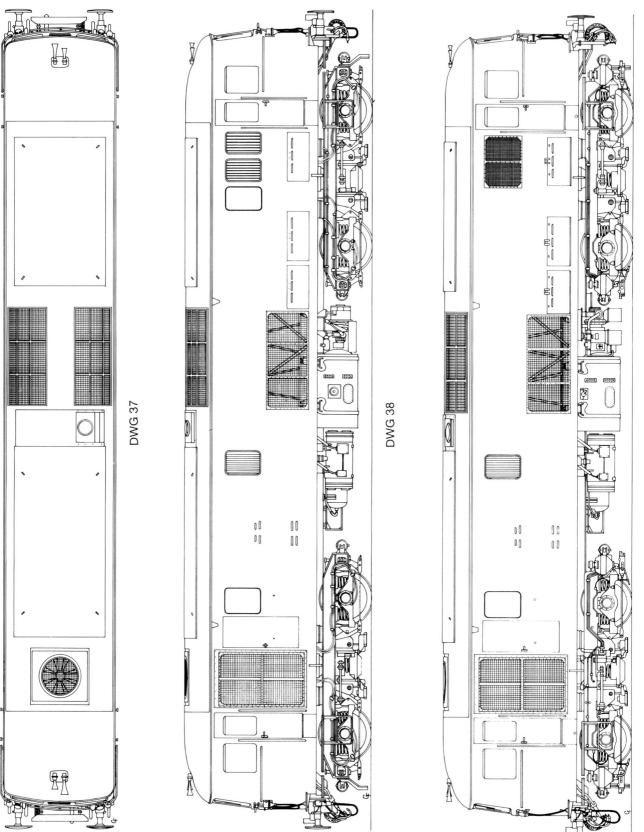

DWG 37

DWG 38

DWG 39

30

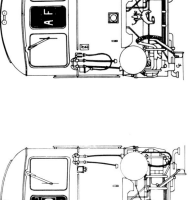

DWG 42A

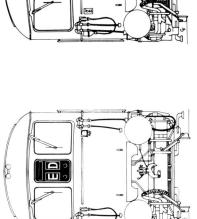

DWG 42

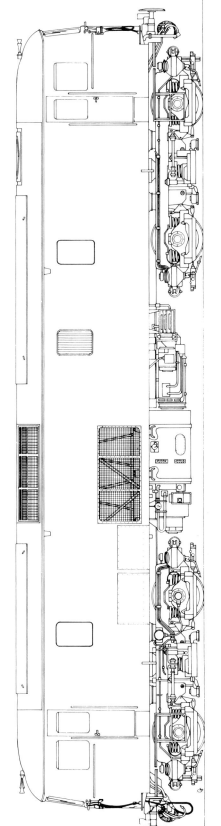

DWG 40

DWG 37
Class 73 roof detail, applicable to all sub classes, No.1 end on left.

DWG 38
Class 73/0 and 73/9 'prototype' fleet (Nos E6001-E6006/73001-73006/ 73901-73906), side elevation. No.1 end (diesel) on left.

DWG 39
Class 73/1 and 73/2 'production' fleet (Nos E6007-E6049/73101-73235), side elevation. No.1 end (diesel) on left. Bogies show modified hinged lid sand boxes.

DWG 40
Class 73/1 and 73/2 'production' fleet (Nos E6007-E6049/73101-73235), side elevation. No. 1 end (diesel) on right. Bogies show original twist top sand boxes.

DWG 41
Class 73/0 and 73/9 'prototype' fleet (Nos E6001-E6007/73001-73006/ 73901-73906), front end, showing the later-installed Oleo pneumatic buffers.

DWG 42
Class 73/1 and 73/2 'production' fleet (Nos E6007-E6049/73101-73235), front end layout.

DWG 42A
Class 73/1 and 73/2 'production' fleet (Nos E6007-E6049/73101-73235), front end layout showing sealed beam headlight.

Note: From 1996 all Class 73/2 had vacuum brake equipment removed.

DWG 41

Class	73/0, 73/9	73/1	73/2
Former Class Codes	72	—	73/1
SR Class Code	JA	JB	JB
Number Range (TOPS)	73001-73006, 73901-73906	73101 -73142	73201 -73235
Former Number Range	E6001-E6006	E6007-E6049	Random from 73/1
Built By	BR Eastleigh	EE Vulcan Foundry	EE Vulcan Foundry
Introduced	1962	1965-67	As 73/2 - 1988
Wheel Arrangement	Bo-Bo	Bo-Bo	Bo-Bo
Weight (operational)	76 tons	77 tons	77 tons
Height	12ft 5⅞in	12ft 5⅞in	12ft 5⅞in
Width	8ft 8in	8ft 8in	8ft 8in
Length (Buffers extended)	53ft 8in	53ft 8in	53ft 8in
(Buffers retracted)	52ft 6in	52ft 6in	52ft 6in
Min Curve negotiable	4 chains	4 chains	4 chains
Maximum Speed	60mph (Note: 3)	60mph (Note: 3)	90mph
Wheelbase	40ft 9in	40ft 9in	40ft 9in
Bogie Wheelbase	8ft 9in	8ft 9in	8ft 9in
Bogie Pivot Centres	32ft	32ft	32ft
Wheel Diameter	3ft 4in	3ft 4in	3ft 4in
Brake Type	Dual, EP	Dual, EP (Note: 4)	Dual, EP (Note: 4)
Sanding Equipment	Pneumatic	Pneumatic	Pneumatic
Heating Type	Electric - Index 66 (Note: 1)	Electric - Index 66 (Note: 1)	Electric - Index 66 (Note: 1)
Route Availability	6	6	6
Coupling Restriction	Blue Star (Note: 2)	Blue Star (Note: 2)	Blue Star (Note: 2)
Brake Force	31 tons	31 tons	31 tons
Nominal Supply Voltage	600-750V dc	600-750V dc	600-750V dc
Engine Type	English Electric 4SRKT Mk II	English Electric 4SRKT Mk II	English Electric 4 SRKT Mk II
Horsepower (Electric)	1,420hp	1,420hp	1,420hp
(Diesel)	600hp	600hp	600hp
Tractive Effort (Electric)	42,000lb	40,000lb	40,000lb
(Diesel)	34,100lb	36,000lb	36,000lb
Cylinder Bore	10in	10in	10in
Cylinder Stroke	12in	12in	12in
Main Generator Type	EE824-3D	EE824-5D	EE824-5D
Aux Generator Type	EE908-3C	EE908-5C	EE908-5C
Traction Motor Type	EE542A	EE546-1B	EE546-1B
Gear Ratio	63:17	61:19	61:19
Fuel Tank Capacity	340gal	310gal	310gal

Note: 1 ETS is only available under electric conditions. A pre-heat system is available on the Class 73/0s.

Note: 2 Multiple coupling conforms to Blue Star for diesel operation, in addition the class can operate in multiple together, and in multiple with Class 33/1 locomotives, as well as selected post 1951 emu stock using the 27 wire waist height jumper connections.

Note: 3 When built class 73/0 max speed was 80mph, and Class 73/1 90mph, now reduced to 60mph.

Note: 4 Modified for air braking only.

Class 73 sub-class differences:

Class 73/0: Prototype electro-diesel locomotive fleet, constructed by BR at Eastleigh Carriage Works; design proved suitable for SR operation, and production fleet was ordered. The 73/0s have an additional jumper cable on the nose end, and grille differences on body sides.

Class 73/1: Production fleet of electro-diesel locomotives constructed by English Electric, mounted on revised bogie design, with side-grille differences from Class 73/0.

Class 73/2: Modified Class 73/1 locomotives for InterCity Gatwick Express operation, later becoming property of Porterbrook Leasing and operating on National Express Group's Gatwick service until replaced by Class 460 EMUs.

Class 73/9: Modified Class 73/0s for Merseyrail 'Sandite' operations.

For the Southern Region, where the principle power source was electric, a dual-power (electric and diesel) locomotive was considered a distinct advantage, having the ability to operate from the third rail electric supply or, if this were unavailable, an on-board subsidiary diesel engine/generator which could provide power for the traction motors.

The basic plans for this style of dual-power locomotive were first considered in the late 1930s, but it was not until the mid-1950s that any firm plans on the dual-power concept were drawn up. Plans advanced in the closing years of the decade and by July 1959 approval was given to construct six prototype dual-power locomotives. The prime power source was simple – straight electric. The auxiliary source adopted was an English Electric 4SRKT diesel engine set to deliver 600hp, traction power being provided by an English Electric generator group. The electric power output was 1,600hp.

The construction contract for the six prototype locomotives, Nos E6001-E6006, was awarded to Eastleigh Carriage Works, where building commenced in 1960. The first completed locomotive emerged on 1st February 1962 carrying the number E6001. The livery applied was BR green with small yellow warning panels. By the end of 1962 all six locomotives were in service, allocated to Stewarts Lane depot in South London, and performing well. An important design feature of the electro-diesel fleet was the installation of electric and diesel multiple-control equipment as well as EMU-compatible jumpers, permitting the locomotives to operate in multiple with any 'blue star'-compatible locomotive or post-1951 electric multiple-unit.

By 1964 the SR was so pleased with its new charges that a repeat order for 43 almost-identical machines was placed, with the contract going to English Electric rather than a BR workshop. The number range allocated to these locomotives was E6007-E6049. The English

Electric contract was fulfilled by the Vulcan Foundry at Newton-le-Willows, the first locomotive arriving on SR metals in October 1965. The body styling of the EE product was practically identical to the BR build except for slight window/louvre alterations, the removal of the multiple-control jumper from the driver's side, and redesigned bogies. Minor internal technical alterations were also incorporated.

Under BR's TOPS numerical classification, the fleet became Class 73. Sub-classes were 73/0 (Nos 73001-73006) for the BR-built locomotives and 73/1 (Nos 73101-73142) for the EE build.

The fleet of 49 locomotives settled down well, operating on all three SR divisions at the head of both passenger and freight services. Their duties remained almost the same until May 1984, when the Gatwick Express service was launched. This originally called for seven of the fleet to be dedicated to the service, though this was increased to 12 and, later, 14. Special rakes of Mk 2 stock were formed with a Gatwick Luggage Van (GLV) coupled at one end and a Class 73 at the other.

Additional work was found for the fleet in 1986-88 when the new Bournemouth stock was under construction and the REP multiple-units were phased out early to donate their electrical equipment to the new type. As a temporary measure, Class 73s were formed with TC stock and used on some Waterloo – Bournemouth services.

When built, the six prototypes were finished in BR green livery. However, when the production fleet emerged, Electric blue was applied, this giving way to standard Rail blue from the late 1960s. The adoption of the 'more yellow' scheme for some classes was extended to the Class 73s in 1983, but, after only a handful had been so treated, full InterCity or 'Main Line' (unbranded InterCity) colours were authorised, this being applied to all locomotives from 1984 to 1988. Following the introduction of independently-funded business groups within BR, other liveries have been applied. Some Class 73/1s appeared in Civil Engineer's 'Dutch' livery, while others were repainted in all-over grey. From 1991 Network SouthEast livery was applied to locomotives owned by this business. Most members of the Class 73/0 fleet retained the all-blue or 'more yellow' format. Following the reintroduction of names on selected classes, the Class 73s have benefited from this addition.

The first of the SR dual power electro-diesel locomotives emerged from Eastleigh Carriage Works in January 1962. This view, taken on 28th January, shows No. E6001 parked in Eastleigh Works yard before operating a test special under diesel conditions to Basingstoke.

BR

During 1991, it was agreed to repaint No. 73101 in full Pullman livery. This was carried out by Selhurst Level 5 depot, and the locomotive was used to operate the VSOE on a special London – Brighton run. It had been intended to repaint the locomotive back into standard colours, but agreement was then reached to retain this distinctive livery.

Over the years, few modifications have been necessary to the Class 73 fleet, but some are worthy of mention. When built, the six prototype machines had oval buffers which were later changed for the conventional Oleo type. Much later, following their introduction on the Gatwick Express service, several '73/1s' suffered electrical fires due to arcing between shoes and bogies, and to overcome this arc shields were fitted. Following the takeover of the Gatwick Express services it was decided in 1988 to dedicate a fleet of 12 locomotives (later 13) specifically for this service, and to re-classify these as Class 73/2. These locomotives, which were given full InterCity colours, were maintained for full 90mph running, whereas the remainder were restricted to 60mph. Class 73/2s later had their vacuum-brake equipment removed. Following the decision to fit headlights to all main-line traction from 1990, all members of the class were fitted. Two Class 73/0 locomotives were later modified for Meseyrail 'Sandite' operation, being re-classified '73/9' and renumbered in the 739xx series.

When the Eurostar operation began, two Class 73s were allocated to this business, both receiving modifications to incorporate Scharfenberg auto-couplers, permitting direct coupling to Eurostar stock. On privatisation this pair were transferred to Eurostar UK ownership.

With the formation of 'shadow' freight companies in the immediate pre-privatisation era, those Class 73s not allocated to Gatwick Express, Eurostar or Merseyrail passed to Mainline Freight, which painted a small number in its aircraft blue livery. Upon full privatisation and the transfer of all freight operations to English, Welsh & Scottish Railway, corporate EWS livery was applied to two locomotives.

By early 2001 the Gatwick Express fleet was being replaced by new Class 460 electric multiple-units, and the '73/2s' face an uncertain future. Two of these locomotives will, however, be retained by Gatwick Express for 'Thunderbird' duties. At the time of writing (May 2001), only a handful of EWS Class 73/1s remain in traffic. Of the surviving '73/0s', one was stored and the other taken over by Merseyrail for Railtrack use, though this and the '73/9s' are seldom used on Merseyside. However, one locomotive (No. 73109) has seen far more use of late, being owned by South West Trains and outbased at Woking as a 'Thunderbird'.

When the production batch of electro-diesels emerged from English Electric a blue livery off-set by a grey base band was adopted in place of the original green. No. E6010 is seen alongside 'West Country' class 4-6-2 No. 34023 *Blackmore Vale* at Waterloo on 16th October 1966.

Colin J. Marsden

At the time of introduction of the electro-diesels the new standard BR rail blue livery had not been instigated and a number of livery variants were recorded. No. E6018 was no exception, painted with full wrap-round yellow ends and a BR electric blue body. The locomotive was photographed heading a rake of TC stock at St Denys on 17th June 1967 forming the 08.45 Waterloo – Lymington Pier service.

John H. Bird

The Class 73 fleet of electro-diesels have operated over the entire area of the former Southern Region and have indeed visited many non-electrified areas of the Southern and other regions, making the Class 73s some of the most versatile locomotives on BR. All-blue liveried No. 73006 is seen near Weybridge on 9th July 1985 with an empty vans train from Southampton bound for Clapham Junction yard.

Colin J. Marsden

Following the introduction of the "Gatwick Express" from May 1984, at first a batch of Class 73/1s were dedicated to this duty. All-blue No. 73109 hurries past Merstham on 26th April 1986 with the 09.00 Victoria - Gatwick service. consisting of a five-vehicle formation of Class 488 stock and a GLV on the rear.

Colin J. Marsden

When new or revised liveries were introduced in the mid-1980s the Class 73s were some of the first to benefit, with many examples repainted with wrap-round yellow ends, large logo and numbers and grey roofs. This livery was later superseded by the InterCity colour scheme. Wrap round yellow liveried No. 73131 passes Newnham on 23rd April 1987 with a vans train bound for Clapham Junction.

Colin J. Marsden

Painted in Gatwick Express livery, with its flag motif on the side, No. 73205 passes Clapham Junction on 4th September 1996 with the 14.00 Victoria – Gatwick. Note that the buckeye coupling is in the raised position – quite normal for these services, as the formations are considered multiple-unit consists.

Colin J. Marsden

Now classified as Class 73/2, No.73201, the former No. 73142, has for many years been the SR's Royal Train locomotive, always being kept in an immaculate condition by Stewarts Lane depot. With a fresh coat of paint No. 73142 *Broadlands* approaches New Malden on 30th July 1986 with the 16.15 Waterloo - Southampton Eastern Docks Royal Train.

Colin J. Marsden

One of the most surprising repaints to any locomotive during the 1990s, was the application of full 'Pullman' livery to No. 73101 *Brighton Evening Argus* in September 1991 by Selhurst Level 5 depot, the 'Pullman' insignia, motifs and numbers being supplied by the VSOE Company. The locomotive is seen here in Selhurst yard after completion.

Colin J. Marsden

In the years 1986-88 the Waterloo-Bournemouth line went through a period of transition with the REP/TC stock gradually being replaced by new Class 442 'Wessex Electric' units. Whilst equipment was salvaged from the REP stock a number of trains were operated by Class 73/1s hauling TC vehicles. On 3rd July 1987 InterCity liveried No. 73107 passes Wimbledon West with the 10.00 Bournemouth - Waterloo service.

Colin J. Marsden

Following the formation of Network SouthEast, under the guidance of Chris Green, the entire South of England railway operating area saw radical change. One of the most criticised at the time was the adoption of a new bright blue, red, white and grey NSE livery, seen here applied to No. 73136 *Kent Youth Music* at Selhurst depot in May 1992.

Colin J. Marsden

At the time of launch of the Eurostar operation between the UK and mainland Europe using Eurostar Class 373 sets, two Class 73s (Nos 73118/130) were converted by Crewe Works to have hinged Scharfenberg auto-couplers enabling coupling to the Eurostar stock for piloting or rescue purposes. The pair were finished in triple grey livery offset by Channel Tunnel segment logos and were officially allocated to Old Oak Common, but in reality they are based at North Pole depot alongside the Eurostar sets, where this view was taken.

Colin J. Marsden

With the launch of the shadow private freight companies, the Class 73s became the responsibility of Mainline Freight, with a very few locomotives repainted in its distinctive but very smart aircraft blue livery. No. 73133 *The Bluebell Railway* displays the livery while on loan to the Torbay & Dartmouth Railway on 25th May 1996 to take part in its Summer Diesel Gala and is seen piloting Class 25 No. D7535 at Waterside.

Colin J. Marsden

Class 74

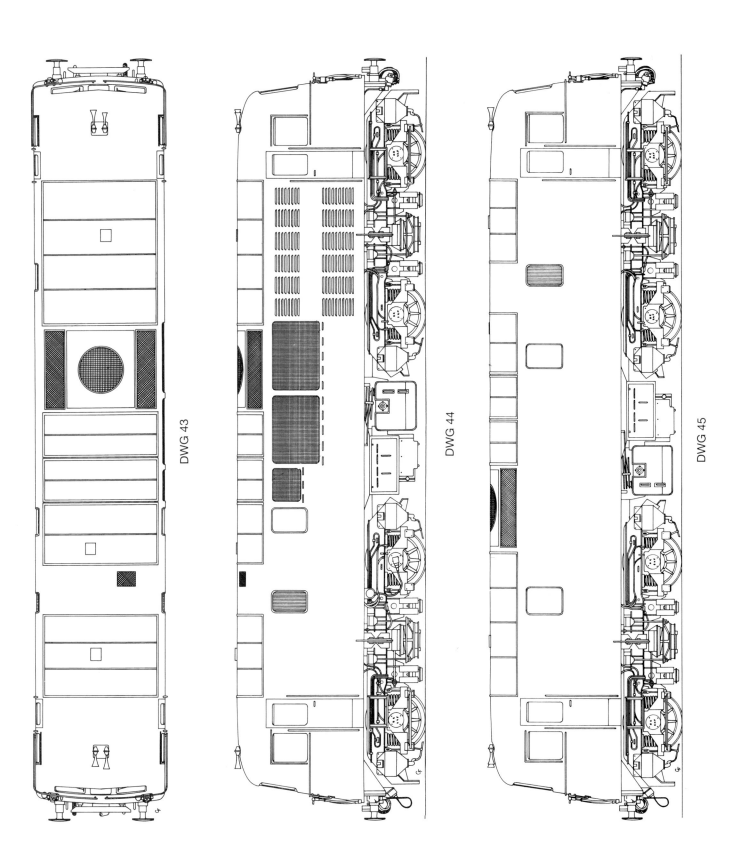

DWG 43

DWG 44

DWG 45

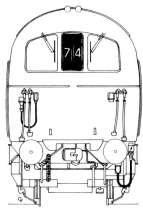

DWG 46

DWG 43
Class 74 roof detail, No. 1 end on right.

DWG 44
Class 74 side elevation, No. 1 end on right.

DWG 45
Class 74 side elevation, No. 1 end on left.

DWG 46
Class 74 front end layout.

Class	74
Number Range (TOPS)	74001-74010
Former Number Range	E6101-E6110 (Note: 1)
Rebuilt by	BR Crewe
Introduced	1966-68
Wheel Arrangement	Bo-Bo
Weight operational	86 tons
Height	12ft 9⅝in
Width	9ft
Length (Buffers extended)	50ft 5¾in
(Buffers retracted)	49ft 3¾in
Min Curve negotiable	4 chains
Maximum Speed	90mph
Wheelbase	37ft 6in
Bogie Wheelbase	10ft 6in
Bogie Pivot Centres	27ft
Wheel Diameter	4ft
Brake Type	Dual
Sanding Equipment	Pneumatic
Heating Type	Electric - Index 66
Route Availability	7
Coupling Restriction	Blue star (Note: 2)

Brake Force		41 tons
Nominal Supply Voltage		600-750V dc
Engine Type		Paxman 6YJXL
Horsepower	(Electric)	2,552hp
	(Diesel)	650hp
Rail Horsepower	(Electric)	2,020hp
	(Diesel)	315hp
Tractive Effort	(Electric)	47,500lb
	(Diesel)	40,000lb
Cylinder Bore		7in
Cylinder Stroke		7¾in
Main Generator Type		EE843
Number of Traction Motors		4
Traction Motor Type		EE532A
Gear Ratio		76:22
Fuel Tank Capacity		310gal

Note: 1   The Class 74s were converted from Class 71 locomotives Nos E5015/16/06/24/19/23/03/05/17/21.

Note: 2   Blue star multiple control equipment fitted for diesel operation. Locomotives also able to operate in multiple (electric) with Class 73, and most post 1951 electric multiple units.

With the coming of the Bournemouth electrification scheme in 1967 the Southern Region (SR) were anxious to exploit to the maximum the use of electric propulsion – however problems prevailed in some locations, such as Southampton Docks and between Branksome and Weymouth where finance was not available for full electrification. The SR with previous experience of dual power traction considered that a powerful electro-diesel would be the answer. At the same time, ten of the Region's E5000 type Class 71 electric locomotives were redundant; after much discussion between the SR, English Electric and the BR Workshops Division a major rebuilding programme for ten straight electric locomotives into 2,552/650hp electro-diesels was authorised. The rebuilding work was carried out at BR Crewe, with English Electric acting as chief sub-contractor. Following rebuilding the fleet was classified Class 74 (SR type HB), and renumbered in the range E6101-E6110. Under TOPS renumbering the fleet became Nos 74001-74010.

The rebuilding of this class was a major undertaking, which called for the entire body to be dismantled down to the frames and then rebuilt. For their new role the main electrical fittings including the booster set were retained, the auxiliary power source being provided by a new Paxman 6YJXL engine of 650hp.

Conversion work at Crewe was a protracted affair with the first machine not arriving on the SR until the end of 1967. All ten locomotives had reached the Region by June 1968. From delivery all locomotives were allocated to Eastleigh depot, and were always used on the South Western Division, where regrettably their performance was not always good, with frequent failures, mainly attributable to the large amount of sophisticated electronics installed. In common with other SR locomotive traction, multiple control jumper cabling was installed, enabling the locomotive to be operated with 1951, 1957, 1963 and 1966 type SR emu stock under electric conditions and blue star restricted locomotives under diesel conditions.

From new the Class 74s were painted in conventional Rail blue livery with full yellow warning ends, the only significant change being the alteration of the number sequence during the early 1970s when TOPS renumbering was introduced.

With the changing traction requirement of the SR and the fleet's record of misbehaviour, the Class 74s were doomed, with the entire fleet being withdrawn by December 1977. All locomotives were eventually broken up.

Very few external modifications existed within the class, except for some members being fitted with a revised cab ventilation system, which required a small covered grille on the cab-side corner posts.

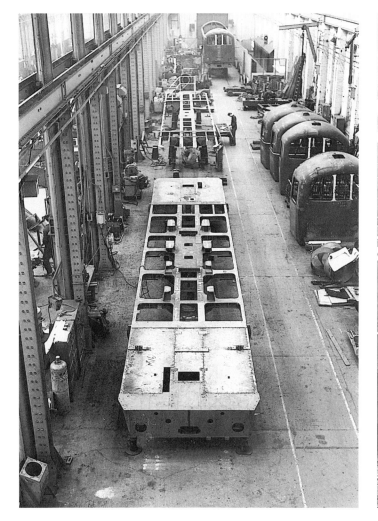

The rebuilding of the ten redundant 'HA' Class 71 electric locomotives into dual-power Class 74 electro-diesel locomotives was performed by BR Crewe Works. The rebuilding was a major undertaking and was tantamount to building a new locomotive. These two views show the Erecting Shop with the left picture illustrating the new frames being assembled and the old cabs stored for re-use on the right. The illustration, right, shows the assembly line in an advanced stage with six locomotives taking shape.

Both: Author's Collection

The Class 74s were always used on the South Western Division's tracks radiating from Waterloo and their normal duties comprised of Waterloo – Southampton Docks and Waterloo – Bournemouth passenger/ van trains. On 8th July 1977 No. 74004 approaches Surbiton with the 07.30 Weymouth Quay – Waterloo boat train, which the electro-diesel would have operated from Bournemouth.

Colin J. Marsden

Front 3/4 study of the first locomotive of the fleet, No. E6101, rebuilt from electric locomotive No. E5015. The addition of waist height air and control jumpers permitted these locomotives to operate in multiple with each other, Class 73/1s, Class 33/1s and selected post-1951 EMUs. No. E6101 is seen in the works yard at Crewe.

Colin J. Marsden

One of the regular duties for the Class 74s was at the head of the frequent Waterloo – Southampton Docks Ocean Liner boat trains, the stock for which was normally stabled at Clapham Junction. In July 1976 No. 74002 is seen at Clapham Junction with empty stock bound for the adjacent yard, on its return to London after forming a down boat train.

Colin J. Marsden

There are very few illustrations available of Class 71 and 74 locomotives together, due to their different operating areas. However this view has been found showing electro-diesel No. E6108 and electric No. E5014 standing in the works yard at Eastleigh in 1968. The modification differences are quite noticeable.

Colin Boocock

Front 3/4 view of Class 74, taken from the No. 2 or diesel end. The nose-mounted air and control jumper connections are clearly visible in this view.

Colin J. Marsden

The main operating stronghold for the Class 74s was on the Waterloo – Southampton Docks boat trains, where the locomotives used their 650hp diesel engines to provide traction between Southampton and the dockside. No. 74010 poses
in Southampton New Docks during September 1977.

Colin J. Marsden

In addition to working the main line services on the South Western section, the Class 74 locomotives were often used on
empty stock diagrams between Waterloo and carriage sidings at Clapham Junction. On 18th September 1974 No. 74007
passes Vauxhall with the 09.57 Waterloo – Clapham Junction ecs train.

John Scrace

Class 76

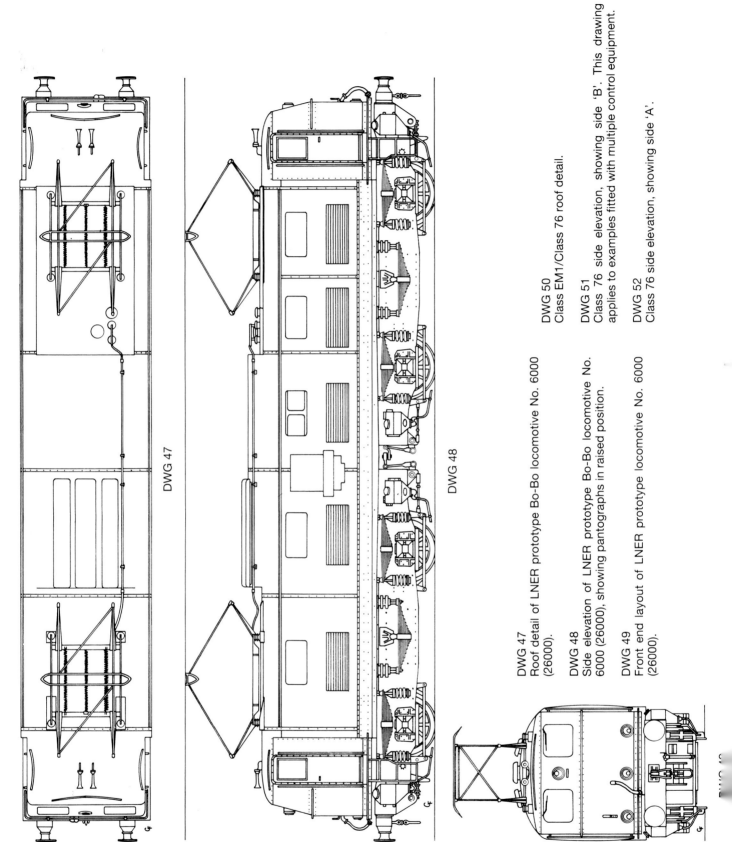

DWG 47

DWG 48

DWG 47
Roof detail of LNER prototype Bo-Bo locomotive No. 6000 (26000).

DWG 48
Side elevation of LNER prototype Bo-Bo locomotive No. 6000 (26000), showing pantographs in raised position.

DWG 49
Front end layout of LNER prototype locomotive No. 6000 (26000).

DWG 50
Class EM1/Class 76 roof detail.

DWG 51
Class 76 side elevation, showing side 'B'. This drawing applies to examples fitted with multiple control equipment.

DWG 52
Class 76 side elevation, showing side 'A'.

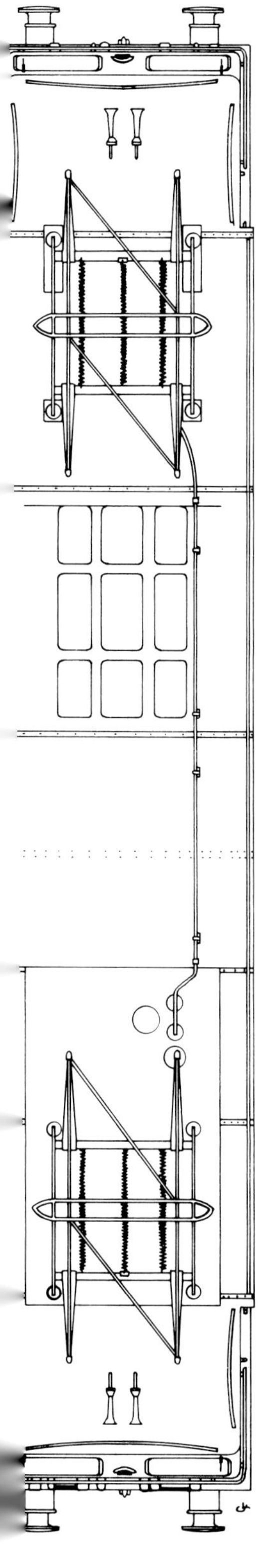

DWG 50

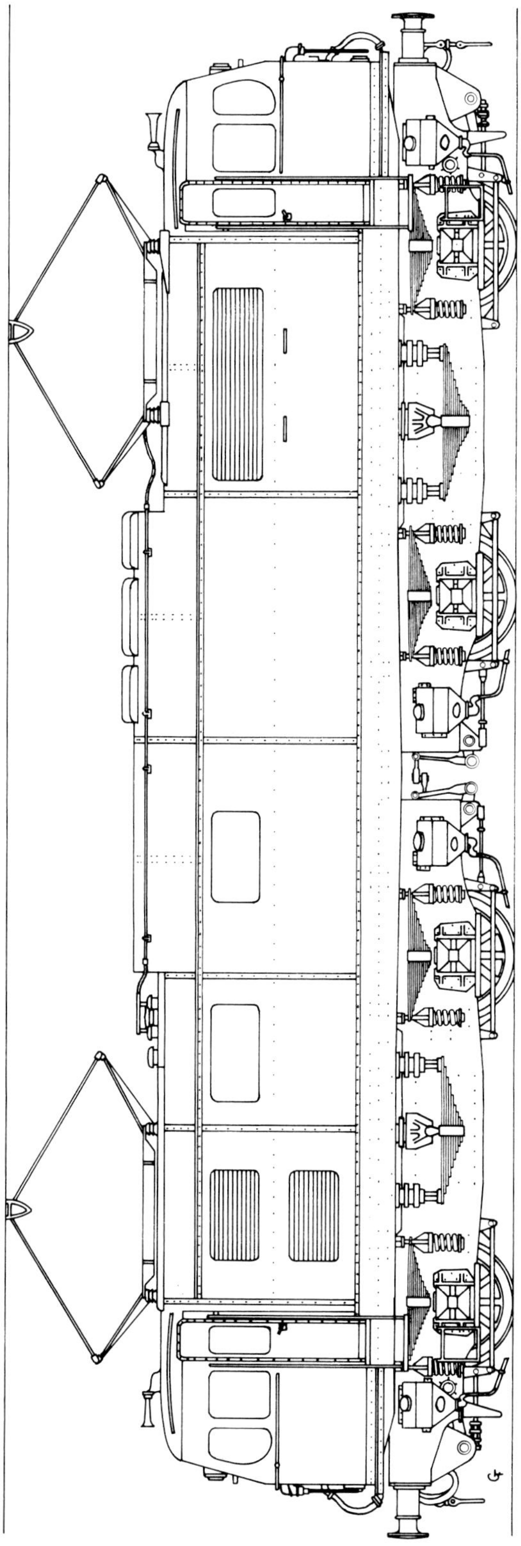

DWG 51

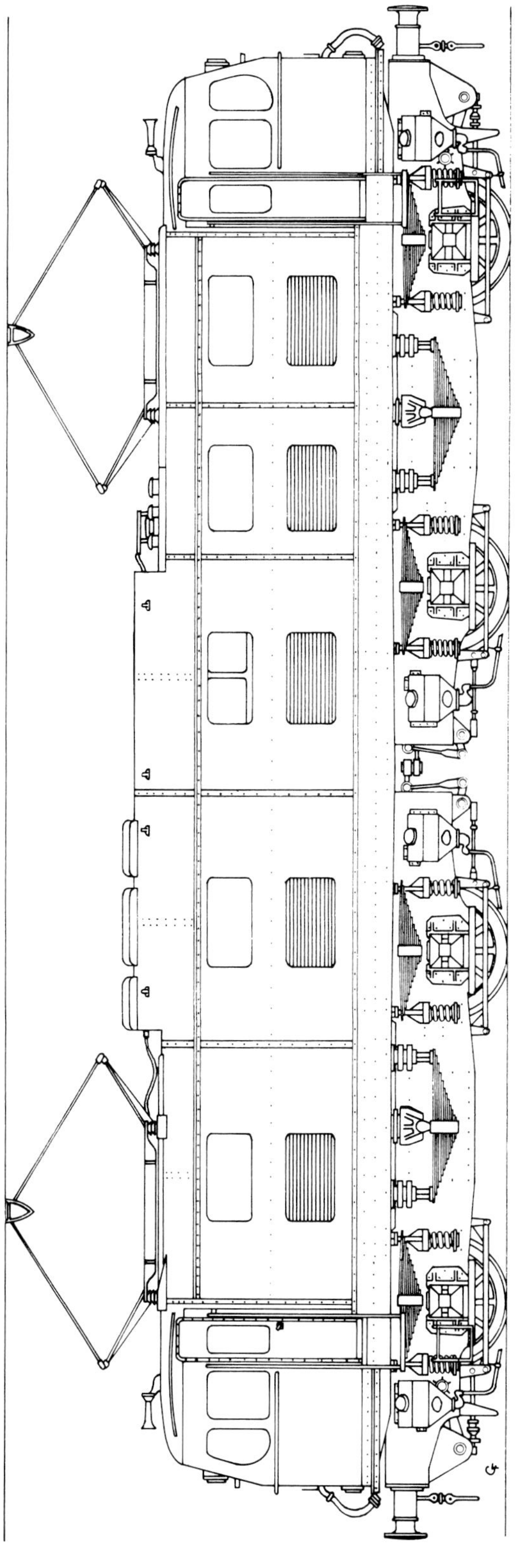

DWG 52

45

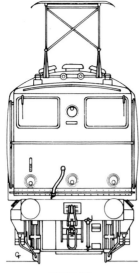

DWG 53

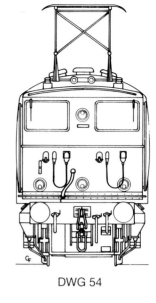

DWG 54

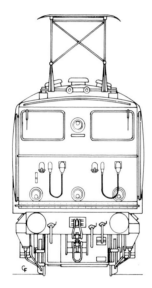

DWG 55

DWG 53
Class 76 front end layout, showing vacuum braking and steam heat pipe, as applicable to locomotives Nos E26046-57.

DWG 54
Class 76 front end layout, showing dual brake equipment and multiple control jumper cables/sockets.

DWG 55
Class 76 front end layout, showing air only braking system and multiple control jumper cables/sockets.

Class	76
Former Class Code	EM1
Number Range TOPS	76001-76057
Former Number Range	E26000-E26057 (Note: 1)
Built by	BR Doncaster and Gorton
Introduced	1941-53
Wheel Arrangement	Bo-Bo
Weight operational	88 tons
Height - pan down	13ft
Width	9ft
Length	50ft 4in
Min Curve negotiable	6 chains
Maximum Speed	65mph
Wheelbase	35ft
Bogie Wheelbase	11ft 6in
Bogie Pivot Centres	23ft 6in
Wheel Diameter	4ft 2in
Brake Type	Vacuum, Dual or air (Note: 2)
Sanding Equipment	Pneumatic
Heating Type	Steam - Bastian & Allen (Note: 3)
Route Availability	8
Coupling Restriction	Within class (Note: 4)

Brake Force	43 tons
Horsepower	1,868hp
Tractive Effort	45,000lb
Number of Traction Motors	4
Traction Motor Type	MV 186
Control System	Electro-Pneumatic
Gear Ratio	17:70
Pantograph Type	MV Cross Arm
Nominal Supply Voltage	1,500V dc overhead
Boiler Water Capacity	210gal (if fitted)

Note: 1   The original locomotive of this build was numbered 6701 when built in 1941. This was altered to 6000, and then into the main fleet.

Note: 2   This fleet was fitted with regenerative braking on the locomotive.

Note: 3   Steam heating equipment was only fitted to locomotives Nos 26000, 26046-26057 (76046-76057), and removed after passenger services stopped on the MSW line.

Note: 4   Multiple control facilities were fitted to locomotives Nos 26006-16/21-30 (76006-10/21-30).

It was the intention of the London & North Eastern Railway (LNER) for many years to invest in electrification of the cross-Pennine route between Sheffield and Manchester via Woodhead, as well as the branch from Penistone to Wath, and onwards from Sheffield to Rotherwood. Plans put forward during the 1920s/30s were gradually shelved and it was not until 1939 that financial approval was eventually given for the project, work starting almost immediately. The power system chosen for the scheme was 1,500V dc overhead. Concurrent with ground work commencing, the LNER works at Doncaster, under the auspices of Gresley, commenced production of a Bo-Bo electric locomotive. The locomotive bearing the LNER No. 6701 was completed in 1941 before the railway had any electrified tracks, therefore in order to test locomotive No. 6701 it was hauled across the Pennines to Manchester and used for a short period on the Manchester South Junction & Altrincham line, before returning to the LNER for storage.

After the end of world hostilities in 1945 the LNER were not able to recommend Pennine electrification immediately, and to avoid the prototype locomotive, by now renumbered 6000, laying idle any longer it was loaned to the Netherlands Railway in 1947.

By 1950, when electrification of the Pennine route was at an advanced stage, orders were placed for locomotives of two different types, classified EM1 and EM2. The EM1 fleet conformed almost identically to the original LNER locomotive and were constructed at the LNER works at Gorton near Manchester with electrical equipment supplied by Metropolitan-Vickers. A total of 57 EM1 locomotives were built, numbered 26001-26057. The fleet commenced operation in February 1952. At the end of the same year, the prototype locomotive was returned from Holland, and after extensive modification at Doncaster, entered service as EM1 No. 26000. This locomotive was named *Tommy*, a name bestowed upon it by European serviceman. After entry into service a total of twelve EM1 locomotives were named, all after creatures in Greek mythology.

From 1954 until July 1981, when the 1,500V dc route closed, this fleet operated the line, giving a good reliability figure. Over the years few modifications were carried out to the fleet, the most noticeable externally being the fitting of multiple control jumpers to 30 locomotives. Later in their careers several examples had their vacuum train brake equipment replaced by air brake only equipment.

Throughout its life the prototype locomotive remained identifiable by a slightly different front end and side design, which is documented in the accompanying drawings.

Under the BR five-figure TOPS renumbering system the EM1 fleet became Class 76 carrying the Nos 76001-76057. A small amount of renumbering occurred in later years when grouping of like brake fitted examples was made.

When built LNER No. 6701 was finished in LNER apple green livery which was carried until the early 1950s when black was applied. All production examples were completed in black which was later amended to BR locomotive green. After Autumn 1967 all repaints were carried out in standard BR blue with full yellow ends.

After closure of the 1,500V dc network all locomotives were sold for scrap, except No. 76020 (26020) which was saved by the National Railway Museum at York, who now have the locomotive painted in original lined black livery.

The pioneer LNER Bo-Bo 1,500V locomotive, built for the Manchester – Sheffield – Wath electrification poses in the works yard at Doncaster soon after construction in 1941. It will be noted that the locomotive is finished in LNER lined green livery and has one of its pantographs in a raised position.

Author's Collection

The 1950 order for Class EM1 locomotives was effected by Gorton Works, where the body shell of the first completed example is seen under high voltage electrical tests, which according to the sign on the front was carried out at 5,000V.

Author's Collection

When introduced the Class EM1 locomotives were painted in black livery, this later giving way to BR locomotive green, and subsequently, BR rail blue. Adorned in black livery and looking rather shabby, No. 26023 heads a heavy mineral train across the Pennines in 1957.

BR

During the 1960s traffic flows over the MSW electrified lines were intense with some 80 per cent of the locomotive fleet normally being rostered each day. On 14th July 1964 No. 26023 pauses in the loop at Penistone whilst sister locomotive, No. 26029, passes with a mineral train. Both locomotives are painted in green livery with a small yellow warning panel.

Colin J. Marsden

One of the main areas for 1,500V dc operation was around Penistone where the lines from Wath and Darnall parted company. Passing through the station on 24th July 1964 is No. 26054 at the head of the usual coal train. This locomotive was one of the batch equipped for passenger operation with steam heating, which is identified by the steam heat pipe on the buffer beam.

Colin J. Marsden

Many of the new 1,500V locomotives were, after completion, stored at Ilford depot in East London, with some locomotives operating trials in the London area using the ER(GE) 1,500V dc system. With only one pantograph in the raised position No. 26002, painted in black livery, stands at Shenfield on 12th November 1950 with the 12.18pm test train bound for Ilford.

L. Price

Throughout the 1970s and early 1980s a sizable row of Class 76 locomotives could be found each evening and at weekends stabled at Wath depot, a servicing shed used jointly by dc electric and diesel traction. This general view of the shed taken in 1977 shows nine Class 76 locomotives stabled in one line, while two Class 37s and a Class 47 stand outside the shed.

Colin J. Marsden

It was not uncommon to find the Class 76 locomotives operating in pairs over the MSW route at the head of long and heavy freight trains. On 3rd September 1980, Nos 76025 and 76016 pull away from the photographer at Valehouse with a westbound coal train.

Brian Morrison

The locomotives fitted with multiple control jumpers were those usually used in pairs, as the two locomotives could be controlled by one driver. A pair of mu fitted examples, equipped with air-only train brake equipment, approach Valehouse with a westbound merry-go-round train. The leading locomotive is No. 76010.

Brian Morrison

Class 77

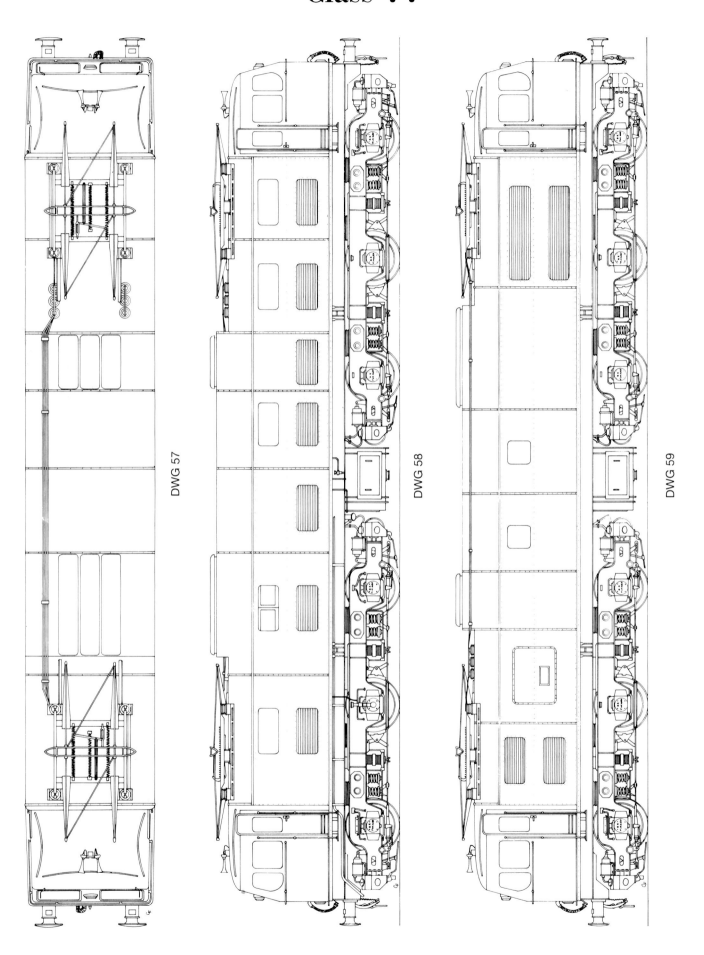

DWG 57

DWG 58

DWG 59

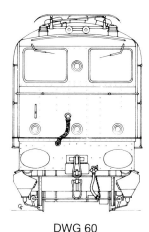

DWG 60

DWG 57
EM1/Class 77 roof detail.

DWG 58
EM1/Class 77 side 'A' elevation. No. 1 end on left.

DWG 59
EM1/Class 77 side 'B' elevation. No. 1 end on right.

DWG 60
EM1/Class 77 front end elevation.

Class	77	Brake Type	Vacuum (Note: 1)
Former Class Type	EM2	Sanding Equipment	Pneumatic
Number Range	E27000-E27006	Heating Type	Steam - Bastian & Allen
Built by	BR Gorton	Route Availability	8
Introduced	1953-54	Coupling Restriction	Not multiple fitted
Wheel Arrangement	Co-Co	Horsepower	2,300hp
Weight	102 tons	Tractive Effort (maximum)	45,000lb
Height - pan down	13ft	Number of Traction Motors	6
Width	8ft 10in	Traction Motor Type	MV 146
Length	59ft	Control System	Electro-Pneumatic
Min Curve negotiable	6 chains	Gear Ratio	17:64
Maximum Speed	90 mph	Pantograph Type	MV Cross Arm
Wheelbase	46ft 2in	Nominal Supply Voltage	1,500V dc Overhead
Bogie Wheelbase	15ft 10in		
Bogie Pivot Centres	30ft 6in		
Wheel Diameter	3ft 7in		

Note: 1   This fleet were fitted with regenerative braking on the locomotive.

Following early experience with the prototype LNER 1,500V dc locomotive, when the ride characteristics gave cause for concem, it was decided to opt for a Co-Co locomtive for use on passenger duties for the Trans-Pennine electrified route. Under original plans it was envisaged that a fleet of 27 Co-Co locomotives would be required, however in light of operational experience with the EM1 Bo-Bo fleet and subsequent bogie modifications, which permitted a speed increase, the production fleet of Co-Co locomotives was reduced to just seven. Under the electric locomotive classification system this fleet became Class EM2, which was later amended to BR Class 77. The number range allocated was E27000-E27006.

Power and control equipments were supplied by Metropolitan Vickers, while construction was effected by the Gorton Works of BR in 1953-54. One of the major structural changes on this fleet to the earlier EM1 type was the fitting of the buffing and draw gear onto the bodywork and not the bogie frame.

From their introduction this small fleet of main line electric locomotives were always deployed on the Manchester - Sheffield - Wath line. However, when during the late 1960s, BR decided to withdraw the passenger services, and reroute the line's passenger duties via the non-electrified Hope Valley route, the class was withdrawn. Although removed from service there was plenty of life left in these machines and BR offered the entire fleet for sale. After only a short period on the market the Netherlands Railway (NS) became interested and purchased all locomotives, which were shipped to Holland and rebuilt to their requirements. To cover NS operations only six locomotives were needed, the seventh, No. E27005 being broken up for spares. Once in service the six NS locomotives were allocated numbers in the 1501 - 1506 series and proved very reliable, remaining in traffic until late 1986. Two locomotives of the fleet have been saved by the preservation movement and returned to England. No. E27000 *Electra* is now preserved at the MRC, Butterley, while No. E27001 is on display at the Greater Manchester Museum of Science & Industry.

When in BR service the locomotives were painted in Electric blue when constructed, this later being amended to BR green. All seven examples of the class were named in association with gods of mythology.

The larger and more powerful Class EM2 locomotives were designed for the Trans-Pennine passenger services and were indeed seldom seen on freight duties. No. 27004 *Juno* is seen near Penistone in June 1964 at the head of a Manchester – Sheffield Victoria service.

Author's Collection

The fleet of seven Class EM2, later BR Class 77 locomotives, were constructed at the former LNER works at Gorton, near Manchester, and received all their classified maintenance at the same location. Painted in BR green livery No. 27001 *Ariadne* is seen outside Gorton Works in 1966.

Colin J. Marsden

Displaying the main line black livery No. 27003, later to be named *Diana,* slowly pulls the 2.10pm service to Marylebone out of Manchester London Road on 18th March 1955.

John Faulkner

With a splendid array of BR and pre-Nationalisation stock behind, No. 27001, still un-named, heads a Manchester – Sheffield working near Oughty Bridge in the summer of 1957.

Author's Collection

During the early 1960s, in the railway's attempt to improve its aesthetic image, new liveries were applied, including a shade known as electric blue, to many electric locomotives. No. 27002 *Aurora* is seen outside Reddish depot after repainting into the new scheme.

L. Price

One of the major exhibits at the British Railway's Traction Exhibition at Willesden in May/June 1954 was brand new No. 27002, delivered direct from the builder's works at Gorton. With pantograph raised the locomotive is seen on 27th May 1954.

BR

As detailed in the introductory text, after their useful life in Britain and their premature withdrawal, the entire fleet was sold to the NS – Nederlandse Spoorwegen – where the locomotives were rebuilt to NS standards at Utrecht. The former No. 27000 *Electra*, disguised as NS No. 1502, is seen at Hoorn on 15th March 1986 with the RT&P 'EM2 Electra Special' from Hook of Holland, Utrecht and Amsterdam.

John Tuffs

After their demise on NS two examples were returned to England for preservation, NS Nos 1502 and 1505, the former BR Nos 27000 *Electra* and 27001 *Ariadne*. NS No. 1502 is seen on display at the Basingstoke Rail Event on 26/27th September 1987.

Colin J. Marsden

In the autumn of 1988 No. 27000 *Electra* was repainted by its owners, the EM2 Preservation Society, into BR green livery. The locomotive is seen at London Waterloo on display at the Ian Allan Network Day on 1st October 1988.

Colin J. Marsden

Class 80

DWG 61

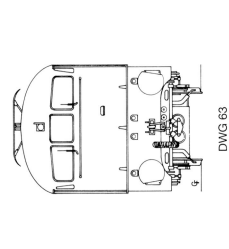

DWG 63

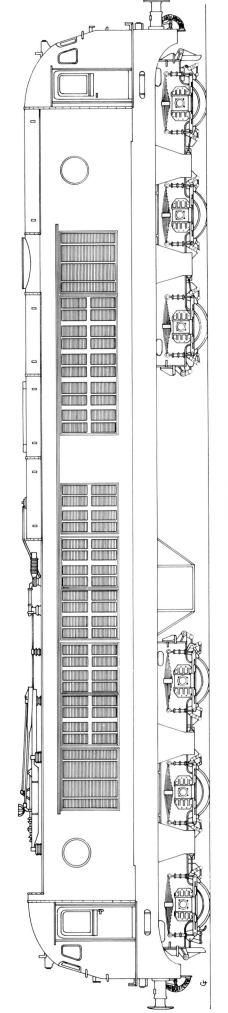

DWG 62

DWG 61
BR/MV prototype 25kV electric locomotive No. E1000 (E2001) roof detail.

DWG 62
BR/MV prototype 25kV electric locomotive No. E1000 (E2001) side elevation.

DWG 63
BR/MV prototype 25kV electric locomotive No. E1000 (E2001) front end detail.

Class	80	Sanding Equipment	Pneumatic
Number	E2001	Heating Type	Electric
Original 1957 Number	E1000	Route Availability	7
Former Number	18100 (Note: 1)	Multiple Coupling Restriction	Not multiple fitted
Rebuilt by	Metropolitan – Vickers	Horsepower	2,500hp
Introduced (Original)	1952	Tractive Effort	40,000lb
Introduced Rebuilt	1958	Number of Traction Motors	4
Wheel Arrangement	A1A-A1A	Traction Motor Type	MV
Weight	109 tons	Control System	LT Tap Changing
Height - pan down	12ft 10in	Gear Drive	Direct spur, single reduction
Width	8ft 8¼in		
Length	66ft 9¼in	Gear Ratio	21:58
Min Curve negotiable	4 chains	Pantograph Type	Stone-Faiveley
Maximum Speed	90mph	Rectifier Type	Mercury Arc
Wheelbase	53ft	Nominal Supply Voltage	25kV ac
Bogie Wheelbase	15ft		
Bogie Pivot Centres	37ft 6in		
Wheel Diameter	3ft 8in		
Brake Type	Vacuum		

Note: 1   This locomotive was rebuilt from prototype gas-turbine No. 18100, and used for training on the LM 25kV AC system.

The first of the 25kV ac overhead electric classes was in many ways an unusual locomotive, being originally built as a gas-turbine by Metropolitan-Vickers in 1952. As a gas-turbine, No. 18100 the locomotive was operated on the WR until being made redundant in 1958.

After electrification of the London Midland Region main line was authorised and traction orders placed, it became apparent that there would be a long wait before any operational hardware would be available. Following much deliberation it was decided to contract Metropolitan – Vickers to rebuild the former gas-turbine No. 18100 into a 25kV ac electric locomotive, enabling training and overhead equipment testing to take place at an early date. At the time of the conversion decision, No. 18100 lay dumped at Dukinfield near Manchester, from where it was hauled to the MV works at Stockton-on-Tees. The rebuilding work was major and consisted of the removal of the former gas-turbine power unit, auxiliary combustion equipment, dc power equipment, fuel tanks and control equipment. In their place ac power, control, transformer and rectifier units were installed. The cabs were also heavily rebuilt to remove the previously fitted GWR style right-hand driving layout. The roof also had to be modified to accommodate the pantograph. Another structural modification worthy of note was the trimming of the buffers to bring the machine within the required gauge in terms of width. To provide traction power for the new electric locomotive, four of the original six traction motors were retained, as were some of the auxiliary

machines such as traction motor blowers, vacuum brake exhauster, air compressor and cooling equipment. During the rebuilding work a very small staff room was incorporated at No. 1 end, which was intended as a training classroom.

The pioneer LM ac electric locomotive, finished in main line black livery off-set by a silver body band, was released from Metropolitan-Vickers in Autumn 1958, still carrying its gas-turbine number 18100. After initial testing in the Styal area the machine was renumbered to E1000 and put to work on the Manchester – Crewe line between Mauldeth Road and Wilmslow. After a short period as No. E1000 the locomotive was renumbered to E2001.

After some twelve months of being the only 25kV ac electric locomotive in service, the production classes started to enter traffic spelling the end for No. E2001, and after mid-1961 the locomotive saw little use. During the autumn of 1961 No. E2001 was sent north to Scotland where it was used on the Glasgow electrified area for equipment testing, but by Christmas the locomotive was returned to the London Midland Region, being stored at various locations such as Crewe, Goostrey and finally Rugby. For a period in 1964 No. E2001 did see some further use, when deployed as a training locomotive at Rugby, but after only a few months the machine was again stood down. By early 1968 the locomotive was deleted from stock, but lay for an extended period in sidings at Market Harborough and Rugby before being sold to J. Cashmore Ltd of Tipton for scrap in 1972.

Few physical body alterations were carried out to gas-turbine locomotive No. 18100 when its was rebuilt into 25kV prototype locomotive No E1000, later E2001. This view shows the locomotive after conversion, with the pantograph at the far end. Note the empty underframe between the bogies, and the trimmed buffers.

GEC Traction

No. E1000 (E2001) only operated as an electric locomotive for a short period, as when sufficient numbers of production 25kV locomotives were available all training and testing was concentrated on these types. No. E1000 is seen heading a rake of Mk 1 stock on the Styal line during 1961.

Author's Collection

An illustration taken only a few days after release from the Metropolitan-Vickers works, shows the prototype electric locomotive lined up for an official photograph, although still carrying its original gas-turbine number, 18100.

Author's Collection

Former gas-turbine locomotive No. 18100 cab layout, as revised for electric operation. The train and locomotive brake valves are located on the left, with the power controller in the middle foreground.

Colin J. Marsden

Class 81

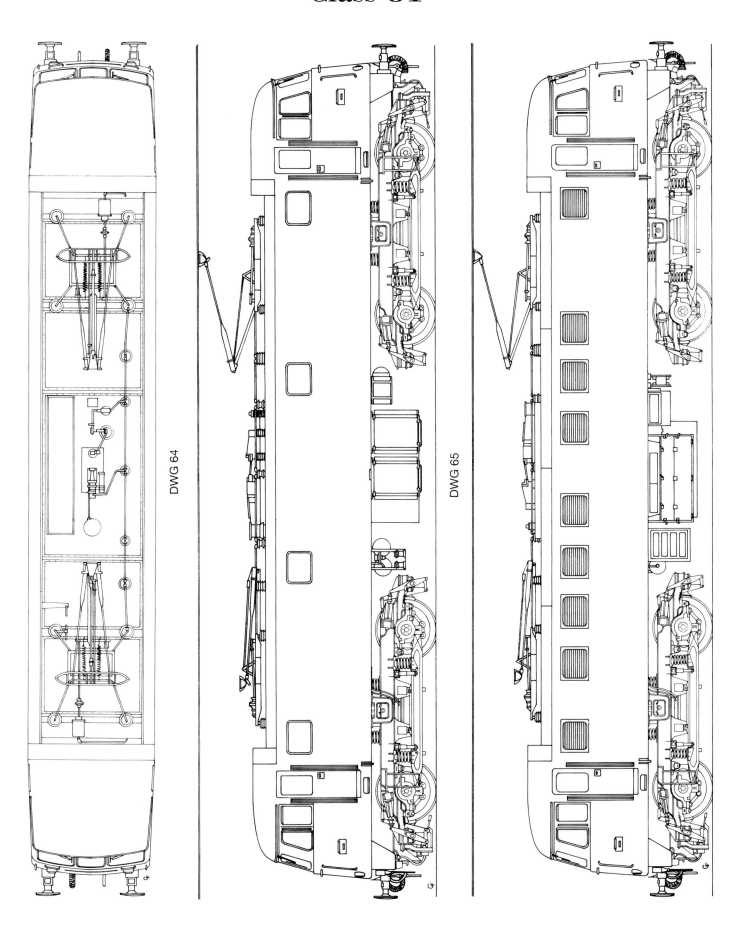

DWG 64

DWG 65

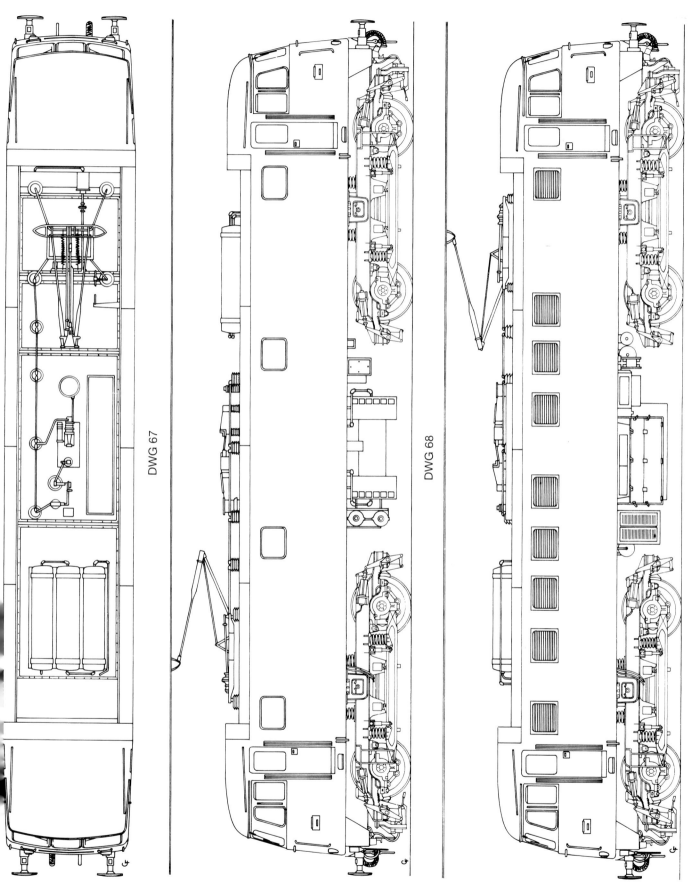

DWG 67

DWG 68

DWG 69

DWG 70

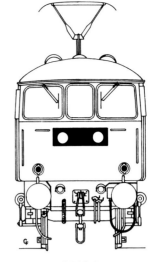

DWG 71

Class	81
Former Class Code	AL1
Number Range (TOPS)	81001-81022
Former Number Range	E3001-E3023, E3096-E3097 (E3301-E3302)
Built by	BRC&W Ltd
Introduced	1959-64
Wheel Arrangement	Bo-Bo
Weight	79 tons
Height - pan down	13ft 0⁹/₁₆in
Width	8ft 8¹/₂in
Length	56ft 6in
Min Curve negotiable	4 chains
Maximum Speed	100mph (Note: 1)
Wheelbase	42ft 3in
Bogie Wheelbase	10ft 9in
Bogie Pivot Centres	31ft 6in
Wheel Diameter	4ft
Brake Type	Dual (Note: 2)
Sanding Equipment	Pneumatic
Heating Type	Electric - Index 66

Route Availability	6
Coupling Restriction	Not multiple fitted
Brake Force	40 tons
Horsepower (continuous)	3,200hp
(maximum)	4,800hp
Tractive Effort (maximum)	50,000lb
Number of Traction Motors	4
Traction Motor Type	AEI 189
Control System	LT Tap Changing
Gear Drive	Alsthom Quill, single reduction
Gear Ratio	29:76
Pantograph Type	Stone-Faiveley
Rectifier Type	Silicon (Note: 3)
Nominal Supply Voltage	25kV ac

Note: 1 The maximum speed of this class was reduced to 80mph in 1986.

Note: 2 When built vacuum only brakes were fitted.

Note: 3 When built mercury arc rectifiers were fitted.

DWG 64
AL1/Class 81 roof detail, showing as-built condition with two pantographs.

DWG 65
AL1/Class 81 side 'B' elevation, showing as-built condition with two pantographs. No. 1 end on right.

DWG 66
AL1/Class 81 side 'A' elevation, showing as-built condition with two pantographs. No.1 end on left.

DWG 67
Class 81 roof detail, after refurbishment with one pantograph. No. 1 end on right.

DWG 68
Class 81 side 'A' elevation, after refurbishment with only one pantograph, and angled rain water strip on cab side roof. No. 1 end on right.

DWG 69
Class 81 side 'B' elevation, after refurbishment with only one pantograph, and angled rain water strip on cab side roof. No. 1 end on left.

DWG 70
AL1/Class 81 front end layout, showing two pantographs and vacuum only train brake equipment.

DWG 71
Class 81 front end layout, showing revised layout with dual brake equipment and modified route indicator panel.

The pioneer order for 25kV ac 'production' locomotives was spread amongst several major builders. Numerically the first series No. E3001 onwards, was the AL1 fleet which consisted of 23 Type 'A' (passenger), and two Type 'B' (freight) locomotives. Construction was carried out by the Birmingham RC&W Co., who were acting as chief sub-contractor to AEI. The mechanical portion, designed by BRC&W, was a load bearing structure, being formed of girder steel, plated in medium gauge sheet. The body structure had full width cabs at either end, and housed all electrical equipment in lockable compartments in the between cab section on one side of the body, the other side housing a between cab walkway. The between cab roof section was lower than standard height to accommodate the pantographs, which were electrically arranged to be able to receive power at either 6.25kV or 25kV depending on the area in which the locomotive was used, although the 6.25kV system was never used.

The first of the production ac classes, the AL1s, started to emerge at the end of 1959 when No. E3001 was released from the BRC&W works at Smethwick, and transferred to the Styal line for active testing. This view shows No. E3001 a few days after release from BRC&W prior to testing. Note that only one pantograph, that for 25kV operation, is raised, and that one of the ventilation louvres at the far end is of a modified type.

Author's Collection

The two body sides of the Class AL1, later Class 81, were totally different, one having four windows, and the other accommodating nine ventilation grilles. When introduced the Type 'A' locomotives were numbered in the E3001-E3023 range, while the Type 'B' locomotives were numbered E3301-E3302, later amended to E3096-E3097. Under the TOPS renumbering system the entire fleet became Nos 81001 -81022.

When constructed the livery applied was Electric blue, with white cab roof and window surrounds. Over the years yellow warning panels were progressively added, and later BR standard Rail blue was carried with full yellow ends.

When introduced the class were fitted for vacuum train brake operation only, this being suppiemented by air brake equipment in the late 1960s, at which time the redundant 6.25kV pantograph was removed.

Until the introduction of second generation electric classes during the mid-1960s the AL1s, in company with the other pilot electric types, were to be found operating over all parts of the LM electrified network, heading both passenger and freight traffic. In latter years members were allotted to Glasgow Shields Road depot, however their diverse operations took them all over the electrified network right to the end of their operating careers. Major withdrawals of the fleet commenced during 1988, with the fleet being eliminated by mid-1991.

When built the Class AL1s had four-character route indicator panels. These were replaced by black screens and white marker 'cut-outs' during the mid-1970s. In later years the redundant indicator boxes were plated over and two sealed beam marker lights fitted.

Although the Class 81s are now a part of railway history, one member of the class, No. E3003 (81002), has been preserved at the Barrow Hill Railway Museum.

From their introduction the ac classes have received the majority of their classified overhauls at the BR/BREL workshops at Crewe where special facilities for their maintenance was provided. This mid-1960's view shows four Class 81s and a Class 40 diesel receiving maintenance at Crewe.

BR

In common with all main line locomotives yellow high-visibility warning panels and later, full yellow ends were progressively applied from the mid-1960s. Whilst adorned with just a small yellow warning panel most locomotives retained a white cab roof which gave a very pleasing appearance. Hauling a rake of Mk1 and Mk2 stock No. E3003 is seen heading south on the West Coast Main Line in October 1968.

BR

Traversing the up slow line at Wolverton, Class 81 No. 81017 heads a Bescot – Willesden Yard 'Speedlink' freight service on 27th July 1988. In the background part of Wolverton Works can be seen.

Michael J. Collins

Displaying the standard BR rail blue livery No. 81007 is seen at Euston with a rake of empty coaching stock on 3rd October 1981. By this time the locomotive had been refurbished with only one pantograph (at the far end), and dual brake equipment.

Colin J. Marsden

The Class 81 fleet finished their working days allocated to Glasgow Shields depot, being used on all sections of the LM/Sc electrified network. On 28th April 1984 No. 81017 fitted with sealed beam marker lights, is seen at Stafford with the 13.26 relief from Euston to Glasgow Central.

Michael J. Collins

Class 82

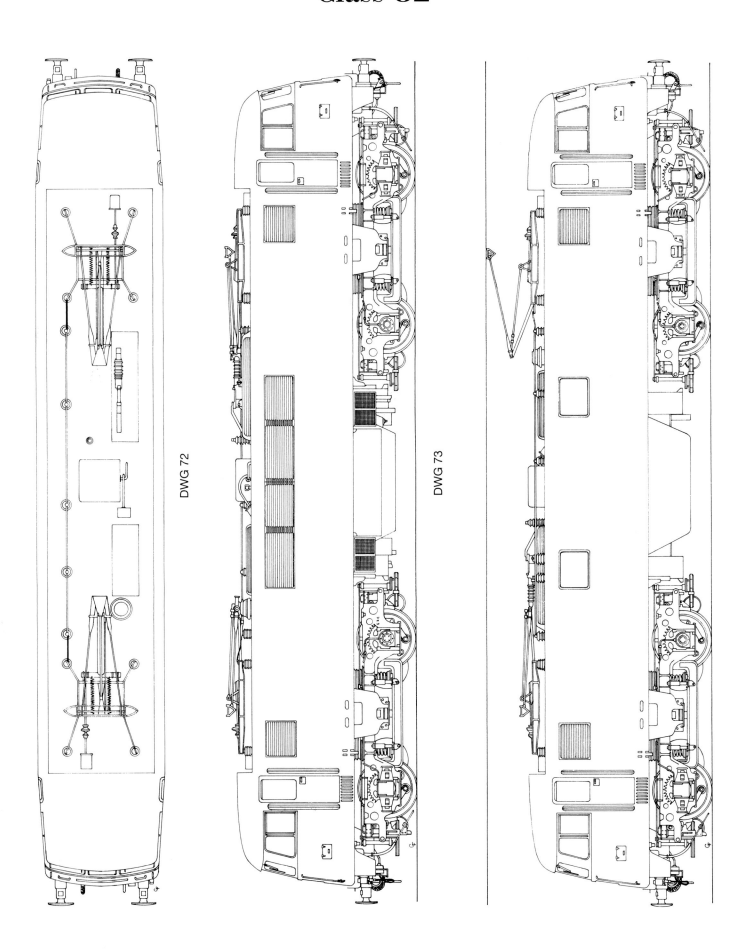

DWG 72

DWG 73

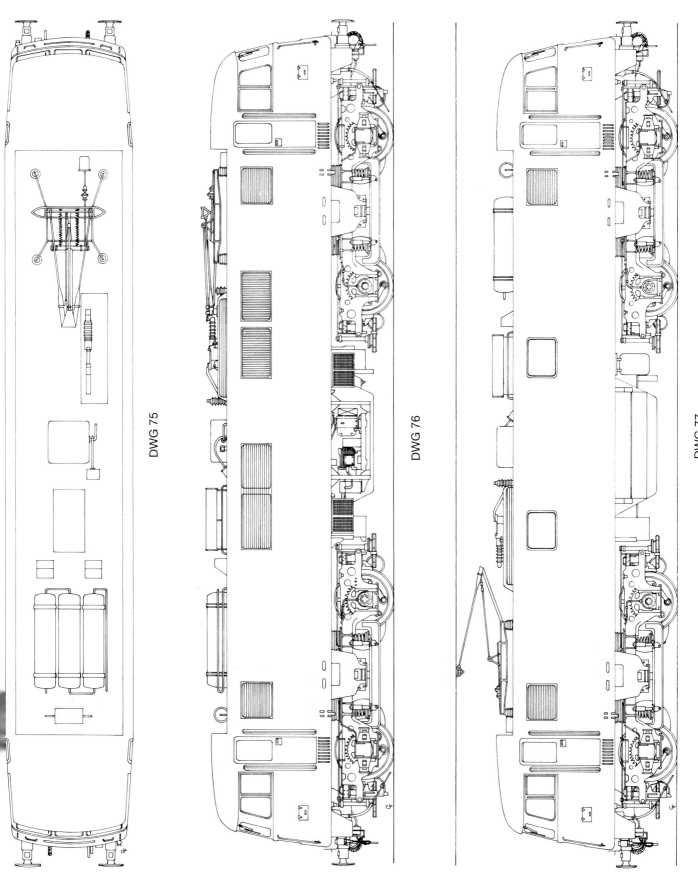

DWG 75

DWG 76

DWG 77

DWG 78

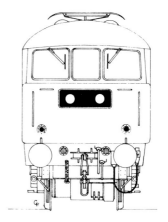

DWG 79

Class	82
Former Class Code	AL2
Number Range (TOPS)	82001-82008
Former Number Range	E3046-E3055
Built by	Beyer, Peacock
Introduced	1960-61
Wheel Arrangement	Bo-Bo
Weight	80 tons
Height - pan down	13ft 0⅝in
Width	8ft 9in
Length	56ft
Min Curve negotiable	4 chains
Maximum Speed	100mph (Note: 1)
Wheelbase	40ft 9in
Bogie Wheelbase	10ft
Bogie Pivot Centres	30ft 9in
Wheel Diameter	4ft
Brake Type	Dual (Note: 2)
Sanding Equipment	Pneumatic
Heating Type	Electric - Index 66
Route Availability	6
Coupling Restriction	Not multiple fitted

Brake Force		38 tons
Horsepower	(continuous)	3,300hp
	(maximum)	5,500hp
Tractive Effort	(maximum)	50,000lb
Number of Traction Motors		4
Traction Motor Type		AEI 189
Control System		HT Tap Changing
Gear Drive		Alsthom Quill, single reduction
Gear Ratio		29:76
Pantograph Type		Stone-Faiveley
Rectifier Type		Silicon (Note: 3)
Nominal Supply Voltage		25kV ac

Note: 1   Class 82 locomotives remaining in service after 1986 were restricted to 40mph for ecs duties in the London area.

Note: 2   When introduced the Class 82s were fitted for vacuum braking only.

Note: 3   When built mercury arc rectifiers were fitted.

DWG 72
AL2/Class 82 roof detail, showing as-built condition with two pantographs.

DWG 73
AL2/Class 82 side 'A' elevation, showing as-built condition with two pantographs, No. 1 end on left.

DWG 74
AL2/Class 82 side 'B' elevation, showing as-built condition with two pantographs, No. 1 end on right.

DWG 75
Class 82 roof detail, after refurbishment with one pantograph. No. 1 end on left.

DWG 76
Class 82 side 'A' elevation, after refurbishment with revised louvre position. No. 1 end on left.

DWG 77
Class 82 side 'B' elevation, after refurbishment with one pantograph. No. 1 end on right.

DWG 78
AL2/Class 82 front end detail, showing the as-built condition with vacuum only train braking.

DWG 79
Class 82 front end detail, showing dual brake fitment.

Under the original ac orders a fleet of ten Type 'A' (passenger) locomotives was ordered from AEI/ Metropolitan-Vickers, who sub-contracted mechanical construction to Beyer, Peacock of Gorton, Manchester. Under the ac locomotive classification system this fleet became Class AL2 and allocated numbers in the range E3046-E3055. Under the later BR TOPS numbering system the fleet became Class 82, being numbered 82001-82008. The first locomotive of the build emerged in May 1960, and immediately took up trial running on the Styal line in Manchester.

The external appearance of this fleet closely followed the style of the previously detailed Class AL1 design, but the construction method was significantly different, incorporating a separate underframe and body. At the design stage it was envisaged that weight might be something of a problem, and to overcome this much alloy and glass fibre was used.

The between cab layout was almost identical to the Class AL1, and the cab layout conformed to the BTC standard style adopted for all the ac builds of the 1960s. Two pantographs were again fitted from new, as was vacuum-only train brake equipment. During the early 1970s, when air braking was being more frequently introduced, the entire fleet was refurbished to provide dual brake equipment, at the same time the redundant 6.25kV pantograph was removed and the space taken by the additional air braking reservoirs.

When constructed, one side of the locomotive had six grilles, while the other had two windows and two grilles. After refurbishing during the early 1970s the louvred side was largely altered to incorporate an additional vent panel to improve internal ventilation.

After introduction the AL2 fleet was allocated to Longsight depot in Manchester, and displayed the standard Electric blue livery, offset by white cab roofs and cab window surrounds. Over the years standard Rail blue livery with full yellow warning ends was applied.

The AL2 fleet performed extremely well on the West Coast Main Line and were well liked by the train crews. However by 1982-83 the majority of the fleet was deemed as surplus to requirements and stored, eventually being withdrawn. However Nos 82005 and 82008 were retained until 1987 for empty stock duties in the London area, being allocated to Willesden. No. 82008 is now preserved at Barrow Hill.

Once sufficient electric traction was available electric services were introduced progressively as the various routes were energised. Taken only a short time after the switching on of the Crewe – Liverpool section on 1st January 1962 an electrically hauled Inter-regional express approaches Liverpool Lime Street headed by a Class AL2 and an AL1 locomotive.

BR

6th March 1967 was a big day in the annals of BR modernisation. During that morning the Official Opening of Birmingham New Street station took place, coupled with the introduction of the new high speed electric timings between London, Birmingham and the Midlands, bringing to an end the eight-year modernisation programme. One of the first workings to the new schedule was the 10.27 Manchester Piccadilly – Euston via Birmingham, seen here leaving New Street behind Class 82 No. E3054.

Author's Collection

The Class 82 locomotives in their refurbished state provided the LM with a reasonably satisfactory fleet of power units, and indeed prior to the full availability of Class 86 and 87 locomotives, were to be found at the head of crack InterCity services. On 25th October 1981 No. 82005 passes Castlethorpe with the Sundays Only 10.50 Euston – Liverpool service.

Michael J. Collins

With its No. 2 or pantograph end leading, and the locomotive's 'B' side nearest the camera, No. 82008 arrives at Willesden Yard on 12th May 1980 with empty newspaper vans from Birmingham.

Colin J. Marsden

During the early years of ac passenger operation on the WCML, double heading of services was not uncommon. Here, Class AL2 No. E3047 pilots Class AL5 No. E3073 at Stafford with an express service bound for London.

Norman E. Preedy

Class 82 No. 82002 used for ecs duties in the London area was repainted into InterCity livery to match the coaching stock during the late 1980s. Looking rather dilapidated after passing through the acid coach washer at Willesden Brent Sidings the locomotive is seen posed inside Willesden DED. Note the cab-shore telephone aerial on the front end to the right of the driver's window.

Colin J. Marsden

Class 83

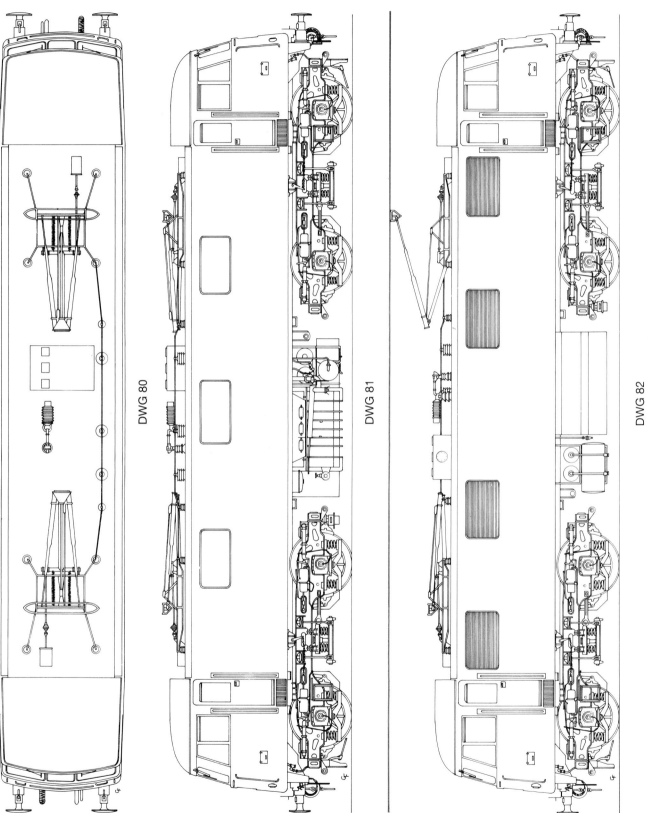

DWG 80

DWG 81

DWG 82

way. Side ventil
by four louvre
three windows
provide an addi
window positio

Vulcan Found
locomotives in
being handed
'A' locomotive
later. The Type
1961 and alloca

In 1960 the
from the BTC
advanced powe
was eventually
of a silicon re
equipment. Alt
final machine
locomotive, as
BTC agreed to
'A' example, wh
provide adequa
this locomotive
grille equipmen

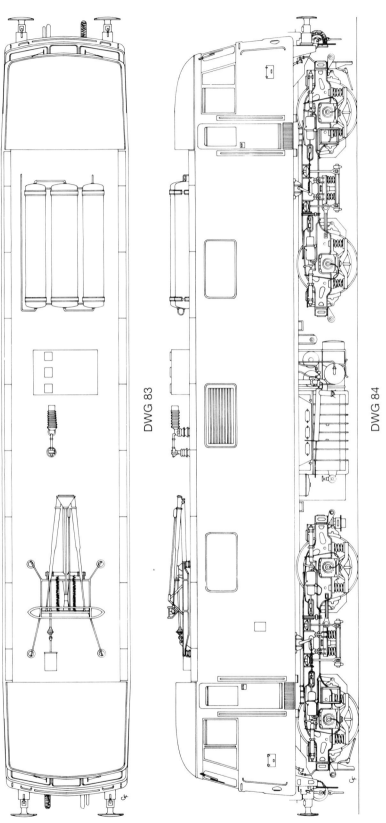

DWG 83

DWG 84

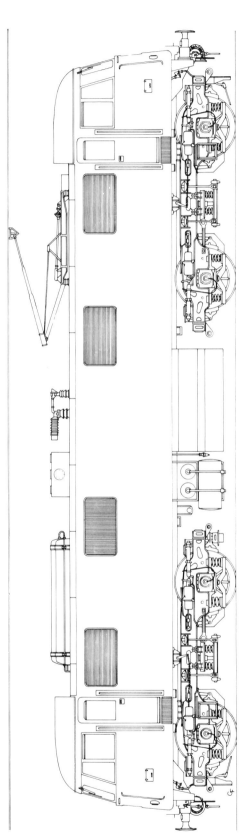

DWG 85

The constru
mechanical
shows four l

DWG 80
AL3/Class 8
two pantogra

DWG 81
AL3/Class 8
with two pan

DWG 82
AL3/Class 8
with two pan

DWG 83
Class 83 ro
graph. No. 1

As detailed in the text, two of the AL3 build were designated as Type B or freight locomotives and numbered E3303 and E3304. After a short period these two locomotives were standardised and renumbered E3098 and E3099 respectively. No. E3304 is illustrated at Allerton.

GEC Traction

Class
Former Class
Number Rang
Former Numb

Built by
Introduced
Wheel Arrang
Weight
Height – pan
Width
Length
Min Curve ne
Maximum Sp
Wheelbase
Bogie Wheelk
Bogie Pivot C
Wheel Diame
Brake Type
Sanding Equi
Heating Type

The Class AL
divided as tw
later amende
contract for tl
sub-contracte
Foundry at Ne
   The main a
constructed 1
being an inte

Although looking the same as the production batch the final AL3, No. E3100 was constructed as an English Electric test-bed to evaluate new advances in traction equipment. After release from Vulcan Foundry No. E3100, was the subject of extensive road and performance tests for both BR and English Electric. Here it is seen with a motley train of engineering test vehicles including three further Class AL3 locomotives all under power, used to draw high current out of the overhead line equipment.

Author's Collection

After the majority of Class 83 locomotives were withdrawn from service as surplus to requirements, three machines, Nos 83009/12/15 were retained for ecs duties in the London area, being maintained by Willesden electric depot. No. 83009 is seen at Euston on 30th December 1985 with stock for the 20.30 Glasgow mail train.

Michael J. Collins

As the final Class 83 locomotives were only used for ecs movements their external condition left something to be desired, as their frequent usage through coach washing plants turned their body sides nearly white. No. 83009 sporting its 1980's-added 'X' arm pantograph, stands at Stonebridge Park on 9th April 1988.

Michael J. Collins

In their closing years the Class 83 fleet became used more frequently on secondary passenger or special duties. Here, No. 83010 is seen at Mitre Bridge Junction, Willesden after arrival with a troop special. At this point the ac electric gave way to diesel traction for the remainder of the journey to Aldershot.

Colin J. Marsden

Class 84

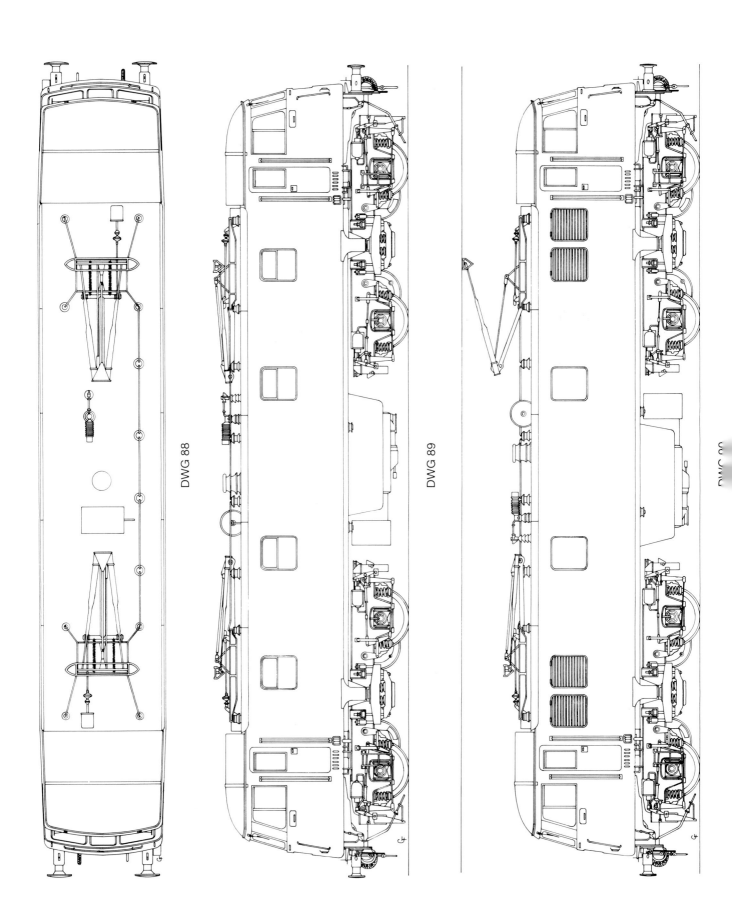

DWG 88

DWG 89

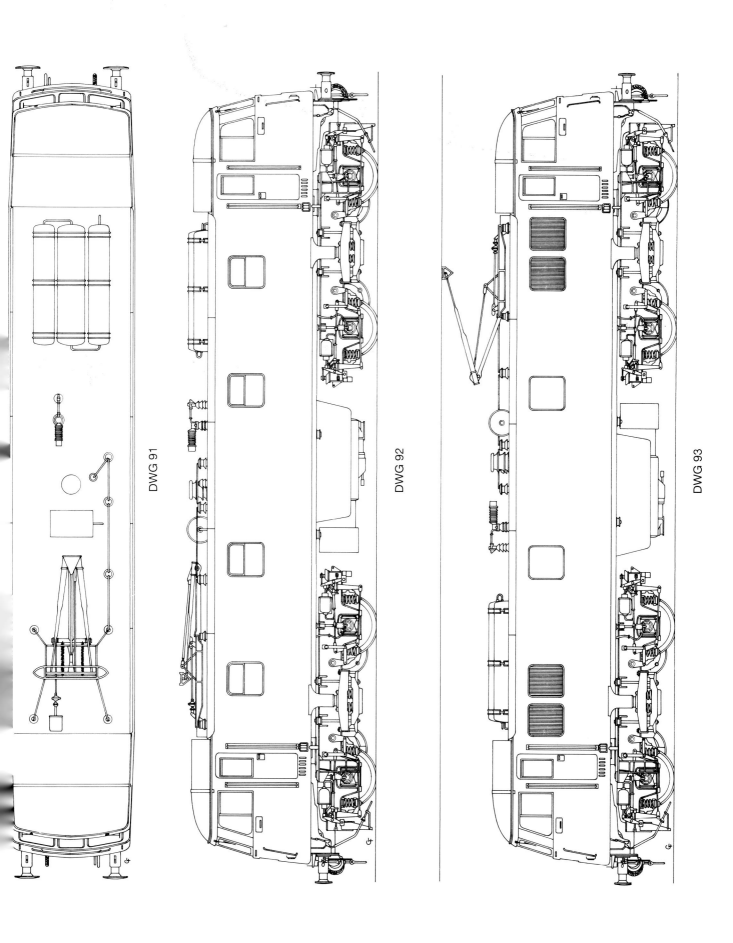

DWG 91

DWG 92

DWG 93

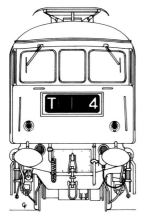

DWG 94

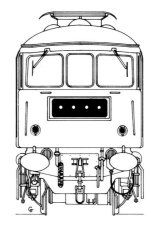

DWG 95

Class	84
Former Class Code	AL4
Number Range (TOPS)	84001-84010
Former Number Range	E3036-E3045
Built by	North British Locomotive Co. Ltd
Introduced	1960-61
Wheel Arrangement	Bo-Bo
Weight (operational)	77 tons
Height - pan down	13ft 0⅝in
Width	8ft 8¼in
Length	53ft 6in
Min Curve negotiable	4 chains
Maximum Speed	100 mph
Wheelbase	39ft 6in
Bogie Wheelbase	10ft
Bogie Pivot Centres	29ft 6in
Wheel Diameter	4ft
Brake Type	Dual (Note:1)

Sanding Equipment	Pneumatic
Heating Type	Electric - Index 66
Route Availability	6
Coupling Restriction	Not multiple fitted
Brake Force	38 tons
Horsepower (continuous)	3,300hp
(maximum)	4,900hp
Tractive Effort (maximum)	50,000lb
Number of Traction Motors	4
Traction Motor Type	GEC WT 501
Control System	HT Tap Changing
Gear Drive	Brown Boveri
Gear Ratio	25:74
Pantograph Type	Stone-Faiveley
Rectifier Type	Silicon (Note: 2)
Nominal Supply Voltage	25kV ac

Note: 1   When built vacuum only brakes were fitted.

Note: 2   When built mercury arc rectifiers were fitted.

DWG 88
AL4/Class 84 roof detail, showing the as-built condition with two pantographs. No. 1 end on left.

DWG 89
AL4/Class 84 side 'B' elevation, showing original layout.

DWG 90
AL4/Class 84 side 'A' elevation, showing original layout with one pantograph (raised).

DWG 91
Class 84 roof detail, after refurbishment with only one pantograph.

DWG 92
Class 84 side 'B' elevation, after refurbishment with only one pantograph. No. 1 end to right.

DWG 93
Class 84 side 'A' elevation, after refurbishment with only one pantograph. No. 1 end is on the left.

DWG 94
AL4/Class 84 front end layout, showing as-built condition with vacuum only train braking equipment.

DWG 95
Class 84 front end layout, showing modified design with dual brake equipment.

The ten locomotives classified by the BTC as AL4 were of Type 'A' and constructed by the North British Locomotive Co. of Glasgow, who acted as chief sub-contractor to GEC who were awarded the main contract. NBL decided to opt for an integral structure using entirely steel members, unlike other competitors who used light-weight fibre glass for some components.

The construction of this fleet commenced in mid-1959, with the first member being handed over to the BTC in March 1960. The style of the product and its livery closely followed previous types, but incorporated a slightly recessed route indicator panel, giving an immediate method of recognition. Also oval buffers were used in place

of the usual round type. The between cab layout was as on previous types, with equipment on one side and a walkway on the other. The walkway side sported four aluminium framed drop light windows, the only openable equipment room windows fitted to any ac electric locomotive type. On the equipment side four grille panels and two glazed windows were provided. The number range allocated was E3036-E3045, under the later TOPS numbering system the fleet becoming Nos 84001-84010.

Following introduction and allocation to Manchester Longsight problems were soon encountered with both rough riding and failures of the main power equipment. In April 1963 the entire fleet were temporarily removed from service and sent to Dukinfield where remedial work was carried out by GEC. Regrettably, even after the class re-entered service electrical problems still ensued, which eventually led to nine of the fleet being stored at Bury from 1967, the tenth example, No. E3043 being allocated to the Rugby M&EE testing station for extensive trials.

It seemed that the AL4 fleet were doomed to be some of the shortest lived electric locomotives. However, after authorisation for the extension of the WCML electrification to Scotland there was a need for additional traction, and this requirement was fulfilled by refurbishing the Class AL4 fleet at Doncaster, a job which was completed in 1972. During the refurbishment dual brake equipment was fitted, and the redundant 6.25kV pantograph removed. At around the same time the type became classified under the TOPS numerical system as Class 84.

Many of the previous problems were overcome by the refurbishing, but others were soon identified, mainly involving the traction motor drives. Expenditure on the fleet was largely curtailed during the mid-1970s, as the BRB could not authorise any further financial investment in the class. By 1977 the first withdrawals were made, with the final member being withdrawn in 1980.

Thankfully, two members of the class were saved from scrap. No. E3044 (84009) was rebuilt as a mobile load bank for the M&EE department, and used for testing new overhead line equipment and No. E3036 (84001) which is now owned by the National Railway Museum, York. The mobile load bank, renumbered ADB968009 was withdrawn from use in Autumn 1992.

The North British built Type AL4, later Class 84, locomotives were always recognisable from their early sisters by having oval buffers, a recessed route indicator panel and drop light windows on one side. Locomotive No. E3037 is seen on display at the 1960 Institute of Transport Congress exhibition at Marylebone. Members of GEC and the BTC pose in front of the new locomotive for this official photograph.

GEC Traction

In common with the 'first' of all new types of locomotive the pioneer Class AL4, No E3036, was the subject of extensive testing once handed over to the BTC. The locomotive is seen here at the head of a rake of Mk 1 maroon coaches during a test run on the Styal line.

Author's Collection

With its distinctive North British Locomotive Co. diamond shaped builder's plate below its cast aluminium numbers, No. E3044 is seen at Manchester Piccadilly. The 'A' side of the locomotive is nearest the camera.

Norman E. Preedy

After withdrawal the majority of Class 84s were disposed of quite quickly, however No. 84008 was retained at BREL Crewe Works until 1988, although in a rather dilapidated condition. The locomotive is viewed on 25th September 1985. Note that the cast BR logo was still in position.
Colin J. Marsden

In their later years the Class 84 fleet were allocated to Crewe electric depot, but maintenance was provided by any of the LM ac electric servicing depots, only the most major repairs being returned to the owning depot. On 7th December 1974 No. 84009 poses inside Willesden depot.
Norman E. Preedy

In the months prior to their withdrawal the Class 84 fleet were deployed on several railtours. On 16th September 1978 No. 84002 was used on the 'AC/DC' tour from Birmingham to Sheffield, which travelled via the Woodhead route and also used Class 76 traction. From Birmingham to Manchester motive power was provided by No. 84002 seen here at Stockport.
Norman E. Preedy

Class 85

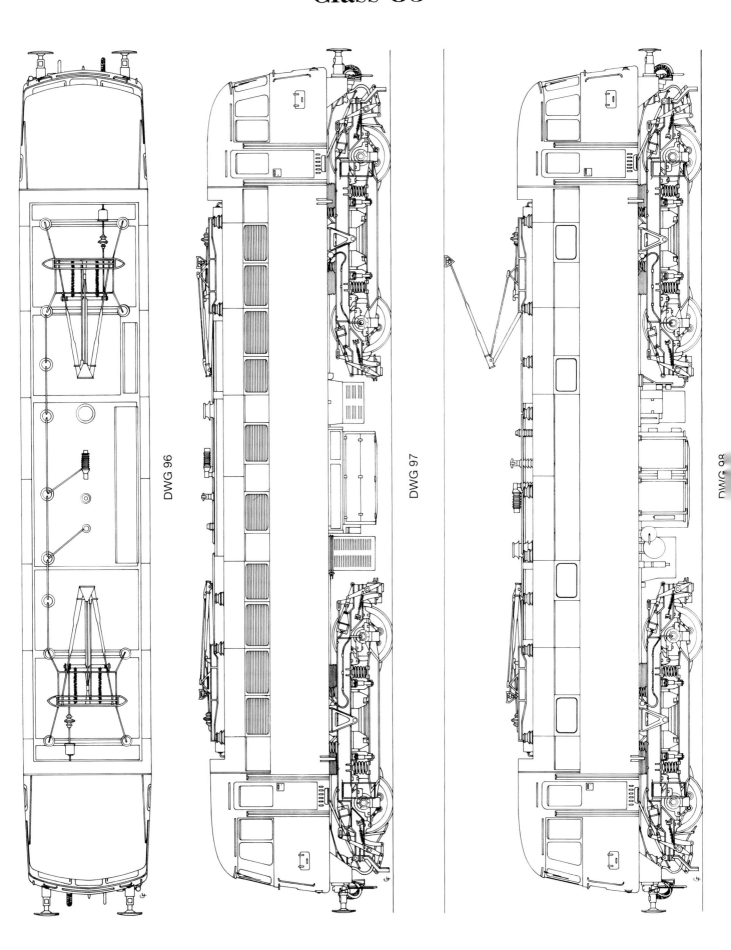

DWG 96

DWG 97

DWG 98

86

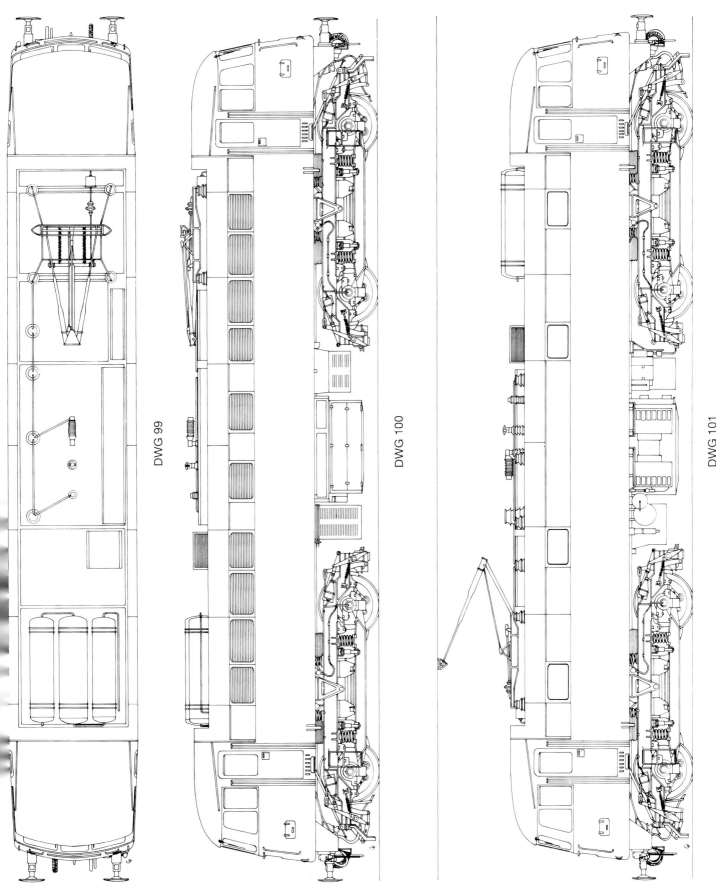

DWG 99

DWG 100

DWG 101

87

DWG 102

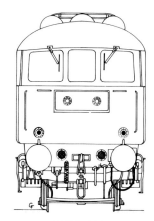

DWG 103

Class .	85
Former Class Code	AL5
Number Range (TOPS)	85001-85040, 85101-85114
Former Number Range	E3056-E3095
Built by	BR Doncaster
Introduced	1961-64
Wheel Arrangement	Bo-Bo
Weight (operational)	83 tons
Height - pan down	13ft 0⁵/₈in
Width	8ft 8¹/₄in
Length	56ft 6in
Min Curve negotiable	6 chains
Maximum Speed	100mph (Note: 1)
Wheelbase	42ft 3in
Bogie Wheelbase	10ft 9in
Bogie Pivot Centres	31ft 6in
Wheel Diameter	4ft
Brake Type	Dual (Note: 2)
Sanding Equipment	Pneumatic
Heating Type	Electric - Index 66
Route Availability	6

Coupling Restriction	Not multiple fitted
Brake Force	41 tonnes
Horsepower (continuous)	3,200hp
(maximum)	5,100hp
Tractive Effort (maximum)	50,000lb
Number of Traction Motors	4
Traction Motor Type	AEI 189
Control System	LT Tap Changing
Gear Drive	Alsthom Quill, single reduction
Gear Ratio	29:76
Pantograph Type	Stone-Faiveley
Rectifier Type	Silicon (Note: 3)
Nominal Supply Voltage	25kV ac

Note: 1   From 1986 some locomotives were restricted to 80mph .

Note: 2   When built vacuum only brakes were fitted.

Note: 3   When built mercury arc rectifiers were fitted.

On Class 85/1 locomotives the ETS equipment was isolated for use on Railfreight services.

DWG 96
AL5/Class 85 roof detail, showing original layout with two pantographs.

DWG 97
AL5/Class 85 side 'A' elevation, showing original layout with two pantographs and straight style rain strips above cab door/window. No. 1 end on left.

DWG 98
AL5/Class 85 side 'B' elevation, showing original layout with two pantographs and straight style rain strips above cab door/window. No. 1 end on right.

DWG 99
Class 85 roof layout, showing refurbished locomotive with one pantograph. No 1. end on left.

DWG 100
Class 85 side 'A' elevation, showing refurbished layout, with only one pantograph, and angled rain water strip above cab door/windows. No. 1 end on left.

DWG 101
Class 85 side 'B' elevation, showing refurbished layout, with only one pantograph, and angled rain water strip above cab door/windows. No. 1 end on right.

DWG 102
AL5/Class 85 front end layout, showing original style with only vacuum train brake equipment.

DWG 103
Class 85 front end layout, showing revised design with dual brake equipment.

The main contractor for the 40 strong AL5 fleet was BR Workshops Division, who allocated the assembly work to its Doncaster Works. Power, control and technical equipment was supplied by GEC/AEI. When introduced this fleet were allocated numbers in the E3056-E3095 range, which later, under the TOPS numbering scheme, was amended to 85001-85040.

On this fleet the base underframe was formed out of seven box sections, onto which the cab ends, and lower sections of the body were assembled, forming a trough-like fabrication. The lightweight top section of the body was then mounted onto the base. One feature of this fleet was that the complete upper section between the cabs was removable and eased access for maintenance.

The internal between cab layout closely followed the previous designs with equipment on one side and a walkway on the other. On the equipment side ten body side louvres were positioned while the walkway side incorporated four glazed windows. When introduced two roof-mounted pantographs were installed, but in later years, after dual brake equipment was fitted the second pick-up was removed in favour of additional air reservoirs.

The Doncaster 'Plant' Works commenced production of this class in early 1960, completing the first locomotive in October, when No. E3056 was exhibited at the Electrification Conference Exhibition held at Battersea in South London After a few early teething troubles the AL5s, later Class 85s, settled down to give good all-round service. spending most of their lives allocated to Crewe Electric Depot.

After being introduced painted in standard Electric blue livery, the fleet was repainted into corpoate BR Rail blue during the mid-1960s, incorporating full yellow warning ends.

The Class 85s remained in service until mid 1991. after inroads had been made into the fleet progressively from 1989. During 1989 13 locomotives were modified by Crewe depot into freight-only locomotives, having their maximum speed reduced and train heat equipment removed. These locomotives were reclassified as Class 85/1 and numbered in the series 85101-85114. Towards the later years of the locomotives' operation they became more extensively used on freight duties, mainly in the northern section of the WCML, while a small number were dedicated to empty stock movements in the London and Manchester areas.

Few major structural changes befell the class after construction, but one front end change worthy of note was the replacement of the four-character route indicator boxes with sealed beam marker lights during the early 1980s.

No. 85006 (85101) was saved from scrap and is now preserved at the Barrow Hill Museum.

Of the five original 'prototype' AL classes introduced, only one fleet, the AL5s were constructed by a BR workshops – Doncaster, who employed AEI/EE as the chief sub-contractor. No. E3079, a 1963 built locomotive, is seen heading the 4.20pm Liverpool Lime Street – Euston express past Runcorn on 30th March 1965.

BR

Although all were introduced without a yellow warning panel front end, this was soon applied, and by the end of 1965 all examples had this addition. With a splendid mixture of maroon liveried LMS/BR coaching stock behind, No. E3087 pulls off the Nuneaton line at Rugby on 14th September 1966 with the 10.00 Liverpool – Euston service.

Author's Collection

During the early 1970s the entire Class AL5 fleet were refurbished by Doncaster Works, when amongst other work, dual brake equipment was installed and the dual voltage power equipment removed, leaving only one roof-mounted pantograph. No. 85025 is seen near Basford Hall, Crewe on 16th July 1985 heading the 09.10 Willesden – Warrington 'Speedlink' service.

John Tuffs

Although not diagrammed for use on crack express duties towards the end of their careers, the Class 85s were often seen at the head of InterCity rakes operating on both the London Midland and Scottish regions as late as the early 1990s. On 25th October 1981 No. 85001 passes Castlethorpe with the 09.50 Liverpool Lime Street – Euston.

Michael J. Collins

With its pantograph end leading, and the locomotive's 'A' side nearest the camera, No. 85028 passes Sandon between Stafford and Crewe with the 11.15 Euston – Manchester service on 20th June 1985.

John Tuffs

The final duties for the Class 85s were for the Railfreight sector, which took the machines to all parts of the 25kV electrified network, and indeed during 1988 members of the fleet traversed the North London Line connection to the ER with examples being recorded at Temple Mills and Stratford. On 4th June 1979 No. 85010 is seen struggling up Shap Bank at Greenholme with a 'Cartic' train bound for Scotland.

Colin J. Marsden

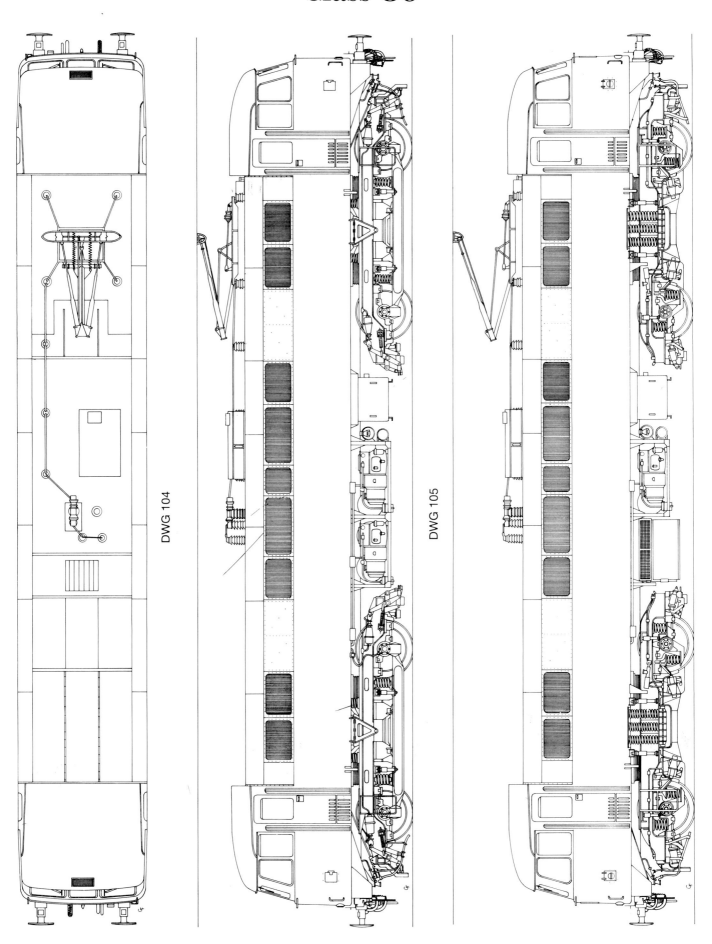

DWG 104

DWG 105

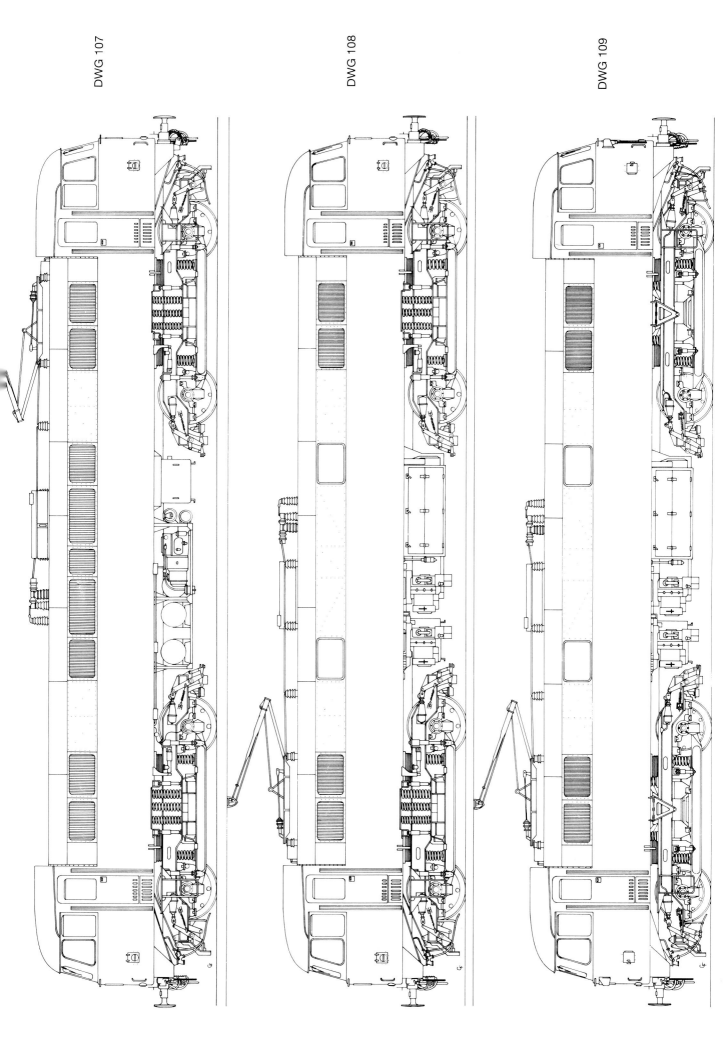

DWG 107

DWG 108

DWG 109

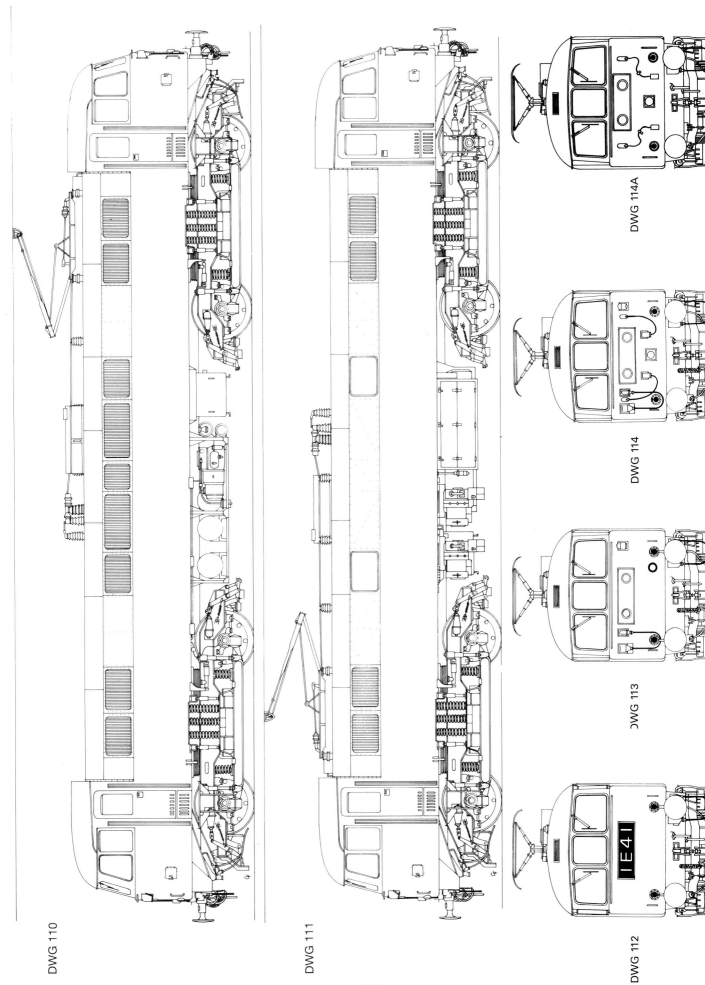

DWG 110

DWG 111

DWG 112

DWG 113

DWG 114

DWG 114A

DWG 104
Class 86 roof detail, No 1 end on left.

DWG 105
Class 86 side 'A' elevation, showing original as-built condition, drawing also applicable to Class 86/0. No. 1 end on left.

DWG 106
Class 86/1 side 'A' elevation, No. 1 end to left.

DWG 107
Class 86/2 side 'A' elevation, showing top hinged sand boxes. No. 1 end on left.

DWG 108
Class 86/2 side 'B' elevation, showing top hinged sand boxes. No. 1 end on right.

DWG 109
Class 86/3 side 'B' elevation, showing side hinged sand boxes. No. 1 end on right.

DWG 110
Class 86/4, 86/6 side 'A' elevation. No. 1 end on left.

DWG 111
Class 86/4 side 'B' elevation. No. 1 end on right.

DWG 112
Class 86 front end layout, showing original as built condition.

DWG 113
Class 86 front end layout, showing headcode box fitted with sealed beam marker lights, quartz headlight and multiple control jumpers.

DWG 114
Class 86 front end layout showing the style fitted with marker lights, central headlight, multiple control jumpers and Time Division Multiplex (TDM) equipment. Some locomotives now have conventional jumpers removed with blanking plates fitted.

DWG 114A
Class 86 front end, showing central high-intensity headlight and revised TDM jumpers.

Class	86/1	86/2	86/4	86/6 (86/5)†
Former Class Code	AL6	AL6	AL6	AL6
Number Range	86101-86103	86204-86261	86401-86439*	86601-86639*, 86501†
Former Number Range	Note: 1	Note: 1	Note: 1	Note: 1
Built by	EE Ltd	EE Ltd & BR Doncaster	EE Ltd & BR Doncaster	EE Ltd & BR Doncaster
Introduced (Note: 2)	As 86/1 1972	As 86/2 1972-75	As 86/4 1984-87	As 86/6 1990, 86/5 2000
Wheel Arrangement	Bo-Bo	Bo-Bo	Bo-Bo	Bo-Bo
Weight (operational)	87 tons	85 tons (Note: 3)	83 tons (Note: 3)	83 tons
Height - pan down	13ft 0⁹/₁₆in	13ft 0⁹/₁₆in	13ft 0⁹/₁₆in	13ft 0⁹/₁₆in
Width	8ft 8¼in	8ft 8¼in	8ft 8¼in	8ft 8¼in
Length	58ft 6in	58ft 6in	58ft 6in	58ft 6in
Min Curve negotiable	6 chains	6 chains	6 chains	6 chains
Maximum Speed	110mph	100mph (Note: 4)	100mph	75mph
Wheelbase	43ft 6in	43ft 6in	43ft 6in	43ft 6in
Bogie Wheelbase	10ft 9in	10ft 9in	10ft 9in	10ft 9in
Bogie Pivot Centres	32ft 9in	32ft 9in	32ft 9in	32ft 9in
Wheel Diameter	3ft 9¼in	3ft 9¼in	3ft 9¼in	3ft 9¼in
Brake Type (Note: 5)	Dual§	Dual§	Dual	Dual§ (86/5 Air)
Sanding Equipment	Pneumatic	Pneumatic	Pneumatic	Pneumatic
Heating Type	Electric - Index 74	Electric - Index 74	Electric - Index 74	Isolated
Route Availability	6	6	6	6
Coupling Restriction	TDM fitted	TDM fitted	TDM fitted	TDM fitted
Brake Force	40 tons	40 tons	40 tons	40 tons
Horsepower (continuous)	5,000hp	4,040hp	3,600hp	3,600hp
(maximum)	7,860hp	6,100hp	5,900hp	5,900hp
Tractive Effort (maximum)	58,000lb	46,500lb	58,000lb	58,000lb
Number of Traction Motors	4	4	4	4
Traction Motor Type	GEC G412AZ	AEI 282BZ	AEI 282AZ	AEI 282AZ
Control System	HT Tap Changing	HT Tap Changing	HT Tap Changing	HT Tap Changing
Gear Ratio	32:73	22:65	22:65	22:65, 86/5 - 18:70
Pantograph Type	Brecknell Willis	Brecknell Willis/AEI	Stone Faiveley/AEI	Stone Faiveley/AEI
Rectifier Type	Silicon Semi Conductor	Silicon Semi Conductor	Silicon Semi Conductor	Silicon Semi Conductor
Nominal Supply Voltage	25kV AC	25kV AC	25kV AC	25kV AC

*Not consecutive numbering
†Class 86/5 regeared Class 86/6 operated by Freightliner
§Many dual braked locomotives now have vacuum system removed

Note: 1 The Class 86 original numbers were E3101-E3200, renumbering was carried out at random, as modification work was effected.

Note: 2 The Class 86s were originally introduced in 1965-66.

Note: 3 A number of Class 86/2s and 86/4s have ballast weights which increase their weight by 1 ton.

Note: 4 Class 86/2s Nos 86209/24/25/31 were in the 1980s fitted with Brecknell Willis high speed pantographs, thus increasing the top speed to 110mph.

Note: 5 Locomotives fitted with rheostatic brake equipment.

The AL6 or Class 86 fleet of 100 ac locomotives represents the BRB's second generation of main-line electric traction. The order for the fleet was placed in 1963 for English Electric/AEI to supply power/control equipment, with mechanical construction divided between English Electric's Vulcan Foundry and the BR workshops at Doncaster.

The basic design for the fleet was based on the previous first generation types, but much of the internal equipment was revised, both to introduce new technology and to improve the layout. External body alterations included revision of the cab end design to incorporate a flat lower body panel, and raked back front screen section. The equipment side of the locomotive incorporated nine ventilation grilles, whilst the cab-to-cab walkway side was fitted with four grilles and two glazed windows.

As there was no intention to equip the AL6 fleet for dual voltage operation (6.25kV and 25kV), only one pantograph was fitted from new.

A total change from previous ac locomotive practice came in the traction equipment, which on this design consisted of axle hung traction motors. At the design stage it was considered these would give improved ride characteristics over the previously used frame-mounted type, but in practice this was far from the case. Unfortunately traction motor and bogie problems later led to serious bogie frame fractures and concern over track damage. To overcome such problems, 'Flexicoil' suspension was fitted on an experimental basis from the early 1970s, and subsequently to the entire fleet, as were SAB resilient wheelsets.

In the early 1970s, when consideration was being given to the next generation of ac traction, three Class 86s were rebuilt as Class 87 test-beds, being installed with Class 87-type bogies, incorporating fully spring-borne traction motors, as well as much revised electrical equipment.

When introduced, the AL6 design was painted in Electric blue livery with white cab roofs and window surrounds, the first few examples being devoid of yellow warning panels. Over the years the Electric blue gave way to corporate Rail blue with full yellow ends. After introduction of the various new business sectors, InterCity colours appeared in various guises, with the 'Swallow' livery being applied from 1988. Also in 1988, one locomotive, No. 86401, was painted in Network SouthEast livery, and another in a mock 1960s Electric blue scheme.

As the sectorisation of BR spread during the late 1980s and early 1990s, in advance of privatisation, further livery variations emerged, including Railfreight triple grey and Rail express systems red.

The area of operation of this fleet has changed considerably over the years. When first introduced, the class operated entirely on the West Coast Main Line, being allocated to Willesden. Their operating range first increased in the mid-1970s following electrification of the route north of Crewe to Glasgow. In the mid-1980s, after the East Anglia electrification was complete, Class 86s were deployed on Liverpool Street – Norwich duties, being allocated initially to Ilford and later to Norwich.

With the privatisation of the railway in the 1990s, the Class 86 fleet was split between the passenger and freight operators, with Virgin Trains having a sizeable allocation for West Coast and CrossCountry services, while Anglia Railways operate a fleet for Norwich – London services. On the freight side, locomotives are operated by EWS and Freightliner. All the private operators have repainted locomotives in their respective house colours and many have effected local modifications, such as the revised fire protection on Anglia locomotives.

Following various modification programmes, five sub-classes now exist within the Class 86 fleet:

86/1: test-bed locomotives for Class 87;
86/2: general passenger fleet fitted with Flexicoil suspension and GEC 282BZ traction motors;
86/4: locomotives operated by EWS for Royal Mail or charter traffic and fitted with Flexicoil suspension and GEC 282AZ traction motors;
86/5: a single locomotive operated by Freightliner, fitted with revised gearing;
86/6: locomotives used by Freightliner with electric train supply equipment isolated.

As with all main line classes, headlights have been fitted in recent years, and the redundant four-character route indicator boxes plated over or removed, being replaced by sealed-beam marker lights. During the mid-1980s, Time Division Multiplex (TDM) jumpers of the RCH style were fitted to most examples of the fleet, as were multiple-control jumpers to the Class 86/4 and 86/6 sub-classes, although from mid-1992 these were removed as the TDM system became more satisfactory.

Following resurrection of the railway naming policy in the 1970s, most Class 86s now carry a name, the majority being to the standard cast style.

By early 2001 only two members of the class had been withdrawn, both after receiving collision damage, and it is likely that Class 86s will remain in traffic for many years to come. However, their use on West Coast Main Line and CrossCountry passenger traffic is likely to cease around 2003-4, when new Class 220, 221 and 390 sets will have entered service.

Following the decision to order a large 'production' batch of 25kV locomotives for LM operation in 1964, constructional contracts were placed with both English Electric/Vulcan Foundry and the BR workshops at Doncaster to build a total of 100 locomotives. This view shows the main production line at Vulcan Foundry, with six locomotives in various stages of assembly.
Colin J Marsden

When the first batch of Class AL6 locomotives were released from Vulcan Foundry a number of major tests were carried out, including an investigation into wheel slip/slide problems as, when built, no such automatic correction equipment was fitted. No. E3161, without a yellow warning panel front end stands at Rugby in Summer 1965 during wheel slip/slide tests. Note the water hose pipes along the solebar and front of the locomotive used to induce wheel slip/slide.

GEC Traction

By the time the Class AL6 locomotives had been introduced into regular service the small yellow warning end had been adopted as standard, and applied to all new locomotives after August 1965. No. E3146 heads a long unfitted freight through Bletchley on 18th June 1966.

John Faulkner

With its No. 2 or pantograph end leading, No. E3193 passes Wembley station during early 1966 with a Euston – Manchester express service.

GEC Traction

Clearly displaying the underframe and bufferbeam equipment layout, No. E3136 is seen at the head of a Ford Motor Company car train bound for Halewood from the Ford works at Dagenham. This locomotive was one of the BR Doncaster built examples.

Colin J. Marsden

Another train operated by the Ford Motor Company between Dagenham and Halewood was a daily parts service, which was diesel hauled between Dagenham and Willesden, and electrically hauled forward. On 14th February 1967 No. E3185 slowly departs from Willesden with the northbound service.

Author's Collection

After the introduction of new electric operated Anglo-Scottish "Electric Scot" services from 1974 the Class 86 locomotives were used alongside the newly introduced Class 87s on the new fast InterCity services. On 9th February 1983 Class 86/2 No. 86257 *Snowdon* passes Grayrigg with the 07.23 Glasgow/07.06 Edinburgh – Birmingham service.

Colin J. Marsden

Following the abolition of four-character route indicator displays during the mid-1970s the Class 86s, in common with other types, had the equipment plated over, with two marker lights fitted in the former indicator position. On 27th March 1982 Class 86/2 No. 86251 *The Birmingham Post* approaches Nuneaton with a Manchester – Euston service.

Colin J. Marsden

After the electrification of the East Anglian lines to Ipswich and onto Norwich the Class 86s became stable power for these accelerated services. Sporting full InterCity livery, No. 86220 *The Round Tabler* stands at Colchester on 5th April 1990 with a Liverpool Street – Norwich working.

Colin J. Marsden

Showing InterCity livery, headlight, sealed-beam marker lights and TDM jumpers, (then) West Coast Class 86/2 No. 86212 *Preston Guild* stands at Manchester Piccadilly at the head of the 10.00 to Euston on 27th February 1990. Behind the locomotive is a DVT, which would usually be leading the train when heading in a southerly direction, but which could not be used due to a jumper problem. No. 86212 now operates on CrossCountry services.

Colin J. Marsden

Following privatisation of the rail industry, a sizeable number of Class 86/2s came under the operational banner of Virgin Trains, which undertook a major repainting operation from mid-1997. No. 86245 *Caledonian* arrives at Stoke-on-Trent station on 6th September 1999 with the CrossCountry 13.17 Manchester Piccadilly – Birmingham International.

Colin J. Marsden

EWS was not slow to apply its distinctive maroon and gold livery to its locomotives. The first to be repainted was No. 86261, seen from its pantograph end, equipment side at Bounds Green on 20th February 1997. This locomotive is used for Royal Mail or charter train workings.

Colin J. Marsden

It is quite amazing what a different livery does for a locomotive design; viewed from its pantograph end, equipment side, Class 86/2 No. 86218 *NHS 50* shows off the Anglia Railways turquoise colour scheme at Norwich. This operator has revised the fire protection arrangements, with tanks now being located on the roof at the non-pantograph end, while a cab ventilation grille is located in the former route indicator box.

Colin J. Marsden

Freightliner adopted an all-over dark green livery, offset by wraparound yellow ends, as its corporate livery under privatisation, with locomotive running numbers applied in full on front ends and the Freightliner name at roof height. Class 86/6 No. 86631 is shown at Crewe Basford Hall, the main centre for Freightliner operations.

Colin J. Marsden

Class 87

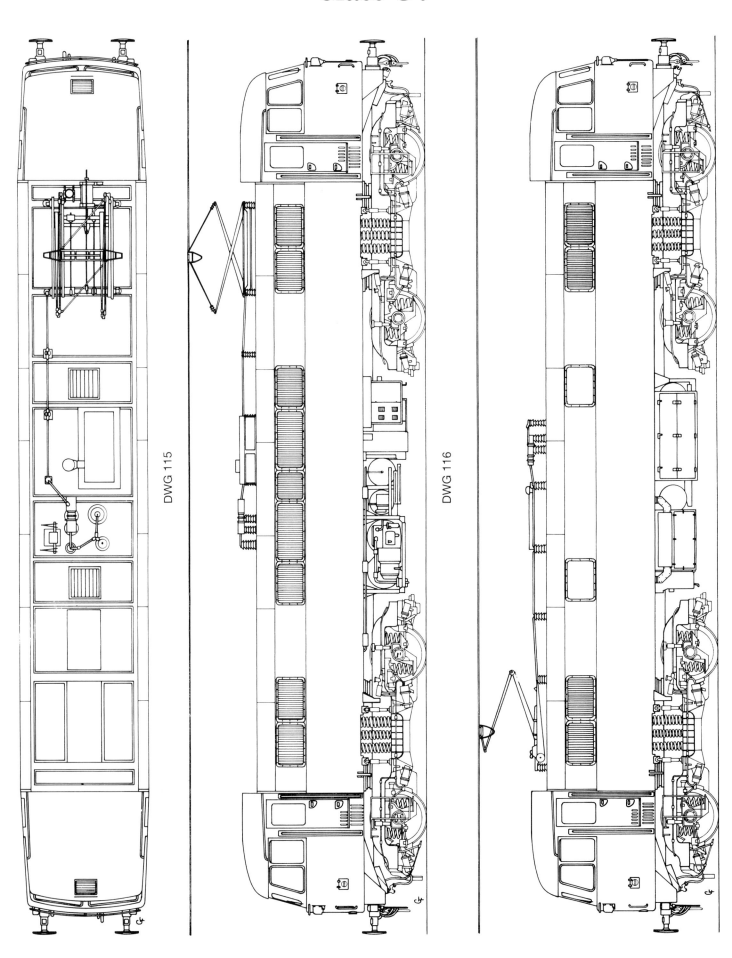

DWG 115

DWG 116

DWG 118

DWG 115
Class 87 roof detail, fitted with original cross arm pantograph. No. 1 end on left.

DWG 116
Class 87 side 'A' elevation, showing original cross arm pantograph. No. 1 end on left.

DWG 117
Class 87 side 'B' elevation, showing the Brecknell Willis High Speed pantograph. No. 1 end on right.

DWG 118
Class 87 front end layout, showing original layout.

DWG 119
Class 87 front end layout, showing Time Division Multiplex (TDM) jumpers.

DWG 119A
Class 87 front end layout, showing the removal of the jumper cable equipment.

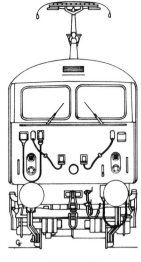

DWG 119

DWG 119A

Class	87/0	87/1
Number Range	87001-87035	87101
Built by	BREL Crewe	BREL Crewe
Introduced	1973-74	1977
Wheel Arrangement	Bo-Bo	Bo-Bo
Weight	83 tons	79 tons
Height - pan down	13ft 1¼in	13ft 1¼in
Width	8ft 8¼in	8ft 8¼in
Length	58ft 6in	58ft 6in
Min Curve negotiable	4 chains	4 chains
Maximum Speed	110mph	75mph
Wheelbase	43ft 6⅛in	43ft 6⅛in
Bogie Wheelbase	10ft 9⅛in	10ft 9⅛ in
Bogie Pivot Centres	32ft 9in	32ft 9in
Wheel Diameter	3ft 9½in	3ft 9½in
Brake Type	Air	Air
Sanding Equipment	Pneumatic	Pneumatic
Heating Type	Electric - Index 95	Isolated
Route Availability	6	6
Coupling Restriction	TDM fitted	TDM fitted
Brake Force	40 tons	40 tons
Horsepower (continuous)	5,000hp	4,850hp
(maximum)	7,860hp	7,250hp
Tractive Effort (maximum)	58,000lb	58,000lb
Number of Traction Motors	4	4
Traction Motor Type	GEC G412AZ	GEC G412BZ
Control System	HT Tap Changing	Thyristor
Gear Ratio	32:73	32:73
Pantograph Type	Brecknell Willis HS	Brecknell Willis HS
Nominal Supply Voltage	25kV ac	25kV ac

The Class 87 fleet was ordered following the authorisation for electrification of the West Coast Main Line north from Weaver Junction to Glasgow, as the existing fleets of ac electric locomotives, dating from the late 1950s and 1960s, would be insufficient for the new scheme. A batch of 36 locomotives was ordered, classified Class 87, and numbered in the TOPS 87xxx series.

Power and control equipment was supplied by GEC Traction, while mechanical construction was effected by BREL Crewe Works. The physical appearance of the fleet closely resembled the previous types, but this breed had only two front windscreens in place of the time-honoured three. Sealed-beam headlights and marker lights were installed from new. A major departure from previous designs was the use of Flexicoil suspension and frame-mounted traction motors.

The mechanical portion consisted of a fabricated underframe onto which the body was assembled, the upper section of the body and roof being arranged as a removable unit to assist with maintenance. The two body sides were of completely different designs, one having an almost complete bank of air louvres, while

the other had two glazed windows and four louvred panels. With the spread of modern technology, the Class 87 fleet was built with air brake only equipment, although this did preclude operators from obtaining maximum availability from the class when first introduced, as much vacuum-braked stock was still in service. The Class 87s were – and still are – allocated to Willesden electric depot, except No. 87101 which stayed at Crewe for freight operations.

Power collection for the Class 87 fleet was originally by means of one GEC crossed-arm pantograph, but by the mid-1980s these had been replaced by Brecknell Willis high-speed units permitting speeds of up to 110mph.

When introduced in 1973/4 the fleet was painted in conventional Rail blue livery with full yellow ends. This remained as standard until 1984, when various livery experiments were carried out, resulting in the development of the InterCity and Main Line liveries of the late 1980s and 1990s. Soon after the fleet was built, the BR locomotive naming policy was revived, and the Class 87s became some of the first recipients.

The 35 passenger locomotives based at Willesden have been responsible for long-distance passenger services on the WCML, operated until privatisation under the InterCity banner and subsequently by Virgin Trains. Under Virgin operation the entire fleet of Class 87/0s has been repainted in VT red livery.

The final locomotive of the build, allocated No. 87036, was constructed by GEC/BR as a test-bed for the use of thyristors in traction control systems. Due to the many differences on this locomotive, it was decided to number it as a separate sub-class as 87101, to avoid confusion with conventional locomotives. After its release into service No. 87101 was the subject of extensive testing to ascertain the benefits of the installation of modern electronics in traction systems. Much of the data obtained paved the way for the application of GEC thyristor control principles for Class 90 and 91 locomotives. Once its useful life as a development locomotive was over, it commenced operation for the Railfreight business. Upon privatisation it became the property of EWS, which retired the locomotive from use, and at the time of writing in early 2001, it remains stored at Crewe.

Very few structural alterations have taken place since this fleet was introduced, the most noticeable being the installation of RCH-style nose end jumpers used for TDM control, and the removal of the original multiple-unit control boxes.

Following the introduction of the Class 87 electric locomotives, designed principally for Anglo-Scottish services, the majority of long-distance LM/ScR passenger duties have been so hauled. After heavy overnight snow, No. 87013 *John O' Gaunt* heads the 09.37 Carlisle – Euston past Grayrigg on 9th February 1983.

Colin J. Marsden

When introduced the Class 87 locomotives were fitted with a GEC 'X' arm pantograph, however following the decision to increase the LM line speeds over selected routes to 110mph the pantographs have been replaced by the Brecknell Willis High Speed type. Still with an 'X' arm pantograph No. 87017 *Iron Duke* passes Marston Green on 21st October 1984 with the 11.18 Wolverhampton – Euston service.

Michael J. Collins

On a number of occasions members of the Class 87 fleet have been used to haul the Royal Train, this including the Royal inaugural special when the new ''Electric Scot'' service was introduced. On 20th June 1977 No. 87004 (later named *Britannia*) sets off from Carnforth with stock off a Royal Train working.

Martin Welch

The Class 87 fleet were some of the first locomotives to benefit from the revised naming policy of the mid-1970s, and indeed some locomotives have been renamed over the ensuing years. The former *Redgauntlet*, No. 87026, was renamed *Sir Richard Arkwright* in a special ceremony at Preston on 12th October 1982. In this view the locomotive is seen awaiting the special unveiling ceremony.

John Tuffs

From their introduction until 1984 the Class 87 fleet were painted in conventional rail blue livery, however with the introduction of new operating businesses separate livery identities were introduced. In connection with these new liveries Class 87s Nos 87006 and 87012 were repainted in experimental schemes, No. 87006 *City of Glasgow* in all over grey, and No. 87012 *Coeur de Lion* in what is now known as InterCity livery. Both locomotives were repainted by Willesden depot where these illustrations were taken on 11th May 1984.

Both: Colin J. Marsden

Before the introduction of CEM maintenance the only location to carry out major repairs to the Class 87 fleet was BREL Crewe Works, However today, most of the classified overhauls are performed by Glasgow Springburn Works, which follows a short period when overhauls were undertaken at Stratford Major Depot. On 19th February 1991 No. 87032 *Kenilworth* poses inside Springburn Works during a classified repair.

Colin J. Marsden

When painted in their distinctive InterCity livery, hauling a rake of similarly liveried stock the Class 87s look extremely smart. Sporting TDM and multiple control jumpers, No. 87020, named *North Briton*, passes Clifton, near Penrith on 29th March 1990 with the 15.15 Edinburgh – Paddington.

Colin J. Marsden

The final member of the Class 87 build, classified as 87/1 and allocated the number 87101, was the testbed for advanced state-of-the-art traction equipments being developed during the 1970s. The machine is seen here coupled to a M&EE test car wired for a test programme in June 1975.

BR

In an early guise of InterCity livery, with its nameplate bi-secting the white body side band, No. 87006 *City of Glasgow*, departs from Euston on 25th September 1985 with the 09.45 Euston – Glasgow service.

Colin J. Marsden

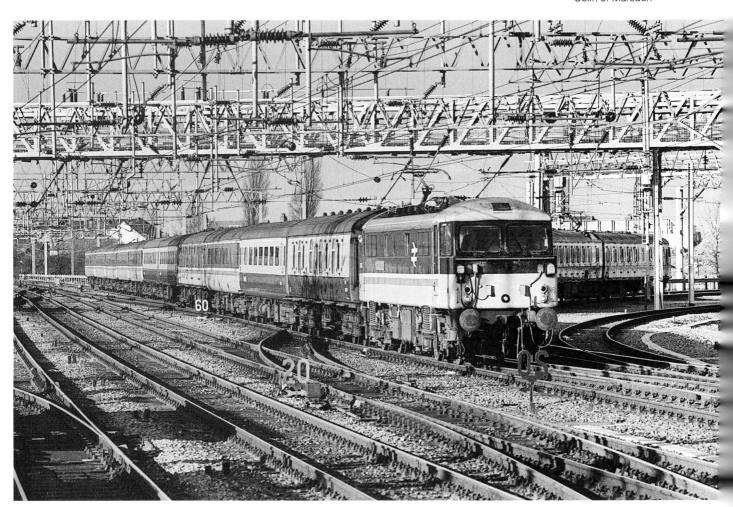

During the period of livery transition, which was a protracted affair, formations of mixed livery coaching stock were a regular sight. InterCity No. 87024 *Lord of the Isles* is seen approaching Crewe on 12th February 1988 with a mixture of InterCity and blue/grey liveried vehicles forming the 13.30 Lancaster – Euston.

Colin J. Marsden

The sole example of Class 87/1, No. 87101 *Stephenson*, stands inside Crewe electric depot, painted in Railfreight livery. Alongside the Class 87/1 is Class 86/6 No. 86602. After this picture was taken, No. 87101 was returned to original rail blue livery and ran thus for a short time before being stored.

Colin J. Marsden

Showing standard InterCity 'Swallow' livery, adopted from 1987, InterCity's 21st anniversary, No. 87026 *Sir Richard Arkwright* stands under the overall roof at Glasgow Central station on 4th June 1996 after arriving with the overnight sleeping car train from London.

Colin J. Marsden

Following Virgin Trains' takeover of the West Coast franchise, the company's red livery was applied rapidly to passenger stock and locomotives. Viewed from its corridor side, No. 87016 *Willesden Intercity Depot* passes Wolverton on 13th September 1999 with the 10.35 Euston – Glasgow Central.

Colin J. Marsden

Class 89

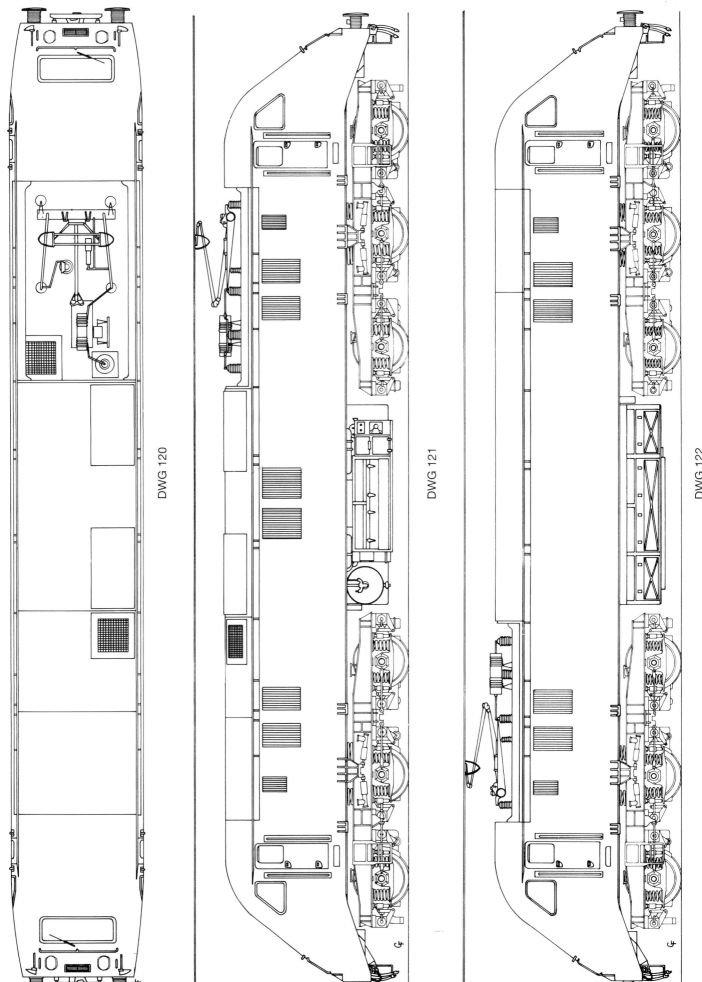

DWG 120

DWG 121

DWG 122

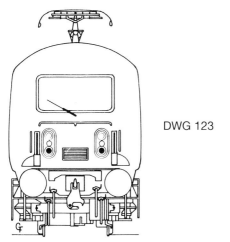

DWG 123

DWG 120
Class 89 roof detail, No. 1 end on right. Drawing shows original buffer design.

DWG 121
Class 89 side 'B' elevation. No. 1 end on right.

DWG 122
Class 89 side 'A' elevation. No. 1 end on left.

DWG 123
Class 89 front end detail.

Class	89	Wheel Diameter	3ft 6¹/₂in
Number	89001	Brake Type	Air
Built by	BREL Crewe & Brush Ltd	Heating Type	Electric - Index 95
Introduced	1987	Route Availability	6
Wheel Arrangement	Co-Co	Coupling Restriction	TDM fitted
Weight	105 tons	Brake Force	50 tons
Height – pan down	13ft 0¹/₂in	Horsepower (continuous)	5,850hp
Width	8ft 11¹/₂in	(maximum)	7,860hp
Length	64ft 11in	Tractive Effort (maximum)	46,100lb
Min Curve negotiable	4 chains	Traction Motor Type	Brush TM 2201A
Maximum Speed	110mph*	Control System	Thyristor
Wheelbase	49ft 6¹/₂in	Pantograph Type	Brecknell Willis HS
Bogie Wheelbase	14ft 5in	Nominal Supply Voltage	25kV ac
Bogie Pivot Centres	35ft 9¹/₄in		

*Designed for 125mph running.

The first electric locomotive to take to the rails with a basic design that was totally different from that of the 1960 BTC modernisation fleets was the prototype Class 89. This class of just one locomotive, No. 89001, was constructed in 1985-87 at BREL Crewe, which acted as a sub-contractor to Brush Traction. The locomotive incorporated advanced traction equipment supplied by Brush Electrical Machines of Loughborough.

The design of the Class 89 was a complete break from previous 25kV ac electric types, featuring a Co-Co wheel arrangement and incorporating streamlined body ends reminiscent of the prototype Class 41 HSDT power cars. The locomotive was constructed as a 'production' demonstrator, with a rating of 5,850hp, which, at the time of its build, made it the most powerful electric locomotive in the UK. Whilst its design was primarily for the high-speed (200km/h) passenger market, the machine had good operating characteristics for slower freight duties. In having the Co-Co bogie arrangement it provided 50 per cent better tractive effort than rival Bo-Bo designs. This tractive effort would have eliminated the need for double heading of many freight services over arduous inclines, but BR engineers still favoured the Bo-Bo configuration, mainly for reasons of dynamic track force.

After construction by BREL Crewe the Class 89 was despatched by rail to Derby, from where it was moved by road to Brush for exhaustive electrical testing. After return to BR tracks the locomotive went back to BREL Crewe, where several modifications were carried out. In mid-1987 No. 89001 was transferred to the Derby-based Engineering Development Unit (EDU), where pantograph, electrical and structural tests took place, as well as the usual 'type tests' carried out on all new designs. In the case of the Class 89, these were effected on the Old Dalby test track. As this line was not at the time electrified, traction was provided by a Class 47 diesel, which propelled the locomotive and test coaches to evaluate high-speed running. After acceptance by BR for mainline trials, the locomotive was temporarily allocated to Crewe Electric depot, from where trials, both north over Shap and southwards to Willesden, were conducted. The performance of the locomotive soon proved to be highly successful.

By October 1987 No. 89001 had clocked up some 10,000 miles of trial running, many of which were at the head of the BREL International demonstration train which was undergoing tests on the WCML at the time. However, due to gauge restrictions, the Class 89 was not permitted to enter Euston. From the end of 1987 the locomotive was transferred to the East Coast Main Line (ECML), being allocated to Hornsey and later Bounds Green, from where driver training was conducted in readiness for ECML electric services. No. 89001 was used on the ECML until May 1988. It was then sent to Derby for preparation prior to being sent together with a Class 90 and 91 to Hamburg for exhibition purposes. After returning to the UK No. 89001 resumed ECML operations, working alongside the Class 91 fleet until 1990, when, due to technical defects, the locomotive was taken out of service and stored at Bounds Green. No. 89001 was finally withdrawn by BR in July 1992, and 'preserved' at the Midland Railway Centre, Butterley.

The folly of such a modern and serviceable locomotive being preserved when the rail industry was short of electric traction was not lost on train operator Great North Eastern Railway, which purchased the machine from its preservationist owners with the aim of returning it to service on the ECML. After spending a long period at Brush, where much new and updated equipment was installed, No. 89001, now painted in GNER blue and red livery, returned to Bounds Green.

To minimise the need for driver training, it was agreed that No. 89001 would operate a fixed diagram on the King's Cross – Leeds/Bradford route in place of a Class 91. Sadly, after a relatively short period, No. 89001 was again in technical trouble with bogie traction faults which required it to be at the Brush works in Loughborough for much of the time between autumn 1999 and autumn 2000. The locomotive did return to service in late summer 2000 only to encounter further problems. GNER has, however, confirmed its intention to return No. 89001 to front-line service.

The cab layout of the Class 89 was totally different from that of any previous ac type, with a deep wrap-round desk incorporating easy-to-observe dials and thoughtfully positioned controls. One novel feature included on the Class 89 was a speed selector switch, whereby the driver could pre-select a required road speed, open the power controller to the 'full' position and let the locomotive's electronics do the rest, regulating the speed to the required figure. This feature worked in both acceleration and deceleration modes. Speed selection equipment was subsequently installed on locomotives of Classes 90 and 91.

The Class 89 was fitted from new with conventional Electric Train Supply (ETS) equipment, buckeye couplers (for the first time on an ac locomotive), and air and rheostatic (locomotive) braking.

When built, No. 89001 was finished in an early version of InterCity livery, later amended to the 1989 scheme. During early 1989 at King's Cross, No. 89001 was named *Avocet* (in recognition of the Royal Society for the Protection of Birds) by the then Prime Minister, Margaret Thatcher. As mentioned above, No. 89001 now displays full GNER livery.

After being the subject of much trial and performance tests the Brush Class 89 was used by BR as part of its exhibit at the 1988 International Rail Exhibition in Hamburg. No. 89001, together with Class 90 No. 90008 and Class 91 No. 91003, stand in the yard of the Railway Technical Centre while being prepared for their visit to Germany.

Colin J. Marsden

Following the return of the Class 89 from Hamburg the locomotive was returned to Bounds Green, from where it commenced operation on the ECML, working with a converted DVT and IC125 formation. One of its regular duties was the 07.18 Peterborough – King's Cross, seen here on 30th August 1988 passing Arlesey near Biggleswade.

Brian Morrison

Whilst working on the ECML the regular northbound commuter service between King's Cross and Peterborough was the 17.36 departure from London, seen here on 10th August 1988 near Welham Green.

Brian Morrison

When the Class 89 emerged from BREL Crewe in 1986 it was fitted with a new design cab layout, not previously seen on a British electric locomotive. This illustration shows the general layout of the No. 2 end cab.

Michael J. Collins

During No. 89001's period of operation on the East Coast Main Line in the late 1980s, its regular workings consisted of commuter services between King's Cross and Peterborough. On 17th February 1989, in full InterCity 'Swallow' livery, it awaits departure from King's Cross with the 17.36 to Peterborough, while HST power cars 43197, 43074 and 43121 make ready for departures to more northerly destinations.

Colin J. Marsden

Although now owned by GNER, the Class 89 still receives any major technical maintenance at the Brush Works in Loughborough. It is seen here receiving bogie and electrical attention in the main erecting shop in the company of a Class 37/6 and a Class 47 on 16th December 1999.

Colin J. Marsden

In its latest guise, with gold GNER letters, the sole Class 89 awaits departure from King's Cross on 9th July 2000 with the 15.40 to Leeds.

Darren Ford

On 10th June 1999, shortly after its return to traffic from preservation, No. 89001 stands at Leeds sporting a white GNER logo with the 09.05 service from King's Cross. On the left is an InterCity 'Swallow'-liveried IC125 operating a Virgin CrossCountry service.

Colin J. Marsden

Class 90

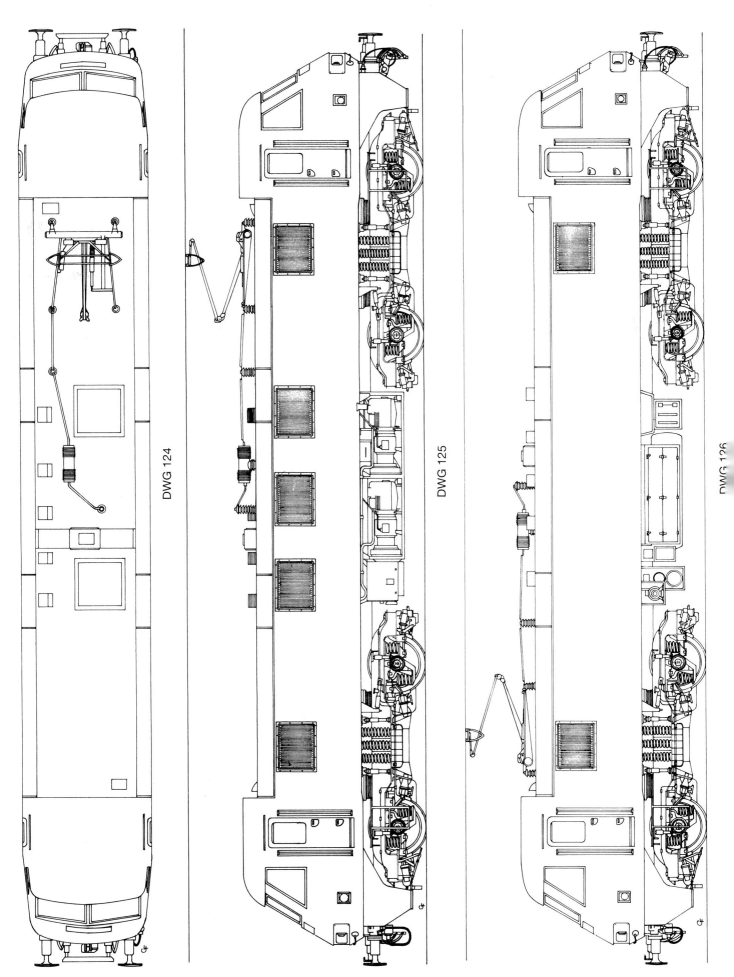

DWG 124

DWG 125

DWG 126

116

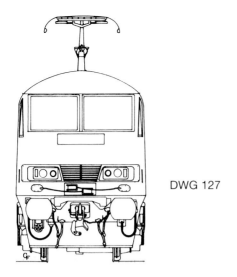
DWG 127

DWG 124
Class 90 roof detail. No. 1 end on right.

DWG 125
Class 90 side 'B' elevation. No. 1 end on right.

DWG 126
Class 90 side 'A' elevation. No. 1 end on left.

DWG 127
Class 90 front end detail fitted with buck-eye coupling and rubbing plate.

Class		90
Number Range	90/0	90001-90040
	90/1	90141-90150
	90/2	90221-90239
Built by		BREL Crewe
Introduced		1987-88
Wheel Arrangement		Bo-Bo
Weight		85 tons
Height - pan down		13ft 0¼in
Width		9ft
Length		61ft 6in
Min Curve negotiable		4 chains
Maximum Speed		110mph
Wheelbase		43ft 6in
Bogie Wheelbase		10ft 9in
Bogie Pivot Centres		32ft 9in
Wheel Diameter		3ft 9½ in
Brake Type		Air (Rheostatic)
Sanding Equipment		Pneumatic
Heating Type		Electric - Index 95
Route Availability		7

Coupling Restriction	TDM fitted
Brake Force	40 tons
Horsepower (continuous)	5,000hp
(maximum)	7,860hp
Tractive Effort (maximum)	43,150lb
Number of Traction Motors	4
Traction Motor Type	GEC 412 BZ
Control System	Thyristor
Gear Ratio	32:73
Pantograph Type	Brecknell Willis HS
Nominal Supply Voltage	25kV ac

Class 90/0 (90001-20/26/28-32/34-37/40): Basic locomotive, authorised for 110mph operation if operated by Virgin or 100mph if operated by EWS.

Class 90/1 (90141-90150): ETS isolated, operated by Freightliner, 90mph.

Class 90/2 (90221-25/27/33/38/39): EWS-owned locomotives, authorised for 110mph operation for use on Royal Mail and ScotRail sleeper operations.

By the mid-1980s BR was seeking new generation electric locomotives for its WCML services, and Government authorisation was sought for a fleet of 50 thyristor controlled state-of-the-art locomotives in 1984. Permission for the build was eventually granted, with construction awarded to BREL Crewe Works, the main equipment sub-contractor being GEC Traction. The locomotives were to be classified 87/2.

The fleet represented a break from previous 25kV ac designs in having steeply raked back cab ends, and, for the first time on a production locomotive type, were fitted with Time Division Multiplex (TDM) multiple-control equipment.

Construction at BREL Crewe commenced in late 1986, with the first locomotive being shown off to the public at a July 1987 open day; numbered 90001, it was not, however, finished until September 1987. During the course of construction the classification was changed from Class 87/2 to 90 as the new product showed virtually no physical or technical resemblance to the earlier build. After completion at Crewe, the first locomotive was transferred to the Railway Technical Centre, Derby, for a major 'type test' programme.

Delivery of the 50 locomotives was a protracted affair, with the final locomotive not being handed over until the end of 1990. The Class 90s were designed for mixed-traffic (passenger or freight) operation. The batch allocated to InterCity was first off the production line, and, once tests had been completed and sufficient stock fitted with TDM had been introduced (together with Driving Van Trailers – DVTs), the locomotives commenced operation on Euston – Birmingham/North West and Anglo-Scottish duties, working in push-pull mode.

Subsequent Class 90s were constructed for the then Railfreight Distribution (RfD) business for use on high-speed long-distance block freight services. By 1992 the allocation of the class was again amended, with a handful dedicated to operating mail and postal services under the Rail express systems (Res) banner.

After the splitting of the railway into businesses prior to privatisation, most of the Class 90s funded by Railfreight were reclassified as Class 90/1, to identify the isolation of their ETS equipment; they were renumbered in the 901xx series. This left InterCity Class 90s Nos 90001-015 allocated to Willesden for passenger work, with the remainder, Nos 90016-025/126-150, based at Crewe for freight work. In the immediate pre-privatisation period in the mid-1990s, the freight locomotives were again split, with Nos 90016-025/126-140 going to Railfreight and 90141-150 to Freightliner. Under the big sell-off, the Railfreight locomotives became the property of EWS and the Freightliner locomotives of the management-owned Freightliner Ltd. Some further renumbering was carried out to return the EWS locomotives to the 900xx series. In very recent times this has been further amended, with 110mph EWS locomotives classified as 90/2 and standard locomotives as 90/0.

During 1990, by which time the ECML was fully electrified, the Class 90s started to appear on some mainline duties from King's Cross, mainly deputising for unavailable Class 91s. From the commencement of the winter timetable in 1991, the class was rostered for ECML services, while, from the commencement of the Summer 1992 timetable, the Res-owned locomotives started to operate van workings over the full length of the ECML.

Even now, in 2001, Class 90s are still seen on the ECML, usually operating on a hire basis to GNER from EWS due to a serious shortfall in the former company's own locomotives.

The Freightliner-owned locomotives have a wide operating range, throughout the WCML and into Essex on block container traffic.

A major feature of the Class 90s from new was the installation of drop-head buckeye couplers with retractable side buffers – essential for high-speed push-pull operation. Although all locomotives were built with this feature, those now operated by EWS and Freightliner have had the equipment removed and many have had the ETS equipment isolated.

When constructed, the first 25 Class 90s received full InterCity livery, with the next 11 emerging in Main Line livery and the final 14 in RfD colours. Following the introduction of the Res red livery, the five locomotives operated by this business were repainted into these house colours. Today the standard livery for passenger locomotives is Virgin red; EWS locomotives are currently in RfD grey, Res red or EWS maroon, while Freightliner locomotives retain grey with Freightliner branding. One odd machine of the fleet is No. 90224, owned by EWS but painted in GNER blue for hire purposes.

The construction contract for the Class 90 build was awarded to BREL Crewe, with the chief sub-contractor being GEC Traction. The first complete Class 90 was finished at Crewe during October 1987, with the various assembly shops effecting the remainder of the build over the next two years. This view of the main shop taken on 12th February 1988 shows locomotive No. 90005 undergoing static tests prior to operating on the main line for the first time.

Colin J. Marsden

Prior to the first Class 90 emerging from Crewe, the classification given to the Class was 87/2, however as these locomotives bore little physical or technical resemblance to the Class 87 fleet it was decided to allocate a different class designation. Prototype locomotive No. 90001 is seen in the advance stages of construction in Summer 1987.

Colin J. Marsden

After completion at BREL Crewe, No. 90001 was transferred to the Engineering Development Unit (EDU) of the Railway Technical Centre, Derby where virtually every item of equipment was placed under a type test procedure. No. 90001 is seen inside the EDU whilst being prepared for an active test programme.

Colin J. Marsden

Throughout early 1988 the Class 90 locomotives were engaged in a major driver training programme involving several hundred staff. One of the driver training runs for Crewe based drivers is seen departing from Crewe on 16th February 1988 behind No. 90003 bound for Carlisle.

John Tuffs

On 29th March 1990, InterCity owned No. 90003 passes near the village of Clifton, south of Penrith with the 10.25 Inverness – Euston service, which the Class 90 would have worked forward from Glasgow.

Colin J. Marsden

Again carrying InterCity livery, No. 90024, which is now owned by Railfreight, but in 1992 was still maintained to main line passenger standards hurries down Hest Bank on 28th March 1990 with the 15.15 Edinburgh – Paddington service. The class 90 would be replaced by a Class 47 diesel forward from Birmingham New Street.

Colin J. Marsden

In far from ideal photographic conditions No. 90006 races through Warrington Bank Quay station on 6th October 1988 with a southbound driver training special.

Brian Morrison

Following the introduction of the Rail express system trading title from October 1991, the new business identity of red and grey, off-set by light blue bands was applied to some traction owned by the business. The first Class 90 to carry the colours was No. 90020, which was named *Colonel Bill Cockburn CBE TD*, and is shown here at Crewe.

Colin J. Marsden

On 30th March 1990, main line liveried Class 90 No. 90033, now renumbered to 90133 starts the climb of Hest Bank with the 07.20 Penzance – Glasgow/ Edinburgh service. This locomotive is now painted in RfD colours.

Colin J. Marsden

For a short period in Spring 1990, Class 90s could be found at the head of coal trains on the East Anglia main line, while driver training on the traction between Ilford and Ipswich was being carried out. On 5th April 1990, No. 90028 hurries towards Colchester with the 14.00 Ipswich – Ilford training special.

Colin J. Marsden

With the last three digits of its number 145 on the front end, Class 90/1 No. 90145 in RfD livery passes Plumpton, north of Penrith on 17th September 1992, with a daily Crewe Basford Hall – Mossend freight.

Colin J. Marsden

Displaying full InterCity 'Swallow' livery, Class 90/0 No. 90019 *Penny Black* stands at Carlisle on 6th September 1991 with the 'First Post' private charter bound for Euston. The train, formed of a Land Cruise charter set, was hired by The Post Office in connection with the naming of a TPO vehicle *The Borders Mail* at Carlisle.

Colin J. Marsden

In immaculate ex works condition, RfD-operated Class 90/1 No. 90126 *Crewe International Electric Maintenance Depot* stands inside the wheel lathe shop at Crewe depot on 18th October 1994 — just three days after it was named at an open day held at the depot. As the Class 90/1s lost their buckeye couplers and Pullman rubbing plates, standard oval buffers have been applied. This locomotive was later renumbered 90026.

Colin J. Marsden

Three Class 90s were painted in international liveries to emphasise the close ties between the UK railways and those in France, Belgium and Germany. The liveries were unveiled at the Freightconnection exhibition held in September 1992. Here the DB-liveried locomotive, No. 90029 *Frachtverbindungen*, stands inside Polmadie depot with a rake of ScotRail-operated sleeper stock. On the right is sister locomotive No. 90027.

Colin J. Marsden

The Class 90s now owned and operated by EWS are emerging painted in its house colours of maroon and gold, offset by a narrow reflective yellow 'safety' band at the base of the body, and yellow warning ends. No. 90031 is shown from its pantograph end.

Colin J. Marsden

The first Class 90 to be painted in Virgin Trains livery was No. 90002, which was used in the high-profile launch of Virgin Trains' takeover of the West Coast franchise on 10th February 1997. The locomotive was named *Mission: Impossible*, using standard cast nameplates. The locomotive is seen on its maiden run at Manchester Piccadilly; note that the buffers are in the retracted position and that the buckeye coupling is in the raised position.

Colin J. Marsden

Class 91

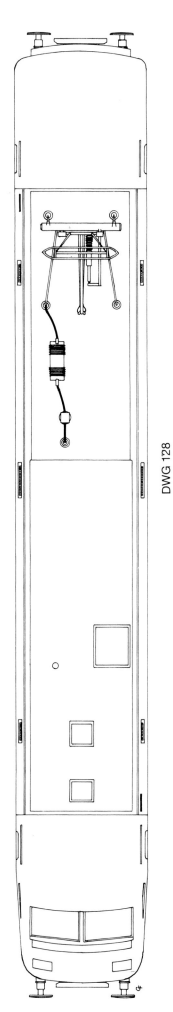

DWG 128

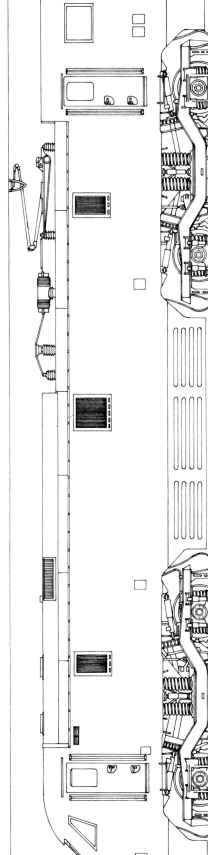

DWG 129

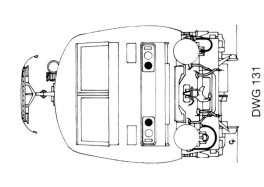

DWG 131

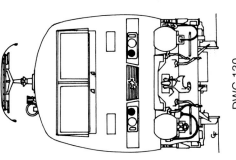

DWG 130

DWG 128
Class 91 roof detail. No. 1 end on left.

DWG 129
Class 91 side elevation. No. 1 end on left.

DWG 130
Class 91 front end detail of No. 1 (raked) end.

DWG 131
Class 91 front end detail of No. 2 (slab) end.

Class		91
Number	91/0	91001-91031
	91/1	91101-91131
Built by		BREL Crewe & GEC-TPL
Introduced		1988-91
Wheel Arrangement		Bo-Bo
Weight		80 tons
Height - pan down		12ft 4in
Width		9ft
Length		63ft 8in
Min Curve negotiable		4 Chains
Maximum Speed		140mph*
Wheelbase		45ft 4½in
Bogie Wheelbase		10ft 11⅞in
Bogie Pivot Centres		34ft 5½in
Wheel Diameter		3ft 3½in

Brake Type	Air (Rheostatic)
Sanding Equipment	Pneumatic
Heating Type	Electric - Index 95
Route Availability	7
Coupling Restriction	TDM fitted
Brake Force	45 tons
Horsepower (continuous)	6,090hp
(maximum)	6,300hp
Traction Motor Type	GEC G426AZ
Control System	Thyristor
Gear Ratio	1 74:1
Pantograph Type	Brecknell Willis HS
Nominal Supply Voltage	25kV ac

*Restricted to 125mph running until full ATP introduced

In 1984, by which time the APT project had virtually been abandoned, the design and indeed implementation of new locomotives and rolling stock for the WCML became of prime importance to the business directors. Thus was born the idea of InterCity 225; each set would consist of a single power car (with cab at each end), a rake of trailer vehicles and a Driving Van Trailer (DVT). Potential builders were invited to prequalify for 'approximately' 25 train sets in the autumn of 1984. Amongst strict guidelines was the requirement that the 'locomotive' should have the ability to haul express passenger services by day and lower-speed sleeper or Freightliner trains by night.

Also towards the autumn of 1984 came authorisation for East Coast Main Line (ECML) electrification. Originally the Class 89 Co-Co design (then under development) was to be used on this line, but soon the InterCity team decided to opt for the IC225 principle for this route, and by early 1985 the IC225 team was formed as an ECML project. By April 1985, under the competitive tendering policy, three firms were invited to submit building tenders – ASEA of Sweden, Brush and GEC Transportation Projects (GEC-TPL). After much deliberation the contract was placed with GEC in February 1986. GEC-TPL was given the complete design, build and test brief, although it sub-contracted mechanical construction to BREL Ltd at Crewe. Under BR's numerical classification the locomotives for this project became Class 91.

Following signing of the contract in February 1986 it was announced that the first locomotive would be rolled out on 14th February 1988 – in just two years. After this announcement the design and construction went full speed ahead, and, despite many problems encountered during construction, the St Valentine's Day roll-out date was met. Many new and novel design features were incorporated in the Class 91, including provision of a streamlined or raked back No. 1 end for high-speed operation, and a slab-fronted No. 2 end for slower-speed operation. One of the most significant changes on this class was in the design of bogie and traction equipment, incorporating frame-mounted traction motors driving an axle-mounted gearbox via a Carden shaft. The disc brake unit is 'off wheel' and fitted on the rear of the traction motor. The Class 91 also incorporated the latest state-of-the-art computer-based electronics for power and brake control.

In common with all new high-speed locomotives, buckeye couplers were fitted, as well as a Time Division Multiplex (TDM) system for remote control from DVT stock.

After the GEC-TPL/BREL Ltd roll-out on 14th February 1988, No. 91001 commenced a series of tests, first from Crewe and then at the Railway Technical Centre, Derby. By late March, No. 91001 was delivered to Bounds Green on the ECML, where test running and training commenced. Due to the protracted deliveries of the purpose-built DVT vehicles, several IC125 (HST) power cars were adapted for TDM operation, and a limited passenger service headed by Class 91s commenced in October 1989. Full use of Class 91s did not begin until 1992.

The initial build of Class 91s was for just 10 locomotives, which were introduced for evaluation running. After many thousands of hours' running, the manufacturers and the BRB then commenced construction of the remaining 21 to make a fleet size of 31. The final locomotive was completed at Crewe in February 1991.

The Class 91s have remained the backbone of the East Coast electrified route, working all non-HST services on the King's Cross – Leeds, Newcastle, Edinburgh and Glasgow corridor. From privatisation the fleet became owned by HSBC Rail and remained hired to the East Coast operator, Great North Eastern Railway. Soon the latter's dark blue and red livery was applied, replacing the original InterCity 'Swallow' colours.

Under their original ownership several locomotives were named, including No. 91029 *Queen Elizabeth II*. Under GNER, names were removed; following concern expressed by public and staff alike, names have been returned, but only in the form of vinyl transfers.

In 2000, major refurbishment of the Class 91s commenced at Adtranz Bombardier Doncaster, with internal equipment being overhauled by Alstom. The work comprised a package of reliability modifications, plus a redesign of the leading cab interior, giving the driver more information and improving his working conditions. Modified locomotives have been renumbered in the Class 91/1 sub-class, retaining the last two digits of their original numbers.

Left: Although constructed at BREL Ltd Crewe works, the Class 91 construction contract was awarded to GEC, who sub-contracted BREL to build the mechanical portion. In September 1990 the body shell of No. 91025 is seen almost complete in the main erecting shop.

Colin J. Marsden

Left, below: The first Class 91 was rolled out of BREL Crewe for the press to inspect on 12th February 1988, two days before the locomotive was handed over to BR for trial running. Looking immaculate No. 91001 stands in the works yard, viewed from its No. 1 end.

Colin J. Marsden

Running slab end forward, No. 91002 passes near Sandy during August 1988 with a southbound test special from Peterborough to Bounds Green. The stock in this train is of the Mk 1 and Mk 2 types.

Brian Morrison

Once sufficient Class 91 locomotives were available a major training and testing operation commenced on the ECML, with a 24 hour per day programme being operated. On 10th August 1988 No. 91004 storms past Sandy with the 12.38 King's Cross – Doncaster training special, the train being formed of test car *Prometheus*, five Mk 3 sleeping cars and a DVT.

Brian Morrison

Much of the staff training on the Class 91s was undertaken at Doncaster. During the evening of 10th March 1989, Nos 91003 and 91006 stand in Doncaster station yard, coupled to a driver training special. The following morning the two locomotives were uncoupled, and operated on their own.

Colin J. Marsden

With a rake of IC125 stock behind, Class 91 No. 91008 hurries through Doncaster on the middle road on 25th April 1989, with the 07.50 King's Cross – Leeds "Yorkshire Pullman" service. This was one of the first ECML services to be taken over by Class 91 traction.

Colin J. Marsden

Leading a full rake of GEC-Alsthom built Mk4 stock, Class 91 No. 91026 pulls towards York through Holgate Bridge Junction on 13th July 1992, while forming the 08.00 King's Cross - Glasgow service.

Colin J. Marsden

Classified works overhauls of Class 91s have always been undertaken at Doncaster Works, where on 2nd May 1995 No. 91007 *Ian Allan* is seen undergoing its first heavy general overhaul. The locomotive is viewed from its 'blunt' end inside the main erecting shop, in company with a Class 86.

Colin J. Marsden

Sporting full GNER livery with vinyl 'nameplate' and showing the revised stainless steel headlight cluster, No. 91026 *York Minster* passes Shipton-on-Beningbrough, north of York, on 20th January 2000 with the 08.30 King's Cross – Edinburgh service.

Colin J. Marsden

In normal circumstances the Class 91s are coupled at the north end of train consists, as demonstrated here by No. 91029 *Queen Elizabeth II*, seen storming through Doncaster on 20th January 2000 with the 11.00 King's Cross – Glasgow service.

Colin J. Marsden

Detail of Class 91 driving cab
1. Park brake on button
2. Park brake indicator
3. Park brake off button
4. Brake overcharge switch
5. Instrument light switch
6. Cab light switch
7. Clip board light switch
8. Cab air treatment switch, heat/vent/cool
9. Cab air treatment switch, high/low
10. Sand button
11. Foot warmer switch
12. De-mister switch
13. Tail light switch
14. Marker light switch
15. Emergency brake plunger
16. Brake controller
17. Bogie brake cylinder gauge
18. Clock
19. Main reservoir gauge
20. AWS alarm
21. AWS indicator
22. Brake pipe gauge
23. AWS isolate warning light
24. Headlight warning light
25. Wheelslip warning light
26. General fault light
27. Tilt warning light
28. Electric train supply (ETS) warning light
29. Line light
30. Pantograph auto-drop light

31. High Speed brake indicator
32. Pre-set speed control
33. Space for ATP
34. Speedometer
35. Noticeboard
36. Driver/guard call button
37. ETS on button
38. Passenger communication override button
39. Pantograph up or re-set button
40. Fire alarm test button
41. ETS off button
42. Fire extinguisher delay button

43. Pantograph down button
44. Loco/shore radio system
45. Headlight switch
46. Drivers' Safety device foot pedal
47. Ashtray
48. Power controller
49. Windscreen wiper control
50. Tractive effort boost button
51. Master switch key socket
52. Master switch
53. AWS re-set button
54. Horn valve

One of the most important days for the electrification of the ECML was on 28th June 1991, when Her Majesty The Queen visited the King's Cross – Edinburgh route, travelled on a Class 91 hauled Mk4 set and named Class 91 No. 91029 *Queen Elizabeth II* prior to departure from King's Cross. On the same day the Queen also named another Class 91, *Palace of Holyroodhouse.* The picture below left shows the Queen unveiling the plate on the side of No. 91029, while the view right, is of the Queen departing from the cab of the locomotive after inspecting the controls, with Sir Bob Reid, the BR Chairman.

Both: Colin J. Marsden

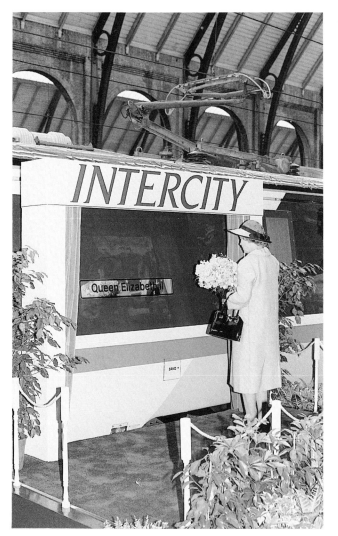

Class 92

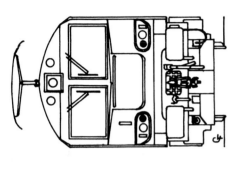

DWG 132

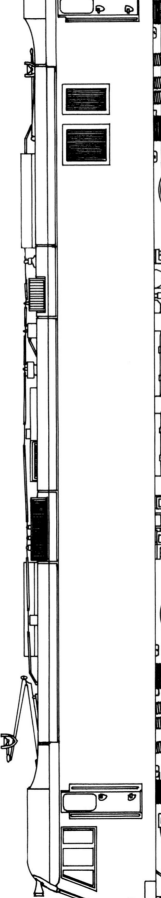

DWG 133

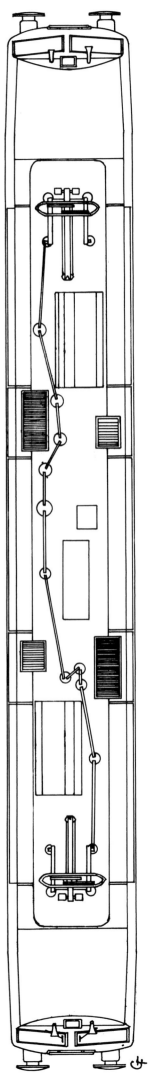

DWG 134

DWG 132
Class 92 front end layout

DWG 133
Class 92 side elevation (same for
both sides of locomotive)

DWG 134
Class 92 roof detail

Class	92		Brake type	Air, rheostatic, regenerative
Number range	92001-92046		Sanding equipment	Pneumatic
Built by	Brush Traction, Loughborough		Heating type	Electric - Index 108
Introduced	1993-96		Route availability	8
Wheel arrangement	Co-Co		Coupling restriction	Within type for multiple working
Weight	126 tons			
Height - pan down	13ft 0in		Brake force	63 tons
Width	8ft 8in		Horsepower (maximum)	
Length	70ft 1in		(Overhead)	6,760hp
Min curve negotiable	6 chains		(Third rail)	5,360hp
Maximum speed	87mph		Traction motor type	Brush
Wheelbase	56ft 6in		Control system	Asynchronous three-phase
Bogie wheelbase	14ft 1in		Pantograph type	Brecknell Willis
Bogie pivot centres	41ft 10$\frac{1}{2}$in		Nominal supply	25kV ac overhead
Wheel diameter	3ft 9in			750V dc third rail

The Class 92 is one of the most sophisticated locomotive types in the world, with the design project going back to May 1988 when various traction alternatives were considered for powering cross-Channel freight trains following the opening of the Channel Tunnel.

Many proposals were put forward by various design/build consortia, but the one which was eventually accepted came from Brush Traction of Loughborough – not altogether surprisingly, as Brush was already building the 'Le Shuttle' Bo-Bo-Bo locomotives for Eurotunnel.

From the outset it was realised that the unique design of the Class 92 would have not only to meet UK operating conditions but also to satisfy the Channel Tunnel authorities and, as originally proposed, mainland European administrations, allowing the locomotives to operate freight and other traffic deep into Europe to avoid the need to change locomotives on the French side of the Channel Tunnel.

The first order for Class 92s was placed on 22nd July 1990 and was for just 20 locomotives, this being followed by three repeat orders for 10, seven and nine identical locomotives to give an eventual fleet size of 46. Of the 'follow-on' orders, nine locomotives were funded by SNCF (French Railways) and seven by European Passenger Services.

The Co-Co Class 92 design was based broadly on the Brush Class 60 diesel design, but encompassed many major structural changes, especially to the ends, which now had to meet Eurotunnel and European railway safety requirements. Even after the design was agreed, serious concern was expressed by the railway trade unions over the design's crashworthiness, its rigidity failing to match that of contemporary French designs.

In common with Brush Traction's usual policy, the Class 92 bodyshells were sourced as complete units, being assembled by Procor of Wakefield; this followed the closure of such fabrication facilities at the Loughborough site. The bodyshells were formed of an underframe, to which the side sections and cab ends were added, the whole being pre-painted prior to road transfer to Loughborough.

Such was the requirement for safety when operating through the Channel Tunnel that the Class 92s had to be designed as virtually two electric locomotives in one shell, with all equipment duplicated to ensure that any normal failure *en route* would not prevent a train from proceeding to at least the far end of the Tunnel.

Construction at Loughborough was carried out in 1992/93, with the first locomotive finished at the end of 1993 and tested at Brush; it was handed over to its operator, BR Railfreight, in February 1994. Delivery of the balance of locomotives was a very protracted affair, with the final machine not being received until early 1996. Although owned by BR Railfreight, SNCF and EPS, all locomotives were operated in a joint pool based at Crewe electric depot.

Such was the complexity of the on-board electronic and control systems that entry into traffic and Railtrack certification took a long time. The first line to see locomotives operational was that through the Channel Tunnel between Folkestone (Dollands Moor) and Calais (Fréthun); later, certification was granted for locomotives to operate between North London and the Channel Tunnel, and eventually, in stages, over the northern sections of the West Coast Main Line, the northern sections of the East Coast Main Line and then the entire West Coast route.

The locomotives are equipped to operate from either a 25kV ac overhead power supply or at reduced traction output from the former Southern Region 750V dc third rail system. Signalling and control systems permit operation with Eurotunnel and SNCF systems. However, operation in France is restricted to the terminal at Calais, this being dictated by the locomotives' lack of French AWS or cab signalling.

The locomotives funded by EPS (now Eurostar UK Ltd) were designed to power overnight 'Nightstar' services from the UK to France, but when this service was abandoned the locomotives became redundant and were operated by UK privatised freight operator EWS, which became the owner of the original Railfreight locomotives. In 2000 the Eurostar UK locomotives were offered for sale, but it is reported few letters of interest were received and the locos are now stored at Crewe.

All locomotives were built carrying the triple grey livery, with their owner's branding applied to the cabsides. Two locomotives (Nos 92001/031) have since been repainted into full EWS maroon/gold livery.

Still showing its cast BR double arrow logo, EWS-owned and operated Class 92 No. 92012 *Thomas Hardy* approaches Otford Junction, off the Maidstone line, on 30th July 1996 with the 13.34 Dollands Moor (08.42 Somain) to Wembley international freight.

Colin J. Marsden

Displaying the SNCF logo below the number, indicating its ownership, No. 92006 *Louis Armand* stands outside North Pole International depot in West London on 14th February 1995 while *en route* from Paris to Crewe, following a period of testing in France. The shoes for collecting current from the third rail are clearly visible in their raised position.

Colin J. Marsden

Carrying the rather shortlived EPS branding, No. 92020, one of the EPS (Eurostar UK) locomotives, is seen at Waterloo International. If all had gone to plan, these locomotives would have been a regular sight at Waterloo International powering 'Nightstar' services from Plymouth, Swansea, Manchester and other northern UK destinations to mainland Europe. The stock destined for these services has now been sold to the Canadian rail operator VIA.

Colin J. Marsden

All members of the Class 92 fleet were named from new, with stick-on letters used; a handful later received cast nameplates, as shown on No. 92022 *Charles Dickens*, which also carried the Railfreight Distribution legend and logo on the bodyside when photographed at Dollands Moor on 15th March 1995.

Colin J. Marsden

What a difference a coat of paint can make. The Class 92 looks a totally different beast in full EWS maroon and gold. Still sporting its Channel Tunnel 'segments', the locomotive now has white stick-on letters for the name, along with large number and EWS branding. No. 92001 is seen at Toton after repainting.

Darren Ford

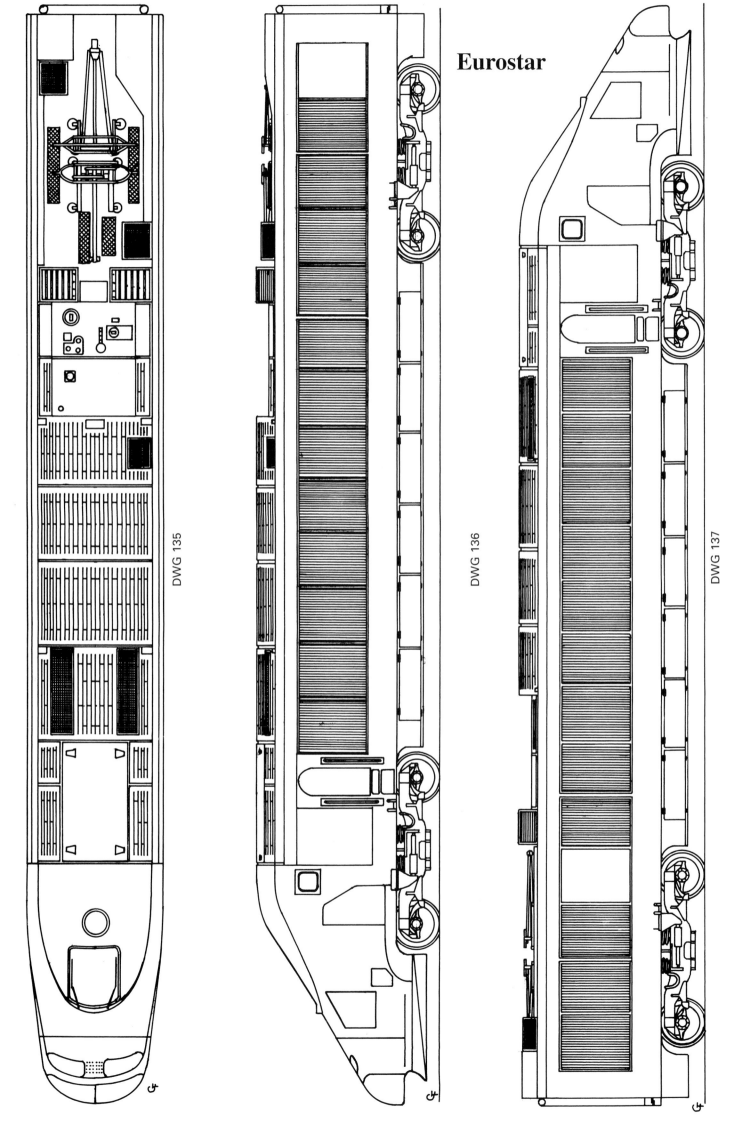

Eurostar

DWG 135

DWG 136

DWG 137

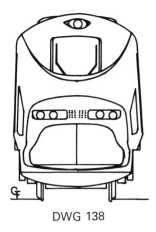

DWG 135
Eurostar power car roof detail

DWG 136
Eurostar power car side elevation, cab end to left

DWG 137
Eurostar power car side elevation, cab end to right

DWG 138
Eurostar cab end

DWG 138

Number range	373001-373022 (Eurostar UK)
	373101-373108 (SNCB)
	373201-373232 (SNCF)
	373301-373314 (Eurostar UK*)
	3999 (spare+)
Built by	GEC Alsthom in France and UK
Introduced	1993-96
Train formation	
(Inter-Capitals)	M, R1, R2, R3, R4, R5, R6, R7, R8, R9 (= half train)
(Regional)	M, R1, R3, R2, R5, R6, R7, R9 (= half train)
Power supply	25kV ac overhead (UK, Eurotunnel, SNCB, SNCF)
	3,000V dc overhead (SNCB)
	750V dc third rail (UK)
	1,500V ac overhead (SNCF¶)
Weight	
(Inter-Capitals)	816.1 tons
(Regional)	682.2 tons
Train length	
(Inter-Capitals)	1,250ft
(Regional)	1,046ft
Seating (half train)	
(Inter-Capitals)	105F/292S
(Regional)	66F/232S
Driving car length	72ft 8in
Saloon R1 length	71ft 8in
Saloons R2-R9 length	61ft 4in
Wheel diameter PC	3ft 0½in
Continuous rating	
(25kV ac)	16,400hp
(3kV dc)	7,638hp
Max speed	186mph (ac power supply)
Brake type	Air, rheostatic and regenerative
Power collection	Brecknell Willis

Inter-Capitals sets

Regional sets

* Originally North of London or Regional sets, now either used by GNER on King's Cross – York route or stored.
+ Power car only.

¶ Set Nos 373201/202/207/208/215/216/223/224/225/226/229/230, to enable SNCF domestic services to be operated.

Sets 373203/204/227/228 are now out of Eurostar control and operating on SNCF domestic services.

Sets 373301-304 are officially on hire from Eurostar UK to GNER; other sets are substituted if maintenance needs occur.

Some of the most impressive trains seen in the UK are the Eurostar sets which operate between the UK and France and Belgium. The Channel Tunnel project, which began with the signing of the Anglo-French Fixed-Link Treaty on 29th July 1987, had progressed enough by the end of 1989 to start the long process of ordering stock. Prior to that, detailed discussions between the three main railway administrations, BR (Britain), SNCF (France) and SNCB (Belgium) had taken place to establish the type of train required.

From the outset it was known that the most desirable option was to equip with French TGV-type trains; the French were keen to follow this path as their trains were highly successful, and this was the most sensible option. The UK, however, favoured a more conventional locomotive-hauled electric train. In the UK the Channel Tunnel operation was led by a separate company, European Passenger Services (EPS), at the time a wholly-owned subsidiary of the BRB. To produce a design which was going to be acceptable to the three countries, a working group – the International Project Group (IPG) – was formed in 1988 to concentrate on both the technical and commercial viability of train designs.

Huge problems existed in developing a Channel Tunnel train which would be capable of working over the railway systems of three countries, as well through the Channel Tunnel: all had their own specific operating and rule structures, and all were loathe to change any principles. The main area of change was the most obvious, that of gauge envelope; on the BR network a very much more restricted space was available between the train and structures compared to mainland Europe, which had followed the UIC or Berne gauge.

Eventually a design consortium was formed of De Dietrich, Ateliers de Construction Electrique de Charleroi (ACEC Transport), BN Division de Bombardier Eurorail, GEC-Alsthom Transportation, Metro-Cammell and Brush. The leading player was GEC-Alsthom, builder of the TGV.

Mechanically, the adopted design not surprisingly followed the French TGV; however, many changes were needed to make it suitable for UK operation, not least to its size, which led to a total redesign of the bodyshells and bogies. To maximise throughput of trains through the Channel Tunnel, long trainsets of 20 coaches were specified. The axle load had to be kept down to the TGV standard of just 17 tonnes, as in France and Belgium the sets would operate over conventional TGV tracks. On power cars, traction motors had to be body-mounted rather than bogie-mounted, which assisted in reducing track wear. An articulated design was eventually accepted, which permitted lower-slung vehicles.

The original contract for Eurostar trains (as they became known) was signed in Brussels on 18th December 1989, for 30 20-vehicle sets. Subsequently a follow-on order was placed, giving a fleet of 31. This number was maintained for just a short while, as, following an agreement for development of north-of-London working, seven extra, shorter (16-car) trains were added. All orders were finalised on 18th December 1991.

Ownership of Eurostars – classified by BR/Railtrack as Class 373 – is complex: Eurostar UK (originally European Passenger Services) owns 18 sets, including seven Regional trains, SNCF 16 sets, and SNCB four sets. Construction of the trains was divided between the participating countries, split by percentage 40:40:20 between the UK, France and Belgium.

The 31 20-car trains each comprise two identical half-train 10-coach formations, with a driving power car and nine passenger saloons, the one coupled to the power car having traction equipment at that end and a power bogie. A full 20-vehicle Eurostar seats 210 First and 584 Standard class passengers, giving a total of 794 seats per train. In addition, 52 tip-up seats are provided.

The Regional sets are each formed of 16 vehicles – two driving and 14 saloons. Total seating is for 578 plus 36 tip-up (114 First and 464 Standard class).

The Eurostar sets are without doubt the most complex trains in the world. By virtue of the routes operated, they have to work from three different power supplies, including both ac and dc obtained from the third rail or overhead systems, as well as operating over four different railway systems. The changeover between the different power supplies is carried out while on the move, with the train running into 'dead' or neutral sections. The action to change power is effected manually by the driver.

It was agreed that the Eurostar sets would be built at various plants in Europe and then joined together as full train consists at either Belfort in France or Washwood Heath in Birmingham.

The first Eurostar was built at Belfort in 1992. Identified as PS1, it was formed of just seven coaches and two power cars, and was delivered for test running in January 1993. Its first powered runs were between Strasbourg and Mulhouse. By June 1993 the set was transferred to the UK for dc tests, arriving on 20th June.

In May 1993, the second pre-service set, PS2 (a full 20-car train), was delivered for testing. After shakedown trials from La Landy (Paris), the set started high-speed running on the Paris – Lille route in July, when, for the first time, a Eurostar reached its maximum design speed of 300km/h (186mph).

The first UK-built train, UK1 (actually formed of Belgian half-sets Nos 3101/3102), was delivered from Washwood Heath to North Pole depot on 31st October 1993.

Eurostar passenger trains started operation from Waterloo to Paris and Brussels in the autumn of 1994, with, at first, two trains per day to each destination. By 2001 this had increased to around 25 departures per day.

Regrettably the Regional or North of London service has never been introduced, as even the projected passenger figures were far lower than originally anticipated. After plans for the Regional service were dropped, the sets were stored at North Pole depot. In 2000 two entered a hire contract with GNER and are now used on selected daytime King's Cross – York services.

When introduced the Eurostar sets were finished in a most distinctive livery of white and blue with full yellow ends. The first change came in 1999 when full-train-length advertising liveries were introduced on a small number of sets (excluding power cars). The two sets normally operated by GNER have been repainted in full GNER dark blue.

There exists one spare power car (No. 3999), which can be used on any set; when not in use, it is usually kept at North Pole.

Led by half-set No. 373005, a test special departs from Ashford via the down loop and approaches Willesborough Crossing on 7th July 1994 bound for Calais Fréthun. The land to the right of the train is now being developed as part of the Channel Tunnel Rail Link project.

Colin J. Marsden

Adjacent to Dollands Moor depot at Folkestone, the line is electrified at both 25kV ac overhead and 750V dc third rail to enable the voltage changeover to be accomplished. On 17th March 1995 the 12.53 Waterloo International - Paris changes to ac power as it approaches Continental Junction led by UK set No. 373016. In the background three Class 92s can be seen in an otherwise empty International yard.

Colin J. Marsden

Running at line speed of 300km/h (186mph), SNCB-owned set No. 373105/106 passes near Haute Picardie on the TGV-Nord route on 9th September 1997 with the 09.23 Waterloo International – Paris Nord service.

Colin J. Marsden

The original 'Windsor' side at London Waterloo was totally rebuilt for the Eurostar operation, with five new 20-vehicle platforms constructed. Winding its way into Waterloo International over the arches which exist virtually all the way from Waterloo to International Junction, SNCF-owned set No. 373209 approaches the terminal with the 06.23 from Paris Nord on 12th June 1995.

Colin J. Marsden

The Royal opening of the Channel Tunnel was held on 6th May 1994, HM The Queen travelling in UK set No. 373004 from Waterloo to the Eurotunnel station at Coquelles, where she met the President of France, François Mitterrand. The historic train, with Union flags on the front and a Royal cipher on the cab doors, passes Polhill.
Colin J. Marsden

Storming towards Lille at 300km/h, UK set No. 373002/001, the doyen of the class, forms the 16.07 Paris Nord – Waterloo International on 12th August 1997. The train is seen passing the emergency spur to/from the Arras line at Roeux.
Colin J. Marsden

Only once has a Eurostar ever been to Cologne, Germany, when on 13th December 1997 North of London set No. 373311/312 took part in an exhibition of high-speed trains at Cologne Deutz station. The following day the set was returned to the UK and is seen passing through Cologne station.
Colin J. Marsden

On only a handful of occasions has a Eurostar set visited Glasgow Central station, one being on the evening of 5th June 1997 when gauge-testing of the sets was carried out in the station area in preparation for possible introduction of a Scotland – Europe through service. The train, with set No. 373308 nearer the camera, is seen awaiting shunting around the station after the close of service.
Colin J. Marsden

With the North of London or Regional Eurostar sets spare and stored and GNER in need of extra stock, a hire deal for two sets commenced in mid-2000 to operate on the King's Cross – York corridor. To conform with corporate identity, the two units were re-liveried in GNER colours. Set No. 373304 is seen at York on 30th May 2000 with stock off the 12.34 from King's Cross.
Colin J. Marsden

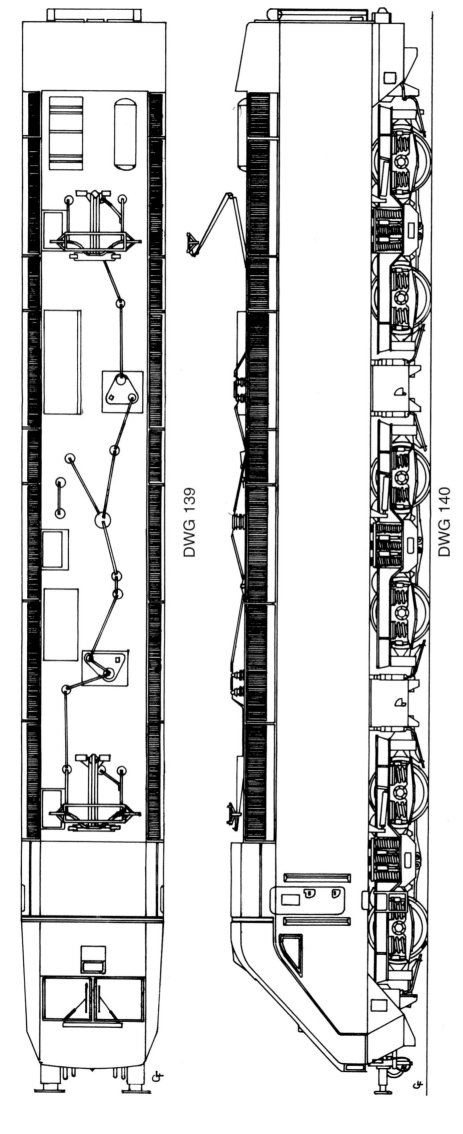

DWG 139

DWG 140

Shuttle Bo-Bo-Bo

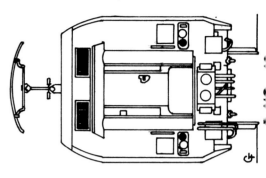

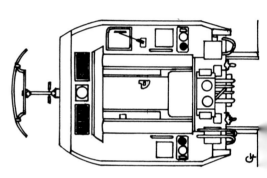

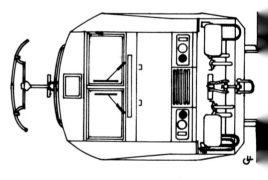

DWG 139
Eurotunnel Shuttle locomotive roof details

DWG 140
Eurotunnel Shuttle locomotive Side A

DWG 141
Eurotunnel Shuttle locomotive front end elevation

DWG 142
Eurotunnel Shuttle locomotives 9001-9040 inner end elevation with driving cab

DWG 143
Eurotunnel Shuttle locomotives 9101-9707 inner end elevation without driving cab

Class	–		Bogie pivot centres	20ft 8in
Number range	9001-9040, 9101-9113, 9701-9707		Wheel diameter	3ft 6in
Built by	Brush Traction, Loughborough		Brake type	Air, rheostatic, regenerative
Introduced	1992-2002		Sanding equipment	Pneumatic
Wheel arrangement	Bo-Bo-Bo		Heating type	Electric
Weight	132 tons		Route availability	–
Height - pan down	13ft 9in		Coupling restriction	Within type using TDM
Width	9ft 9in		Brake force	50 tons
Length	72ft 2in		Horsepower (maximum)	7,725hp
Min curve negotiable	4 chains		Traction motor type	ABB 6PH
Maximum speed	110mph		Control system	Asynchronous three-phase
Wheelbase	50ft 8in		Pantograph type	Brecknell Willis
Bogie wheelbase	9ft 2in		Nominal supply	25kV ac overhead

Although never owned/operated by the erstwhile British Rail or its successors, these three fleets of high-powered Bo-Bo-Bo locomotives have been included as they have now become an important part of the UK rail scene.

The first order for 38 single-ended locomotives was placed with Brush Traction of Loughborough by Channel Tunnel operator Eurotunnel in the late 1980s, during the early phase of tunnel construction work. The locomotives are unique in the UK as they are mounted on three two-axle bogies, giving them a Bo-Bo-Bo wheel configuration, to enable them to operate around very tight curves within the Eurotunnel network.

Constructed to a non-standard gauge envelope, the Shuttle locomotives are thus not allowed to operate outside the Eurotunnel rail network, and run on a loop system between the Cheriton terminal at Folkestone in the UK and the Coquelles terminal at Calais in France.

The locomotive bodies were fabricated at Qualter Hall Engineering of Barnsley and transported by road to Brush at Loughborough for fitting out. In order to meet the very strict safety and operating requirements of the Channel Tunnel, these effectively combine two electric locomotives in one body, so that only the most serious of failures could prevent a Shuttle train from continuing its journey.

Numbered in a new Eurotunnel 90xx series, the original fleet of 38 locomotives, 9001-9038, was delivered to Eurotunnel's French base at Coquelles well before the Tunnel opened, delivery being by road and sea. Following the Tunnel's opening, traffic growth exceeded expectations, and it was decided to order a follow-on

fleet; these would have driving controls only at the leading end (the original locomotives featuring a remote shunting/driver's cab at the slab end). Other modifications to this batch rendered them a separate sub-class and these were numbered in the 91xx series. In late 1999 an order was placed for a further batch of locomotives with a higher power output but to the same body style, and these will be numbered in the 97xx series and used exclusively for Freight Shuttle haulage.

All locomotives are finished in Eurotunnel grey and white. The 90xx machines originally carried a green and blue band at cantrail height, but this is now being replaced by a Eurotunnel livery, developed after the original trading title of 'Le Shuttle' was dropped. Soon after delivery, all 90xx locomotives were given names.

In normal operation, a Bo-Bo-Bo 'Shuttle' locomotive is coupled at each end of a train, with both locomotives operating under the control of the leading driver. If a problem prevails, the on-board train captain can go to the rear of a train and take control of the trailing locomotive to remove all or part of the train from the tunnel. Two types of train are powered by the 'Shuttle' locomotives: Freight Shuttles, which transport lorries, and Tourist Shuttles, which transport motor cars and coaches.

All locomotives are based and maintained in purpose-built accommodation within the Coquelles Eurotunnel terminal, their gauge preventing them from operating outside the Shuttle loop system.

One locomotive has been withdrawn – No. 9030, which was the rear locomotive involved in the Channel Tunnel fire in 1996. No. 9040 was built as a replacement.

Shuttle locomotive No. 9026, showing the original Le Shuttle livery, is seen at the depot at Coquelles, Calais. It is viewed from the raked-back main driving end. Standard buffers and drawgear are carried, as are triangulation headlights. Unlike locomotives authorised for BR or Railtrack use, these machines do not have yellow warning ends.
Colin J. Marsden

Normal train operation sees one Bo-Bo-Bo locomotive coupled at each end of a train, thus ensuring that, in case of emergency, a train can be drawn out of the tunnel in either direction. Under standard operating procedure, both locomotives provide power to trains, with all rolling stock fitted with a TDM multiple-control system. Locomotive No. 9012 is seen at the rear of a lorry shuttle arriving at the UK terminal on 3rd July 1994.

Colin J. Marsden

The second locomotive of the follow-on order, No. 9102, is seen on shed at Coquelles. These locomotives differ from the original build in having driving controls only at the main end; body differences include the omission of the 'blunt'-end side window and headlight. No. 9102 also shows a revised footstep arrangement on its cab side, to avoid there being a large gap between locomotive and platform in the terminal area.

Colin J. Marsden

Fascinating Flow Blue

Schiffer Publishing Ltd

Jeffrey B. Snyder

4880 Lower Valley Road Atglen, PA 19310 USA

To Hazel Hall and Olive Snyder - my grandmothers, with love.

About the Values in This Book

Please note: The value ranges that appear here in the captions for Fascinating Flow Blue are derived from compiled sources and were not supplied by the people acknowledged in the credit lines. The ranges were conscientiously determined to reflect the market at the time this work was compiled. No responsibility for their future accuracy is accepted by the author, the publisher, or the people credited with the photographs.

Please note: A typesetting Error was made in the courtesy lines. Mr. Frederick's first name should read as Gale.

Published by Schiffer Publishing Ltd.
4880 Lower Valley Road
Atglen, PA 19310
Phone: (610) 593-1777; Fax: (610) 593-2002
E-mail: Schifferbk@aol.com
Please write for a free catalog.
This book may be purchased from the publisher.
Please include $3.95 for shipping.

In Europe, Schiffer books are distributed by
Bushwood Books
84 Bushwood Road
Kew Gardens
Surrey TW9 3BQ England
Phone: 44 (0)181 948-8119; Fax: 44 (0)181 948-3232
E-mail: Bushwd@aol.com

Please try your bookstore first.
We are interested in hearing from authors
with book ideas on related subjects.

Table of Contents

Acknowledgments

I wish to express my gratitude to all of the people who made this book possible. Dealers and collectors allowed me into their shops and homes, permitting me to disrupt their lives and clutter their homes and work places with my tangle of equipment. They made this book possible. I offer my thanks to each of these individuals: Gale Frederick, Margot Frederick, and Dan Overmayer; Tom and Valorie Hays; Lynn Trusdell; and Dorothy and Arnold Kowalsky. I wish to give special thanks to Gale Frederick, who kindy loaned me the black background photographs appearing in this text. I would also like to extend my heart-felt appreciation to everyone I encountered over the past six years (and four Flow Blue books) who provided invaluable information, constructive commentary, unfailing support, and friendly encouragement. You all made this a journey well worth taking.

Introduction

This volume strays from the beaten path. Rather than provide a sweeping survey of Flow Blue of all types (as in my previous volumes), from the most expensive and rare on down to the most common examples, this book is focused on the rare and unusual, the highly-coveted, and the best loved. In other words, here is a survey of the Flow Blue most collectors find fascinating. Tea services and children's tea and dinner sets are explored in detail. The body shape names assigned to specific forms (predominantly from the second and third quarters of the nineteenth century) are identified — along with many of the flowing patterns gracing those shapes. Finally, a chapter surveying some of the best-loved and most often sought identified patterns and vessel forms available in Flow Blue rounds out the presentation.

Brush stroke pattern partial child's tea set. 4" high teapot. *Courtesy of Tom and Valorie Hays.* $2200-2500

JAPAN pattern partial tea set with two pots by Thomas Fell & Company. Teapots: 10.5" high and 9.5" high. *Courtesy of Margot Frederick.* $2500+

What Is Flow Blue?

To define terms, "Flow Blue" refers to a technique used to decorate hard, white bodied earthenwares vessels from roughly 1835 on into the first quarter of the twentieth century. Flow Blue decorations were underglaze blue patterns (most often transfer printed onto the ceramic bodies but also applied by hand with a method now referred to as brush stroke), the ink of which was caused to bleed or "flow" into the undecorated portions of earthenware vessels during the glaze firing. The desired "flow" was produced when lime or chloride of ammonia was added into the protective shell of the fire-clay sagger surrounding the wares during that glaze firing.

BEAUTIES OF CHINA sauce tureen underplate. 1" high, 10" in diameter handle to handle. *Courtesy of Gail Frederick and Dan Overmeyer.* $150+

JG printed manufacturer's mark. *Courtesy of Gail Frederick and Dan Overmeyer.*

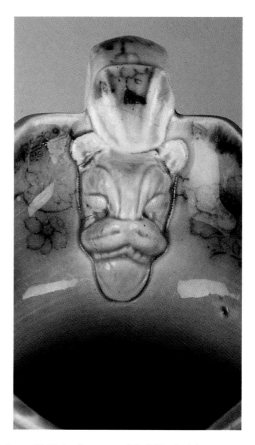

JAPAN FLOWERS milk pitcher with dragon handles, marked "JG" on the base. 6" high. *Courtesy of Gail Frederick and Dan Overmeyer.* $250-350

Two HONG KONG syrups with pewter lids. 8" & 7.25" high. *Courtesy of Gail Frederick and Dan Overmeyer.* Left: $500-700; right: $400-600

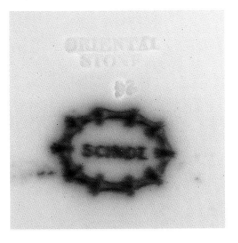

SCINDE plate, printed pattern name mark and the impressed "ORIENTAL STONE" mark used by John and George Alcock, 1839-1846. *Courtesy of Gail Frederick and Dan Overmeyer.*

SCINDE reticulated plate by John and George Alcock, c. 1840. 2" high, 10.75" handle to handle. *Courtesy of Gail Frederick and Dan Overmeyer.* $2000+

Above and right: SHANGHAI dinner plate by Baker. 10" diameter. *Courtesy of Tom and Valorie Hays.* $125+

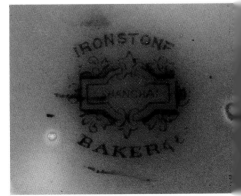

Pearlware and various whitewares were decorated with Flow Blue designs. These strong, white earthenwares were the culmination of English potters' efforts during the late eighteenth and early nineteenth centuries to create an inexpensive, durable earthenware body that would have the clean white surface of Chinese porcelain, if not the translucency. They succeeded with pearlware and continued that success with a variety of whitewares. England's potters, instead of using the names they had given their earthenware bodies, frequently described their early Flow Blue crockery as "china," associating their wares in name with China's fashionable export porcelains. Early Flow Blue patterns also copied the Chinese blue and white porcelain designs, reinforcing this positive association.

LA BELLE handless punch cups and an urn featuring a bone/ivory handled spigot. This set is marked Wheeling Pottery Co. 15" high urn, 3.5" high and 3" diameter cups. *Courtesy of Margot Frederick.* *Urn:* $3000-5000; punch cups: $300-500

Wheeling Pottery Company mark, Wheeling, West Virginia. *Courtesy of Gail Frederick and Dan Overmeyer.*

"There is a certain style of design known as 'flow blue,' which has nondescript patterns, flowers, geometric designs, and which has nothing of beauty or interest to recommend it ..." — N. Hudson Moore. Unidentified rose pattern decorative pitcher with gold gilt at the base. This Middle Victorian period pitcher measures 13.25" high to the spout and 15.5" high to the top of the handle. *Courtesy of Tom and Valorie Hays.* $300-500

LABELLE charger by the Wheeling Pottery Company. 14.5" high. *Courtesy of Gail Frederick and Dan Overmeyer.* $250

Wheeling Pottery Company "WP" printed manufacturer's mark. *Courtesy of Gail Frederick and Dan Overmeyer.*

An unidentified geometric pattern and gold gilt adorns this pewter lid pitcher. 10.5" high to lip. *Courtesy of Tom and Valorie Hays.* $350-500

By 1840, Flow Blue [flown] ceramics were particularly popular in the American market and continued to be produced in England into the first quarter of the twentieth century. This long English production flew in the face of British critics such as N. Hudson Moore, who wrote in his 1903 edition of *The Old China Book*, "There is a certain style of design known as 'flow blue,' which has nondescript patterns, flowers, geometric designs, and which has nothing whatever of beauty or interest to recommend it..." (Perkins 1997)

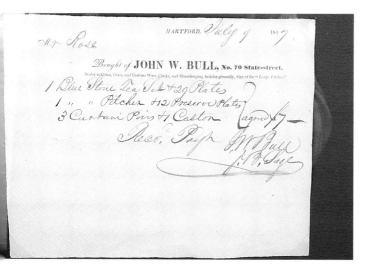

A bill of sale for one John W. Bull of No. 70 State Street, a "Dealer in China, Glass, and Earthen Ware, Clocks, and Housekeeping Articles generally ...", dated July 9, 1847. Among the goods purchased for seven dollars included, "One Blue Stone Tea Set & 29 Plates" and "One Blue Stone Pitcher and 12 Preserve Plates." *Courtesy of Gail Frederick and Dan Overmeyer.*

Above and left: ORIENTAL plate, no manufacturer's mark. 10.5" in diameter. *Courtesy of Tom and Valorie Hays.* $150+

Above and right: ALTHEA compartmented dish by Villeroy and Boch. Compartmented dish with a small section for salt? 3.5" high x 12" wide. *Courtesy of Gail Frederick and Dan Overmeyer.* $350+

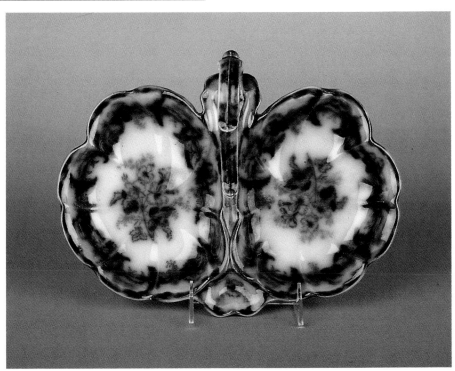

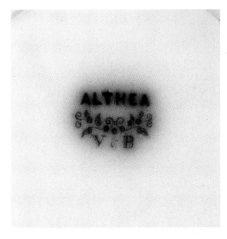

Villeroy and Boch "V.B." printed manufacturer's mark with pattern name. *Courtesy of Gail Frederick and Dan Overmeyer.*

Americans have never been ones to give critics too much of their attention, especially British critics. America's consumers adored the dark blue hazy patterns and purchased Flow Blue by the barrel full. As the nineteenth century progressed, Flow Blue found its way into a variety of households — beginning with the burgeoning middle classes at its introduction and expanding until these wares were available to nearly everyone by the late nineteenth century. While England would always be the largest producer of Flow Blue,

LABELLE jardinier by the Wheeling Pottery Company. *Courtesy of Gail Frederick and Dan Overmeyer.* $350 and up, varies with size from small upwards

LABELLE jardinier pedestal by the Wheeling Pottery Company. *Courtesy of Gail Frederick and Dan Overmeyer.* $2000+

France, Germany, and Holland followed the English lead and produced their own flowing wares. After 1875, American potters began serving up their own renditions of Flow Blue to compete with English and European production. Two of the best known American potteries producing flowing wares were the Wheeling Pottery Company, of Wheeling, West Virginia, and the Mercer Pottery Company of Trenton, New Jersey. (Snyder 1995)

T.J. & J. Mayer, Longport, Opaque Porcelain manufacturer's mark. *Courtesy of Gail Frederick and Dan Overmeyer.*

Often, identifying the manufacturer and the name of the pattern adorning a particular piece of Flow Blue is a simple matter of either turning the plate over or the vase upside down. Transfer printed patterns such as Flow Blue frequently included printed or impressed manufacturers' marks on the bottoms of plates and the undersides of hollowwares. Printed marks were created as part of the overall transfer print and applied at the same time. Impressed marks were pressed into the unfired clay underside or base with a tool reminiscent of a branding iron. Whether printed or impressed, these marks contained the firm's name, initials, symbol, and location — or some combination of these. Often the pattern name is supplied with the mark as well. These marks are one of the best and easiest guides to identifying Flow Blue. However, many small firms either saw no reason to use marks (as they had no name recognition value) or sometimes used marks which have never been identified because of the short lifespan and limited production of the company. Also, be aware that a few firms printed the *name* of the ceramic body or of that body's *shape* rather than the name of the *pattern* on their marks. This may cause some confusion. (Snyder 1994; Hill 1993, 4)

Take care when identifying patterns; there are occasions when a particular pattern name was used by a number of different potters to identify patterns that were very different, one from another. There are at least three Madras patterns and as many as five Osbourne patterns produced by different potters. (King 1997)

The registration mark from the PEKING soup tureen. *Courtesy of Gail Frederick and Dan Overmeyer.* $1500+ for the soup tureen.

In 1842, the English Copyright Act was responsible for the creation of an additional mark to be found printed or impressed into the base of flowing blue wares. A diamond-shaped registration mark was added to the back of pottery as proof that a pattern had been registered and was not to be copied by others, and renewable every three years. Registration mark design changed slightly between 1867 and 1868. From 1842 to 1867, a letter code designating the year of registry was located at the diamond's appex, just below the Roman numeral IV (a code for ceramics). A letter on the diamond's left side indicated the month. From 1868 to 1883, the year code letter was moved to the diamond's right side and the letter code for the month was moved to the base. In 1884, these registration marks were replaced with registration numbers that indicated only the year the pattern was registered in a numeric sequence beginning with Rd. No. 1 in 1884. (For more information on dating and registration marks, *see* Snyder, *Flow Blue* 1992 and *Historic Flow Blue,* 1994.)

Is This Pattern Flown?

BEAUTIES OF CHINA coffee pot by Mellor Venables and Company. Note cylindrical neck as compared with teapot style. 11.5" high. Marked. *Courtesy of Gail Frederick and Dan Overmeyer.* $3000+

Mellors, Vennables & Company "M.V. & Co." printed manufacturer's mark, Burslem, Staffordshire (1834-1851). *Courtesy of Gail Frederick and Dan Overmeyer.*

Some examples of Flow Blue provide very little evidence that the pattern has ever been flown. CHINESE MUSICIANS teapot, no manufacturer's mark. Note that this is an early shape style. 10" high. *Courtesy of Gail Frederick and Dan Overmeyer.* $3000+

Flow Blue patterns range from heavily flown (in some cases the pattern can not be discerned through the haze) down to a mere faint halo effect around the lines of the transfer. Examples of both, and a little of everything in between, may be found in this book. Many heated discussions have resulted from the capricious nature of the flowing effect. Herbert Minton discussed this dilemma in a letter dating back to January 5, 1848, "... as respect all FB (Flown Blue) patterns, we cannot, after taking all the pains in our power, guarantee that all the pieces of the service should be exactly of the same tint and color or degree of flow." (Kowalsky 1997)

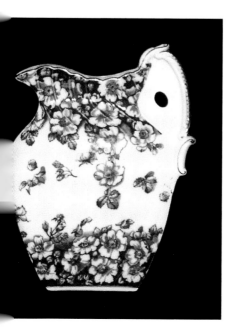

DUCHESS wall plaque, no manufacturer's mark but possibly by Dunn Bennett, c. 1900. *Courtesy of Gail Frederick and Dan Overmeyer.* $500-700

Arnold Kowalsky asserts that a conscious effort was made in latter decades to decrease the flowing effect. He states:

In the late 1870s and onward, taste and circumstances dictated a clear, clean look. To a large extent, floral and art nouveau patterns replaced the romantic and oriental look. The "Flow Blue" (color) took on an almost clear and clean transfer appearance reminiscent of late eighteenth and early nineteenth century blue and white transferware. The difference, however, lay in the rich blue coloring of Flow Blue as opposed to the early soft blue of transferware so well noted and illustrated by Coysh, Whiter, Copeland, and others in their works. (Kowalsky 1997)

The Whiteware Body and Its Assembly

Mason's Patented Ironstone printed manufacturer's mark. You can not say which Mason used this. *Courtesy of Tom and Valorie Hays.*

English potters developed very hard, inexpensive earthenware bodies which were white enough to compete with porcelains produced in China or Europe and were also much better suited to the rigors of overseas travel to foreign markets. These earthenwares were christened with a wide variety of descriptive names emphasizing either their brilliant whiteness or their immense strength. These names included whitewares, semi-porcelains, Spode's "Stone China," and Mason's acclaimed "Ironstone China." (Snyder 1992)

Above and right: SCINDE plate (note panels as opposed to circular plate) by J. & G. Alcock. 10.25" in diameter. *Courtesy of Tom and Valorie Hays.* $125+

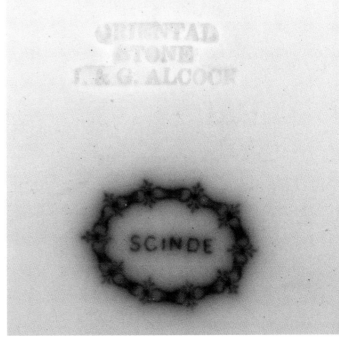

Plates produced in these enduring earthenwares were formed by "jiggering." A pliant, thin disk, or bat, of clay was placed onto the surface of a plaster mold. That plaster mold was in the shape of the upper surface of the plate. The mold was then mounted on a rotating turntable and the clay bat was smoothed down over the surface of the mold with a profile tool bearing a "jiggering" head. The profile tool shaped the underside of the plate and the plate's foot while the upper portion was shaped by the plaster mold. (Hill 1993, 3)

"PAGODA" two handled loving cups, no manufacturer's mark. 6" high, 4.5" wide. *Courtesy of Gail Frederick and Dan Overmeyer.* $300+ each

Whiteware cups were created in a process potters termed "jollying." Here the roles of the plaster mold and profile tool were reversed. A soft clay sphere was placed in a plaster mold attached to the turntable. This time the plaster mold was in the shape of the outside of the cup and the profile tool on a jollying head was pushed into the clay, forming the cup's inside, as the wheel rotated. (Hill 1993, 3)

REEDS & FLOWERS pitchers — the largest pitcher has a pewter lid and the middle-sized pitcher has copper lustre, no manufacturer's marks. These pitchers range from 9.5" high to 7" high. *Courtesy of Tom and Valorie Hays.* Left: $500-750; center: $300-500; right: 250-350.

Hollowwares (teapots, pitchers, gravy boats ...), on the other hand, were cast in molds. To create the mold, the intended shape was first carved in wood. The handles and base were carved from separate pieces of wood. The wooden form was used to produce two part plaster molds from which many hollow forms could be produced. Once created, the two part mold was firmly held together and liquid clay, or slip, was poured into the open end of the mold. Excess slip was poured out of the mold as the slip began to set. This left thin walls of slip to harden into the eventual hollow form. Once the slip was "leather hard," the mold could be opened and the hollow body removed. (Hill 1993, 3-4)

CHAPOO coffee pot by John Wedg Wood, circa 1850 11.5" high. *Courtesy of Gail Frederick and Dan Overmeyer.* $3000+

15

Handles were molded in the same manner. However, slip was not poured away as the handle began to harden. The handles were left solid. In quality wares, the mold seams left behind from the two part mold were smoothed away, leaving handles seamless and smooth. Lesser firms producing inexpensive wares did not remove these seams. Pouring spouts were manufactured using the same molding process. Lids were also molded. Lid finials were created in separate molds and attached later. (Hill 1993, 4)

When the time was right, finials, spouts, and handles were attached to the body of the hollow form with slip. Spouts were attached to teapots only after strainer holes were cut into the body of the pot. Ellen Hill points out that teapot lids also had to be punctured. They needed a so-called "steam-hole," the primary purpose of which was actually to prevent a vacuum from forming as tea was poured. (Hill 1993, 4)

The Transfer Printing Technique, Creating Flow Blue

The transfer printing technique was the principal decorating method used on Flow Blue wares. HOMESTEAD coffee pot, no manufacturer's mark. *Courtesy of Gail Frederick and Dan Overmeyer.* $3000+

While simple designs could be hand painted quickly, cheaply, and directly onto the surface of some early Flow Blue wares, the transfer printing technique was the principal decorating method. This process allowed patterns to be quickly duplicated, transferring the design from an engraved and pigment-coated copper plate to a ceramic vessel via a specially treated paper.

An engraver with an artist's touch was essential to producing beautiful transfer printed patterns. Large pottery manufacturers had their own engravers while the smaller companies purchased patterns from engraving firms.

To create a successful design, the engraver first sketched his pattern and adapted it to fit every piece of crockery in the service. When he was satisfied with the design, the engraver transferred the patterns for the various wares to copper plates. Once transfered, the pattern lines were engraved. When the engraving was complete, burrs raised along the edges of the etched lines were scraped smooth and any areas of the pattern requiring darker shades of color or deeper shadows were etched again. (Copeland 1980, 21)

Trial prints of the new pattern were then pulled onto ceramic bodies to guarantee that, once fired, the final image would be all it was expected to be. If the pattern proved to be correct, the etched copper was plated with nickel, and later steel, to extend the pattern's working life. The nickel or steel plating decreased the chances that the copper plate's surface could be scratched, adding unwanted extra lines to the pattern. (Copeland 1980, 22)

When the pattern was approved, it was up to transferrers to correctly place the central images and border pieces of the print. These women carefully matched joins and arranged prints around spouts, finials, and handles. Then the back of the specially treated paper holding the inky pattern was gently rubbed with a small piece of felt to transfer the design. The paper was then rubbed down with a stiff-bristled brush to ensure that the color had been completely transferred to the porous earthenware biscuit.

Once transferred, the paper was washed away and the biscuit bearing its new design was glazed, placed in a protective fire saggar, and fired. In the case of Flow Blue, appropriate chemicals were added to the saggar during the glaze firing to induce the flow.

The first successful underglaze transfer print color was the deep cobalt blue shown here. This would remain the favorite color for Flow Blue. A soup tureen with an unidentified Oriental pattern by an unknown potter. 12" high, 15.5" handle to handle. *Courtesy of Gail Frederick and Dan Overmeyer.* $2000-3000

The first successful color used in underglazed transfer printing during the eighteenth century was deep cobalt blue. Cobalt blue was the only color which would withstand the high temperatures used during early underglazing and was the mainstay of underglazed transfer printing by 1776.

In 1828 new underglaze techniques allowed black, green, yellow, and red enamels to be transferred. This resulted in prints with two or more colors. The process was expensive, however, with each color requiring its own transfer and a separate firing. The early deep cobalt blue color was replaced with new synthetic blues around 1845. In 1848, multiple color underglazing techniques were further advanced in England, allowing three colors (red, yellow, and blue) to be applied in a single transfer with only one firing. Green and brown were added in 1852.

Flow Blue Pattern Types and Their Embellishments

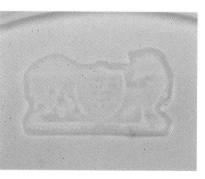

Above, far left and left: CASHMERE dinner plate by Ridgway and Morley, complete with both printed and impressed back marks. 10.5" in diameter. *Courtesy of Tom and Valorie Hays.* $175+

There are two distinctive types of patterns found in Flow Blue. The most common pattern type features a distinct central image and a separate border design. The amount of white space left between the border and center design varies from pattern to pattern and from one decade to another with changing aesthetics. Border designs usually completely cover the rim of a plate or platter. Both the border and center designs conform to plates and platters best and were adjusted to fit hollow forms. Small pieces such as butter pats and cup plates generally received only a small portion of either the center or border pattern for decoration.

MARBLE candlesticks, marked "J. & W." 9" high each. *Courtesy of Gail Frederick and Dan Overmeyer.* $500-650 set.

Sheet patterns, on the other hand, have no separate centers or borders. A single pattern covers the entire object as if it had been covered with a sheet of wallpaper. Sheet patterns came in two distinct varieties: floral patterns and marble patterns. Floral patterns became popular in the 1860s and continued to attract consumers on into the early twentieth century. Evidence suggests that the popularity of Marble patterns was strong early in the nineteenth century. (Hill 1993, 7) Middle class families hoping to climb the social ladder would have liked to decorate their homes with real marble. Most, however, settled for the less costly gently flowing Marble patterns which most often were found decorating chamber sets.

An example of a floral sheet pattern appears on this small lidded pitcher. 6" high, 4.5" high to spout. *Courtesy of Tom and Valorie Hays.* $400-600

MARBLE holder, no manufacturer's mark. Middle class Victorian families who could not afford to decorate their homes in real marble settled for this Marble pattern. *Courtesy of Gail Frederick and Dan Overmeyer.* NP (No Price)

Above and below: JAPANESE polychrome teapot, lidded sugar, and creamer, marked W. & B., featuring polychrome overglaze decoration. *Courtesy of Tom and Valorie Hays.* $1200-1500 set.

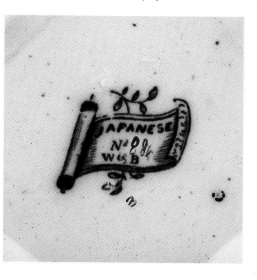

Embellishments to these two distinct pattern types include polychrome painting over or under the glaze, gaudy overglaze painting, ground colors, and gold gilt decoration. Polychrome decorations are hand painted decorations in colors other than blue, which embellish the Flow Blue designs. These may have been applied either over or under the surface of the glaze. Colors under the glaze have an advantage over colors applied over the glaze ... they do not wear off. Overglaze polychrome decorations were painted over the surface of the glaze and were exposed to wear and tear from utensils, fingernails, and wash brushes.

GAUDY STRAWBERRY platter, unidentified manufacturer. 15.5" wide. *Courtesy of Tom and Valorie Hays.* $350+

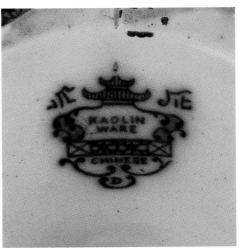

Dimmock's "D" initial manufacturer's mark with pattern name and body ware type identifying name Kaolin Ware. *Courtesy of Gail Frederick and Dan Overmeyer.*

Gaudy ironstone PINWHEEL with copper lustre on a milk or water pitcher, no manufacturer's mark. 9" high. *Courtesy of Gail Frederick and Dan Overmeyer.* $400-600

The term gaudy overglaze painting is frequently applied when colors (other than blue) were added over the glaze to Flow Blue brush stroke patterns. "Gaudy" in this case is derived from the Gaudy Dutch decorative style. (Hill 1993, 11)

Above and left: CHINESE pedestal comport by Thomas Dimmock & Company with green ground and gold trim. 6.5" high x 13" handle to handle. *Courtesy of Gail Frederick and Dan Overmeyer.* $1500+

Above and below: Unique ORIENTAL pattern on a hedgehog (polychrome) used for forcing bulbs by Samuel Alcock. Orange polychrome paint. Commonly found in basalt. 6.5" x 11.5". *Courtesy of Gail Frederick and Dan Overmeyer.* $3000+

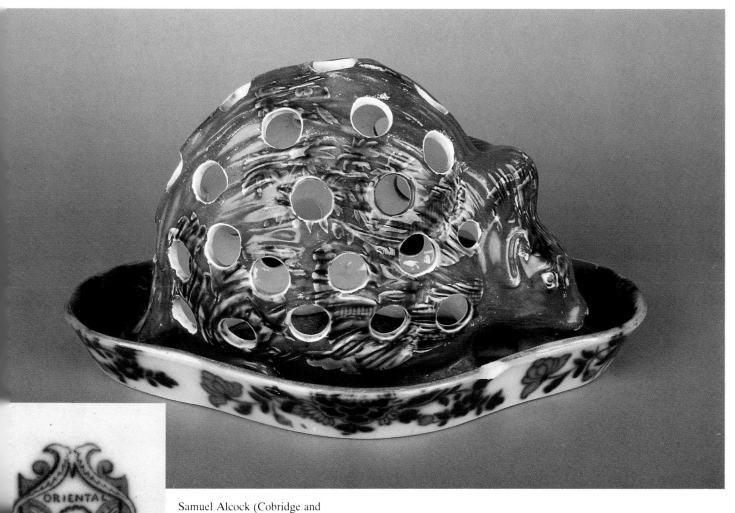

Samuel Alcock (Cobridge and Burslem, Staffordshire, c. 1830-1859) printed "S.A." manufacturer's mark. *Courtesy of Gail Frederick and Dan Overmeyer.*

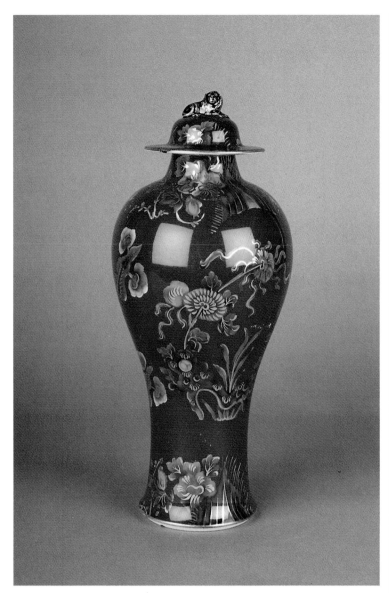

Left and above: Covered jar in an unidentified pattern with red ground and gold gilt. 12.5" high. *Courtesy of Gail Frederick and Dan Overmeyer.* $2500-3500

Unidentified pattern covered jar with red ground and gold gilt. 20.5" high. *Courtesy of Gail Frederick and Dan Overmeyer.* $3000-4000.

"W.B. & Co.," William Brownfield & Company impressed mark from the covered jar. *Courtesy of Gail Frederick and Dan Overmeyer.*

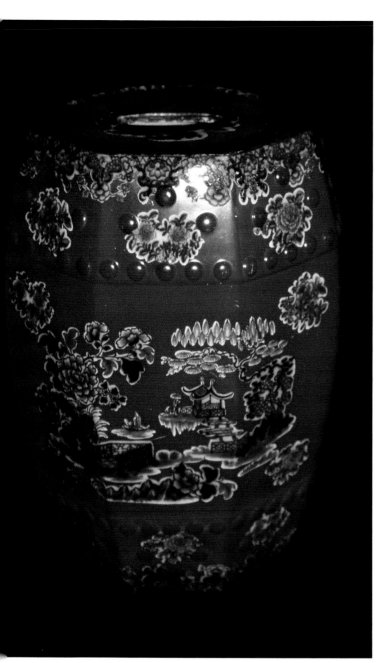

CHINESE pattern garden seat with red ground. 18.5" high. *Courtesy of Gail Frederick and Dan Overmeyer.* $3500+

Flow Blue could be found around the house, adding touches of elegance to any room. The ceramic casing for this clock is decorated in an unidentified Flow Blue pattern with gold gilt. *Courtesy of Gail Frederick and Dan Overmeyer.* $400-600

Three Periods of Flow Blue

Ground colors are found on Flow Blue from time to time. The normally white background has been colored, most often in shades of red or green. Examples of dessert sets, vases, and garden seats with this treatment are sometimes found. (Savage and Newman 1985, 142; Hill 1993, 11)

Gilding, or gilt decoration — frequently gold in color, was applied at times to embellish a pattern. The gilding was applied by hand over the glaze. Gilded pieces were fired again in a "muffle" kiln to set the gilt decoration. This gilt decoration suffered the same fate as overglaze polychrome decoration — it was easily worn away with use and cleaning. (Savage and Newman 1985, 135; Hill 1993, 12)

Above and left: This whey bowl by William Adams of Tunstall is decorated in a Flow Blue stick/sponge and overpaint decoration, c. 1840s-1860s. This blue does flow naturally to a degree. This bowl includes an impressed Adams mark in use by the company from 1800 to 1864. 16.5" in diameter. *Courtesy of Tom and Valorie Hays.* $600-850

23

Brush stroke decorated teapot, no
manufacturer's mark. 9.5" high. *Courtesy of
Gail Frederick and Dan Overmeyer.* $800-
950

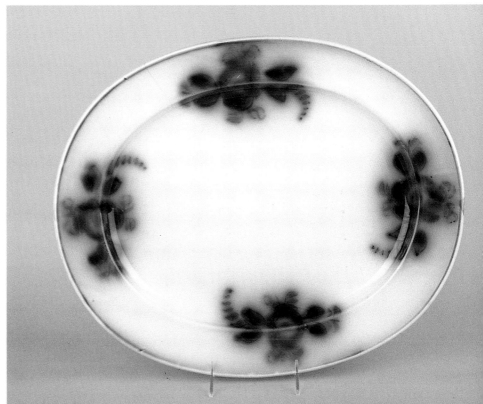

This unidentified oval platter is decorated
with flowing brush stroke patterns. 17.75"
wide. *Courtesy of Tom and Valorie Hays.*
$300+

24

Left: This brush stroke pepper pot (brush stroke pre-dates the Oriental designs) is a rare object. 5.25" high. *Courtesy of Tom and Valorie Hays.* $500+

Above: Davenport printed and impressed manufacturer's marks and Amoy pattern name. Davenport's (Longport, Staffordshire) printed "DAVENPORT" mark was in use in a variety of forms from 1820 to 1860. The impressed anchor mark can often be found with the last two digits of the year located on either side of the anchor. *Courtesy of Tom and Valorie Hays.*

Below: AMOY teapot, lidded sugar, and creamer, by Davenport date to the Early Victorian period. The creamer is hard to find. 9.5" high. *Courtesy of Tom and Valorie Hays.* $1500-1850

SHANGHAE tea set by Jocob Furnival & Company dates from the Middle Victorian period and has a *Ten-Panel Pumpkin* body shape. 8.5" high teapot. *Courtesy of Gail Frederick and Dan Overmeyer.* $1500-1850

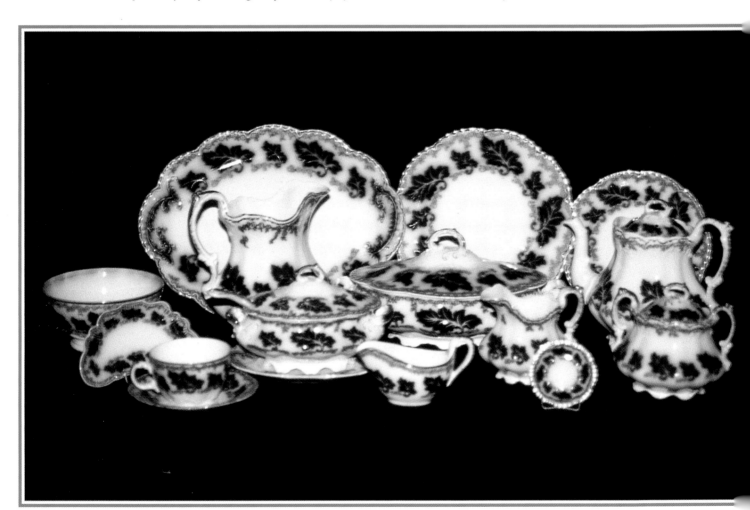

NORMANDY platter, plates, waste bowl, pitcher, covered vegetable bowl, teapot, bone dish, sauce tureen, creamer, covered sugar bowl, gravy boat, and butter pat. These date to the Late Victorian period. *Courtesy of Gail Frederick and Dan Overmeyer.* NP

Flow Blue and its patterns may be organized into three general periods of production: The Early Victorian period from circa 1835 to 1860, the Middle Victorian period from the 1860s through the 1870s, and the Late Victorian period from the 1880s through the early 1900s. The term "Victorian" is used loosely here, bearing in mind that the formidible English Queen Victoria did not take the throne until 1837 and ended her reign in 1901. Pattern designs and themes change recognizably through each period with certain exceptions during transitional years. Brush stroke patterns predate Flow Blue and when found in flowing designs may be considered early decorations. For printed patterns, the following general guidelines apply: during the Early Victorian period Oriental patterns based on imported Chinese porcelains and romanticized scenic patterns were common. Familiar Oriental scenes include the Amoy, Chapoo, Pelew, and Scinde patterns. Through the Middle Victorian period, fancy floral patterns grew in popularity and Japanese motifs appear on the scene. Fusions of the two occurred, combining Japanese designs with flowers, medallions, and ornate borders. Furnival's Shanghae and Hughes Shapoo patterns are strong examples of Middle Victorian decoration. During the Late Victorian period, Japanese, Arts and Crafts, and Art Nouveau designs proliferated. These were simpler, more naturalistic patterns with greater use of white space. These Late Victorian patterns are the most commonly found today. Popular patterns from this period include Conway, Melbourne, Normandy, Osbourne, Touraine, and Waldorf. (Snyder 1995; King 1997)

Recent Vintage Flow Blue

Flow Blue reproductions were first introduced in the 1960s as interest in these antiques grew. In 1963, England's Stevenson pottery produced a flowing floral pattern, predominantly decorating wash sets and associated accessories. From 1939-1969, the Swedish firm Gefle Porcelainworks produced a dinnerware with a flowing grape, vine, and leaf pattern named Viranka. The now discontinued Viranka pattern is considered quite collectible in today's market. Be aware that Flow Blue continues to be produced from time-to-time. (Snyder 1992; King 1997)

CHINESE potpourri jar by Thomas Dimmock & Company. Flow Blue allowed the rising middle class to *appear* to be doing quite well with impressive, yet affordable, wares such as these two potpourri jars. Normally, these came in a set of two with a center vase. 19.5" high. *Courtesy of Gail Frederick and Dan Overmeyer.* $8500+ as a three piece set. Individually, $3000 each.

Thomas Dimmock & Company printed "D" manufacturer's mark was in use from c. 1828 to 1859. *Courtesy of Gail Frederick and Dan Overmeyer.*

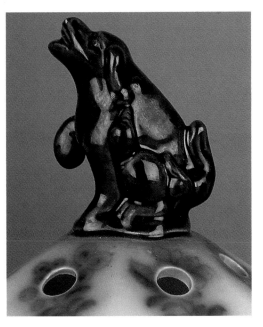

Left: The Foo dog finial on the lid of the potpourri jar. *Courtesy of Gail Frederick and Dan Overmeyer.*

Below: CIRIS pattern potpourri jar with a Wood & Brownfield manufacturer's mark. This impressive form has an inner lid used to hold scent in until one wished to let it out. The outer lid is perforated. The jar has a red ground and gold gilt. 25" high. *Courtesy of Gail Frederick and Dan Overmeyer.* $3000-5000

By the time Flow Blue was introduced, economic opportunities and standards of living were on the rise. The ranks of the Victorian middle class swelled, a middle class intent on climbing the twin social and economic ladders of success. Acquiring wealth and conspicuous consumption were considered proof of a family's virtue and a measure of their success. Until a family had that wealth, *appearing* well-to-do could make all the difference in Victorian social circles.

Flow Blue provided durable, moderately priced services much less expensive than porcelain or bone china, yet tasteful and delicate enough to be used for formal dinners and teas. CHUSAN pattern dining service, the table is set for dinner. *Courtesy of Tom and Valorie Hays.* NP

FORMOSA teapot, covered sugar, and creamer by T.J. & J. Mayer. 8.5" high teapot. *Courtesy of Tom and Valorie Hays.* $1500-1850

T.J. & J. Mayer manufacturer's mark in use from 1843 to 1855. *Courtesy of Tom and Valorie Hays.*

For the middle class, Flow Blue was a godsend, providing durable, moderately priced services much less expensive than porcelain or bone china, yet tasteful and delicate enough to be used during formal dinners and teas. Hosting these affairs was absolutely essential to rising in the Victorian social rankings.

After the middle of the nineteenth century, the dinner party became one of the most reliable methods of drawing and impressing a crowd. This endeavor was not undertaken lightly. Massive tomes were written prescribing every detail. The dinnerwares on which to properly serve the food took up many pages.

Here Flow Blue played its most significant role as a durable ware in a variety of forms offered at prices well within the range of the aspiring middle class. By 1850 ettiquette required large matching services with a number of functionally specific pieces. Flow Blue was produced with the color, the style, and the diversity of form recommended — at a price the aspiring middle class host and hostess could afford.

Above and below: Chinese motifs were considered best for the main course. PELEW dinner plate by Edward Challinor. 10" diameter. The manufacturer's mark was in use from 1842 to 1867. *Courtesy of Tom and Valorie Hays.* $125+

Nested CHUSAN platters ranging from 10.5-13" wide. *Courtesy of Tom and Valorie Hays.* NP

BLUE BELL supper set made in Wales. Shown here with the egg set outside of its container. *Courtesy of Gail Frederick and Dan Overmeyer.*

BLUE BELL complete supper set. Yes, there is a fourth section in the back. *Courtesy of Gail Frederick and Dan Overmeyer.* $3500-5000 complete set.

This rare two-sided egg cup is decorated in an unidentified bird and vase pattern. This clever design holds 2 sizes of eggs. 2" high. *Courtesy of Tom and Valorie Hays.* $250-350 (This is not a napkin ring.)

Left and Below: HONG KONG reticulated round fruit comport. 4.75" high, 9.5" diameter. *Courtesy of Gail Frederick and Dan Overmeyer.* $2000+

Above: SCINDE soup tureen by Alcock. 12.5" x 14" handle to handle, ladle 11.5" long. *Courtesy of Gail Frederick and Dan Overmeyer.* $7000+
Below: Three piece SHELL sauce tureen by Challinor. 5" high x 8" handle to handle. *Courtesy of Gail Frederick and Dan Overmeyer.* $1200-1500

Ladles: ACADIA, 1850-1870, 11.5" long; HONG KONG, 11" long; CARLTON, 11.5" long, SCINDE, 11" long; TUSCON, 10.5" long. Sauce ladle: BLEEDING HEART, 6.5" long. *Courtesy of Gail Frederick and Dan Overmeyer.* Arcadia: $350-550; Hong Kong: $1000+; Carlton: $1000+; Scinde: $2000+; Tuscon: $350-550; Bleeding Heart: $350+.

HONG pattern broth bowl, no manufacturer's mark. *Courtesy of Gail Frederick and Dan Overmeyer.* $400-650

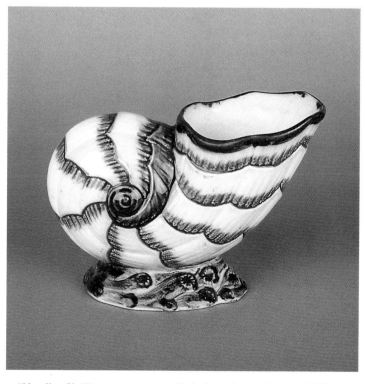

"Nautilus Shell" spoon warmer with feather edge brush stroke.7.5" wide, 4.75" high. *Courtesy of Gail Frederick and Dan Overmeyer.* $1750+

33

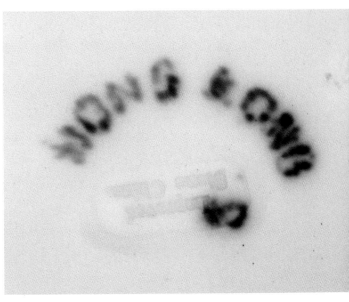

CHUSAN gravy boat — there is an undertray (not shown) that goes with this gravy boat. 9" long handle to spout. *Courtesy of Tom and Valorie Hays.* $250+

Improved Stone China impressed mark on the back of the Hong Kong butter dish. *Courtesy of Gail Frederick and Dan Overmeyer.*

Butter dishes in OREGON by T.J. & J. Mayer (Longport), HONG KONG, and AMOY by Davenport (with insert). 7" diameter, 4.5". 6" high, 8 1/2" diameter. *Courtesy of Gail Frederick and Dan Overmeyer.* $1200-1500 with inserts; $700 without inserts.

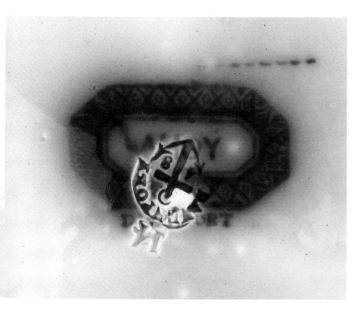

Davenport impressed anchor seal dating from 1848. The numbers 48 on either side of the anchor are the last two digits of the year. *Courtesy of Gail Frederick and Dan Overmeyer.*

Major pieces came and went from the table with each successive course. The impact of the parading dinnerwares themselves was fleeting, however. Small ceramic wares came to the rescue, remaining behind on the table and reinforcing a positive lasting impression. SLOE BLOSSOM mustard pot with a pewter lid, no manufacturer's mark. 3.5" tall. *Courtesy of Gail Frederick and Dan Overmeyer.* $500+

MARBLE master salt; Egg cups: the patterns, left to right: WINDSOR SCROLL, BASKET, BRUSH STROKE, CHEN SI, CHRYSANTHEMUM, UNIDENTIFIED, HINDUSTAN, and BLUE BELL. 2.75" largest, 2" smallest. *Courtesy of Gail Frederick and Dan Overmeyer.* NP

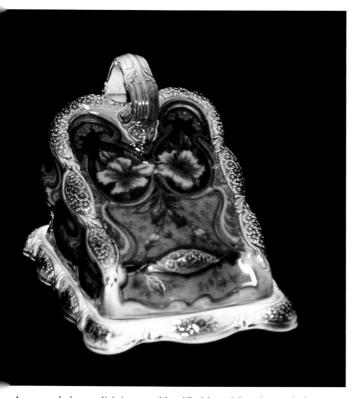

A covered cheese dish in an unidentified Late Victorian period pattern, manufacturer unknown. *Courtesy of Gail Frederick and Dan Overmeyer.* $450-600

During the course of the meal, Flow Blue wares would have been employed to serve the main courses. For a group of twelve, courses for the dinner party could well run to ten courses *before* dessert, coffee, and walnuts. Flow Blue would be used for the soup, game, and main courses. For the main course, dining wares decorated in a Chinese motif were considered best. (Pool 1993, 75)

Six cup plates. (Many were produced by Davenport and several by Clementson.) *Courtesy of Tom and Valorie Hays.* $100 and up.

Twelve butter pats of different patterns. They average 3" in diameter. *Courtesy of Tom and Valorie Hays.* $30-50 each

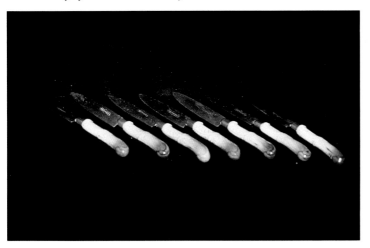

Flow Blue touches were added to knife sets to complement the dinnerware at the table. *Courtesy of Gail Frederick and Dan Overmeyer.* $500+

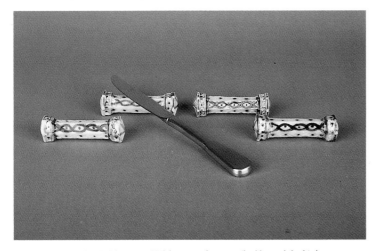

Brush stroke knife rests. With a carving set (knife and fork) it was customary to provide two rests. 3.5" long. *Courtesy of Gail Frederick and Dan Overmeyer.* $500+ for a two piece matched set.

Punch cups: the patterns, left to right: HONG KONG (covered), LAHORE, JAPAN (by Thomas Fell), MANILLA, HONG KONG, AMOY, and AMOY. *Courtesy of Gail Frederick and Dan Overmeyer.* $200+ per cup

HONG KONG covered cup. It is rare to find a covered cup. *Courtesy of Gail Frederick and Dan Overmeyer.*

Punch cups: the patterns, left to right: PELEW, BRUSH STROKE, BRUSH STROKE with two colors. 3.5" high, 3.25" in diameter. *Courtesy of Gail Frederick and Dan Overmeyer.* $200+

Mugs: the patterns, left to right: UNIDENTIFIED, SCINDE, HONG KONG with a handmade wooden lid, WHAMPOA, and TONQUIN (1845). Two handled mugs were love mugs, three handled mugs were conversation mugs. These mugs range from 5" high and 3" in diameter to 2.75" high and 2.5" in diameter. *Courtesy of Dan Overmeyer and Gail Frederick.* NP

Two HONG KONG syrups with pewter lids and different finials on each. 7.25" and 6.75" high respectively. *Courtesy of Gail Frederick and Dan Overmeyer.* $550-750

Rare SCINDE and ARABESQUE ceramic lid pots. Scinde 6" high, Arabesque 5.5" high. *Courtesy of Gail Frederick and Dan Overmeyer.* $1500+ for Scinde; Arabesque: $1100+

Major pieces came and went from the table with each successive course. The impact of the parading dinnerwares themselves was fleeting, however. Small ceramic wares came to the rescue, remaining behind on the table and reinforcing a positive lasting impression. These diminutive combatants in the art of social warfare included a wide variety of butter pats, individual salts, table salts, sugar bowls, and cream and syrup pitchers produced in Flow Blue. (Pool 1993, 75)

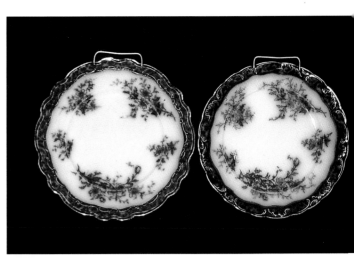

TOURAINE plates, no manufacturer's mark. The Touraine pattern was produced by at least two manufacturers: Henry Alcock, c. 1898 and the Stanley Pottery Company, 1928-1931. *Courtesy of Gail Frederick and Dan Overmeyer.* $35-110, plates vary in price by size.

AMOY cake plate by Davenport. *Courtesy of Gail Frederick and Dan Overmeyer.* $300-500

AMOY dessert dish by Davenport, part of a dessert set. This piece is very rare. *Courtesy of Gail Frederick and Dan Overmeyer.* $700-1000

Dessert services were designed to finish that impressive dinner party with a flourish. The service itself, lavishly decorated with tasteful flowers and fruits and made of the most expensive material a family could afford, consisted generally of comports with varying heights, at least two cake plates, and twelve dessert plates. Once again, the display was as important as the sugary delicacies served. (Godden 1990, 80)

Eventually, the formal dinner drew to a close. Ladies withdrew to the drawing room upstairs for coffee or tea. Gentlemen then passed the port and smoked cigars. Cigars were preferred as these were considered symbols of status and manly wealth. Smoking wares in Flow Blue were produced to accommodate this need as well. (Pool 1993, 77)

Below and right: Unidentified pattern tobacco humidor. 6.5" high. *Courtesy of Dorothy and Arnold Kowalsky.* $1500+

The dinner table, however, was not the only arena where appearances of wealth and success mattered to the middle class. The presence of a complete ceramic "chamber set" in every bed chamber, the latest advance in domestic sanitation, was another cue that a family was moving up in the Victorian world prior to mid-century. All but the most destitute had a couple of chamber pots. However, full wash sets in each bedroom were the very height of gentility; a matching basin and ewer, a soap-dish, and a sponge-dish for private bathing, a cup for brushing teeth, a slop pail, and a chamber pot with a cover to reduce disagreeable scents and spillage. Flow Blue wash sets produced by Minton, Wedgwood, and other firms of all sizes were available. A number were produced in a Marble pattern that was very appealing at the time. By mid-century, a chamber set for every bed chamber would become more common and these sets remained a staple of the earthenware trade. (Larkin 1988, 144)

Right: WINDSOR SCROLLS foot bath pitcher (note protruding hook on side) by an unidentified manufacturer whose initials are "S. & H." 12" high, 13" wide handle to spout. *Courtesy of Tom and Valorie Hays.* $650+

Below: CASHMERE bath set including a wash ewer and basin, footbath, soap dish, and covered tray. *Courtesy of Gail Frederick and Dan Overmeyer.* $10,000+

Another useful piece for the bed chamber: a HONG bed pan by Petrus Regout, c. 1858. *Courtesy of Gail Frederick and Dan Overmeyer.* $1200-1500

Unidentified printed S. & H. manufacturer's mark. *Courtesy of Tom and Valorie Hays.*

"BASKET" toast rack. *Courtesy of Dan Overmeyer.* $400-600

Afternoon tea began in the 1840s in England and soon extended to America. Tea services for five o'clock tea, a ritual in-and-of-itself by the 1860s, were comprised of a teapot, sugar bowl, creamer, cups and saucers, cup plates, a waste bowl, plates, two cake plates, preserve plates, a butter plate, a tray, hot-water urn, spoon holder, and occasionally a syrup or molasses pitcher. Breakfasts and teas could be served on a rotating table in the boudoir as well.

To accomodate the new demand for tablewares of all sorts, manufacturers expanded their production capacities and distribution networks. By the end of the nineteenth century, this expansion would lead to a wide choice of services for all occasions at prices almost everyone could afford. Late nineteenth century Flow Blue reflects this trend with wares exhibiting a wide range of qualities produced by well known and obscure manufacturers from Britain, Europe, and America.

About the Values

Breakfast, tea, and dessert also required their own special wares and decorum. During the first half of the nineteenth century breakfast sets included twelve cups and saucers with larger teacups than would generally be used for other occasions, a sugar dish, a milk pot, teapot, slop bowl, and breakfast plates. Larger sets would include a coffee pot, butter boat, and cake plate. By the end of the nineteenth century, fruit and mush had been added to the breakfast menu, requiring a fruit plate and mush bowl. (Godden 1990, 80-81)

The values in the captions of this book are for Flow Blue wares in mint condition. Values vary immensely according to the condition of the piece, the location of the market, and the overall quality of the design and manufacture. Condition is always of paramount importance in assigning a value. Prices in the Midwest differ from those in the West or East, and those at specialty antique shows will vary from those at general shows. Of course, being in the right place at the right time can make all the difference.

All of these factors make it impossible to create an absolutely accurate price list; however, a useful general pricing guide can be offered. The values reflect what one might realistically expect to pay at retail or auction and are listed in U.S. dollars. Best of luck to you in your search for Flow Blue!

SCINDE pumpkin style tea set. 9 " high teapot, marked. *Courtesy of Gail Frederick and Dan Overmeyer.* $1500-1850 set.

Ironstone Body Shapes Associated With Flow Blue

SCINDE pitchers and creamer, left to right: *Full Paneled Gothic* body shape, 7.25" high; *Classic Gothic* body shape 9.5" high; and *Eight-Panel Pumpkin* body shape, 6" high. *Courtesy of Gail Frederick and Dan Overmeyer.* Left: $850+; center: $1000+; right $450+

The white ironstone ceramic body used in much of Flow Blue production came in many body shapes, styles, or forms. Particular body shapes were sometimes given specific names by their potters. In more recent years, collectors have added names of their own to the list. Naming body shapes provides a convenient means for collectors and dealers to discuss and compare Flow Blue wares in a common language. As of this writing, roughly fifty Flow Blue body shapes with identifiable traits are named. These named body shapes tend to date from the second and third quarters of the nineteenth century. In the future, others are sure to be added.

Many of these shapes also appear decorated in Mulberry. Mulberry, also referred to as "Flow Black," was another flowing motif. Instead of using cobalt, manganese carbonates were used in the transfer inks to create a pur-

plish color. Mulberry tended to be less expensive than Flow Blue and provided an alternative to the standard cobalt blue transfer printed patterns consumers were familiar with. Many of the same manufacturers produced both Flow Blue and Mulberry wares from the 1830s through the 1870s, and frequently used the same patterns as well as the same body shapes. (Stoltzfus and Snyder 1997)

Specific diagnostic features used to identify body shapes include molded body decorations and paneling, base designs, and finial designs. Teapots tend to be the focus of any discussion of body shape as they commonly exhibit all of the specific features associated with a particular shape. Teapots also have several extra features worth noting when studying a particular shape — their handle and spout configurations. While the basic diagnostic features are also found on associated sugar bowls and creamers, they usually can not be found your average dinner plate or soup bowl. Teapots also have the advantage of being common items. Americans ordered tea sets in vast quantities throughout the nineteenth century and even adopted the British tea time ritual in the 1860s. Finally, teapots are are much loved by collectors, in part because they are associated with a warm, pleasant, and civil pastime. (Frederick, et al. 1993, 1)

Other wares which usually display the definitive features of a particular form include soup tureens, sauce tureens, and vegetable dishes. When possible, these are also displayed in this chapter to provide a broader view of a particular shape than is available through the teapots alone.

To date, semi-porcelain shapes in Flow Blue have not been addressed. Each pattern had its own particular teapot shape, making the total numbers of shapes too large to handle. That is a project we mere mortals can gladly hand off to future super-computers after their programmers tire of playing chess. (Frederick, et al. 1993, 2)

Teapot History

Before reviewing shapes based primarily on teapots, a brief teapot history will provide a heightened appreciation for these special, much-loved pots. Tea drinking and teapots originated in China. The earliest tea history is as murky as an overly flown transfer print, but tea drinking is well established by the Han period dating from 206 B.C. to 220 A.D. Whether prepared from roasted black leaves or green leaves, tea was considered a stimulant for scholastic and meditative souls. (Tippett 1996, 6)

The early tea drinkers were among the educated upper classes. In time, tea drinking trickled down to the masses. Trickling down as well were both rituals and special implements necessary for the proper enjoyment of this respected drink.

The first teapots were probably Chinese wine pots with shaped spouts and overhead bail handles. The first were made of bronze and other metals. The early pots and tea bowls were tiny affairs. The pots were smaller than the wine pots they emulated. This small size befit the sophisticated drink and allowed the individual to make his or her own personal brew. In a small pot, the tea was strong — no doubt further enhancing the scholastic and meditative processes. (Tippett 1996, 6-7; Carter 1995, 8)

China had a huge early lead on Europe in technological innovation. The Chinese were producing perfect porcelain two thousand years before the Europeans, for example. Needless to say, Chinese exports were in great demand when their markets opened abroad. International trade spread customs and rituals, and in time tea drinking spread across Asia and then the Arab world by the sixth and seventh centuries A.D. In the sixteenth century, the Portugese were the first

Europeans to reach China. The British, Dutch, and French soon followed and the Chinese set up tight controls over the traffic, routing all international shipping through Canton. (Tippett 1996, 7)

The Dutch first imported tea into Europe in 1610, and with it the Chinese porcelain teapot and tea bowl. These pots were nearly perfect in design. They were broad at the base to keep the pot from tipping over and scalding the drinker. The spouts were large enough not to be clogged by tea leaves. The pots were, however, also small enough to allow everyone to have their own private pot of tea. The accompanying tea bowls were equally small. (Pratt 1982, 104-105)

As the Chinese expanded their international trade and tea production, throughout Europe a mania developed for all things Chinese, and a positive craze developed for tea

Covered tea caddies in an unidentified pattern. 6" high. *Courtesy of Gail Frederick and Dan Overmeyer.* $500-750

Printed back mark, an English imitation of Chinese marks. *Courtesy of Gail Frederick and Dan Overmeyer.*

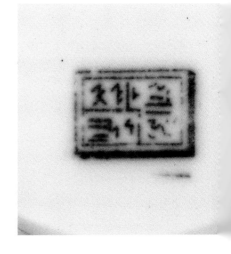

drinking. By the 1720s, tea filled ninety percent of the space in the holds of ships sailing for the West. The tea was exported in wooden crates overseas. Within the crates were those small porcelain teapots and other tea wares essential for brewing and drinking a proper cup of tea. Demand for teapots and tea bowls grew rapidly. By the middle of the 1700s, the East India Trading Company's sales agents were providing the Chinese with Western specifications for decorating the teapots and tea wares packed within the shipping crates. (Carter 1995, 9)

These early teapots and tea wares were limited to the upper classes in the West. The costs of shipping tea and tea sets were enormous and only the rich could afford them. The tea sets were especially desirable since porcelain production techniques had yet to be perfected in England or Europe. (Tippett 1996, 8-9)

It was not long before English and European potters were striving to imitate the immensely popular Chinese export wares. This is evident in the early Flow Blue teapots which almost always feature Oriental patterns and handleless tea bowls. The blue and white coloration also emulated the Chinese decoration.

In time, English and European potters developed their own ideas as to what constituted a well made teapot and how it should be decorated. These changes in form and decorative motifs are evident in the Flow Blue teapots and tea wares produced over many decades.

The tea cup's form was changed in Western hands as well. England's potters enlarged the cup and added a handle to it. The tea bowl was no more, and the new English tea cup was remarkably similar to the familiar English posset cup. The new tea cup form was so successful that by the time tea was England's national drink, the "teacupful" was a standard measure for English cooks. (Pratt 1982, 110)

Body Shapes

The following listings of shapes are organized by the established shape names recognized in the Flow Blue collecting community. If you wish to ascertain whether a particular shape name was provided originally by the potter or much later by collectors and dealers, refer to registration marks, manufacturers' marks, and original registry drawings. If a particular name was given to a blank by a potter, that name will be found in these sources. All other shape names, however, are of more recent vintage.

In this discussion of body shapes, the author has referred to the following texts: *Flow Blue and Mulberry Teapot Body Styles* by Gale Frederick, Valorie and Tom Hays, Ellen Hill, Lou Nelson, and Dan Overmeyer (1993); *Mulberry Ironstone. Flow Blue's Best Kept Little Secret* by Ellen R. Hill (1993); *White Ironstone: A Collector's Guide* by Jean Wetherbee (1996); and, a recent arrival, *White Ironstone. A Survey of its Many Forms* by Dawn Stoltzfus and Jeffrey Snyder (1997). For the detailed information concerning individual potters, the author referred to: *The Dictionary of Blue and White Printed Pottery 1780-1880* (2 vols.) by A.W. Coysh and R.K. Henrywood (1982 & 1989); *Encyclopaedia of British Pottery and Porcelain Marks* by Geoffrey A. Godden (1974); and *Historic Flow Blue* by Jeffrey B. Snyder (1994). All of the date ranges and potter's identification found throughout this book also come from these three sources.

CASHMERE by Francis Morley & Company, *Broad Shoulder* body shape. 8.5" high creamer and teapot. *Courtesy of Gail Frederick and Dan Overmeyer.* $750+ creamer; $1500+ teapot.

Broad Shoulder

The Broad Shoulder shape was produced by Francis Morley & Company (Broad Street, Shelton, Hanley, Staffordshire, 1845-1858) in c. 1850. This shape has eight convex upper panels over eight lower body panels and an eight petal flower finial with a conical bud. The bases are also eight sided. Flow Blue patterns found on this shape include Cashmere and Pheasant.

The Bulbous shape was manufactured by Podmore, Walker & Company (Tunstall, Staffordshire, 1834-1859) in c. 1849. It features a twelve-paneled bulbous body with a recessed rounded base and a fig finial. The Flow Blue Temple pattern and Mulberry Washington Vase and Eagle patterns are associated with this shape.

Bulbous

Bulbous Octagon

TEMPLE teapot with a rounded base, twelve-paneled *Bulbous* shape, with a fig finial, by Podmore, Walker & Company. 9.75" high. *Courtesy of Tom and Valorie Hays.* $850+

Above and right: OREGON teapot, eight-paneled *Bulbous Octagon* body shape. 9.5" high. *Courtesy of Tom and Valorie Hays.* $850+

Left: TEMPLE teapot by Podmore, Walker & Company in the *Bulbous* shape. *Courtesy of Gail Frederick and Dan Overmeyer.* $850+

Bulbous Octagon OREGON tea set by Thomas, John, & Joseph Mayer. Teapot 9.75" high. *Courtesy of Gail Frederick and Dan Overmeyer.* $1500-1850 set.

Bulbous Octagon was manufactured by Thomas, John & Joseph Mayer (Furlong Works and Dale Hall Pottery, Burslem, 1843-1855) around 1845. This shape features an eight paneled body with a recessed eight-sided base and an eight-panel flower finial with a center bud. Flow Blue patterns associated with this shape include Oregon and Formosa.

Classic Gothic

Gothic shapes were inspired by the resurgence of interest in the paneled forms, multiple designs, pointed arches, flying buttresses, and ribbed vaulting of Gothic architecture in the 1830s. Gothic Revival influences included ironstone body shapes for a time. The simple Gothic label registered for these shapes was too broad to provide meaningful descriptions for modern collectors and dealers. Gothic shapes have been provided with additional descriptive terms and appear as Classic Gothic, Full Panel Gothic, and so on to narrow the scope. (Frederick, et al. 1993, 2)

There are five Classic Gothic shapes currently associated with Flow Blue. This first Classic Gothic shape was produced by Edward Challinor (Pinnocks Works and Unicorn Pottery, Tunstall, Staffordshire, 1842-1867) around 1850. Challinor's Classic Gothic has an eight-paneled body with a recessed eight-sided base and a curly mushroom finial. Challinor's Flow Blue pattern associated with this shape is Pelew and his Mulberry patterns include Calcutta and Pelew.

Far right and right: Joseph Clementson manufacturer's mark with the printed "J. Clementson" and Phoenix bird was in use from 1840 onward. An American distributor's mark, "F. J. Blair, Milwaukie, Wis.", also was found on this set. *Courtesy of Tom and Valorie Hays.*

Classic Gothic — Joseph Clementson

CHUSAN teapot, creamer, and sugar bowl by Joseph Clementson in the *Classic Gothic* shape. 9.25" high teapot. *Courtesy of Tom and Valorie Hays.* $1500-1850 set.

Joseph Clementon (Phoenix Works, Shelton, Hanley, Staffordshire, c. 1839-1864) produced his version of the Classic Gothic shape in c. 1845. The shape had an eight-paneled body, a recessed eight-sided base, and an eight-sided pagoda finial. His Flow Blue pattern Chusan and Mulberry pattern Oak & Ivy grace the shape.

Classic Gothic — Davenport

AMOY tea set by Davenport, *Classic Gothic* shape. tea set. 10.5" high. *Courtesy of Gail Frederick and Dan Overmeyer.* $1500-1850 set.

This shape has an eight-paneled body, recessed eight-sided base, and an eight-sided step pagoda finial Classic Gothic shape produced by Davenport & Company (Longport, Staffordshire 1794-1887) around 1845. The Flow Blue Amoy pattern and Mulberry Cyprus pattern adorn this shape.

Classic Gothic — Mellor, Venables & Company

Mellor, Venables & Company (Hole House Pottery, Burslem, Staffordshire, 1834-1851) produced their eight-paneled body, recessed eight-sided base, eight-paneled flower finial Classic Gothic body shape around 1850. The Flow Blue pattern Flow Blue-Mulberry Brush stroke Stripe and Mulberry pattern Beauties of China grace the shape.

Classic Gothic — Podmore, Walker & Company

TEMPLE tea set by Podmore Walker & Co., *Classic Gothic* shape. This set is of special interest because of the lion's head cameo on each handle. 9" high. *Courtesy of Gail Frederick and Dan Overmeyer.* $1500-1850 set.

Podmore, Walker & Company also produced an eight-paneled, recessed eight-sided vase, curly mushroom finial Classic Gothic shape. It was decorated with Flow Blue Temple, Manilla, and Brush stroke patterns and Mulberry Corean and Washington Vase patterns.

Cockscomb Handle

"MORNING GLORY" and "GAUDY BERRY" or "GAUDY STRAWBERRY" overpaint decoration on a pedestaled *Cockscomb Handle* body shape teapot. 10" high. *Courtesy of Gail Frederick and Dan Overmeyer.* $850-1200

"STRAWBERRY" brush stroke pattern pedestaled teapot in the *Cockscomb Handle* body shape. *Courtesy of Lynn Trusdell.* $850-1200

"MORNING GLORY" and "GAUDY BERRY" or "GAUDY STRAWBERRY" overpaint decoration on a *Cockscomb Handle* pedestaled teapot. *Courtesy of Gail Frederick and Dan Overmeyer.* $850-1200

Cockscomb Handle teapot shape decorated with the "BLACKBERRY" brush stroke pitcher with overpaint, no manufacturer's mark. *Courtesy of Gail Frederick and Dan Overmeyer.* $850-1200

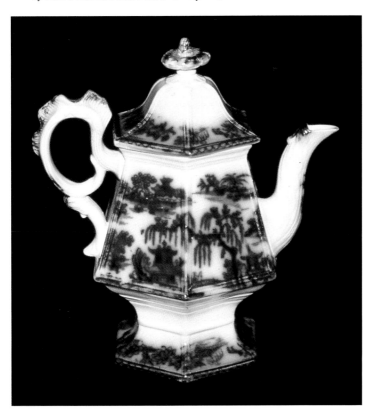

MANILLA teapot by Podmore, Walker & Company in the *Cockscomb Handle* shape. *Courtesy of Gail Frederick and Dan Overmeyer.* $1200-1500

This popular shape was produced in the 1840s and 1850s by a number of firms including Elsmore & Forster (Clayhills Pottery, Tunstall, Staffordshire, 1853-1871), Jacob Furnival & Company (Cobridge, Staffordshire, c. 1845-1870), Thomas Furnival & Company (Hanley, c. 1844-1846), Podmore,

Walker & Company, and Thomas Walker (Lion Works, Tunstall, Staffordshire, c. 1845-c. 1853). The Cockscomb Handle shape has a six-paneled body, a pedestaled base with a six-sided footprint, and most notably an ornate handle with two openings and cockscomb shaped flanges. The Flow Blue patterns adorning this shape include Brush stroke, Gaudy, Manilla, and Simla. The Mulberry patterns found on the "CCH" shape include Corean, Grape & Sprig Brush stroke, Hong, Kansu, Medina, Rose, Scinde, Strawberry Brush stroke, and Wreath.

Columbia

Gaudy Ironstone Flow Blue coffee pot by Edward Challinor in the "*Columbia*" shape. *Courtesy of Gail Frederick and Dan Overmeyer.* $2000+

Edward Challinor produced this shape in c. 1855. It has a many-paneled bulbous embossed body, recessed rounded base, and an apple finial. Flow Blue patterns on Columbia include Gaudy Ironstone and Pelew. The Mulberry pattern associated with this shape is Rose.

Davenport Octagon

Davenport & Company produced this eight-sided body with straight over angled panels, recessed eight-sided base, and onion finial shape around the middle of the nineteenth century. The Amoy Flow Blue pattern and Cyprus Mulberry pattern have been found on this shape.

Eight-Panel Pumpkin

John & George Alcock (Cobridge, Staffordshire, 1839-1846), Samuel Alcock & Company (Cobridge and Hill Pottery, Burslem, Staffordshire, 1828-1859), Ralph Hall (& Co. or & Son, Swan Bank, Tunstall, Staffordshire, 1822-1849), and Podmore, Walker & Company all produced this pattern around 1845. It is also known simply as "Pumpkin." The body is a squat eight-paneled pumpkin shape, the base is recessed with an eight-sided footprint, and the finial is also eight-sided. Flow Blue patterns found on this shape include Manilla, Scinde, and Sobraon. The Mulberry pattern associated with this pumpkin shape is Ning Po.

Flat-Paneled Primary

William Ridgway (Bell Works, Shelton and Church Works, Hanley, c. 1830-1854 — under various names and in several locations William Ridgway produced pottery from c. 1830-1879) produced this shape around 1840. It features an eight convex panel body over eight flat panels, a recessed eight-sided base, and an eight-sided pagoda finial. William Ridgway decorated this shape with the Pagoda Flow Blue pattern.

SOBRAON *Eight-Panel Pumpkin* shape teapot, no manufacturer's mark. *Courtesy of Gail Frederick and Dan Overmeyer.* $850+

PAGODA pattern, *Flat-Paneled Primary* shape teapot, sugar, and creamer by William Ridgway. 9" high teapot. *Courtesy of Tom and Valorie Hays.* $1500-1850 set.

Full Panel Gothic — William Adams & Son

Full Panel Gothic — James Edwards

William Adams & Son produced this shape, also known by the descriptive name "Lighthouse," in c. 1850. This shape features an eight-paneled body, single ridge eight-sided base, and an eight-sided banded pyramid finial. The Flow Blue pattern Jeddo and Mulberry patterns Athens and Jeddo cover this shape.

Full Panel Gothic — J. & G. Alcock, J. & S. Alcock, Jr.

SCINDE teapot in the *Full Panel Gothic* shape produced by the Alcocks. *Courtesy of Gail Frederick and Dan Overmeyer.* $1200+

The partnerships of John & George Alcock (1839-1846) and John & Samuel Alcock, Jr. (Cobridge, Staffordshire, c. 1848-1850) produced their version of this shape around mid-century. Their Lighthouse version included an eight-paneled body, a single ridge eight-sided base, and an eight-sided banded pyramid finial. The Flow Blue Scinde and Mulberry Vincennes patterns grace the Alcock's shape.

Above and right: COBURG *Full Panel Gothic* teapot by James Edwards. The registration date, according to the mark and the very unusual written date, is October 26, 1846. 8" high. *Courtesy of Tom and Valorie Hays.* $850+

James Edwards (Dale Hall, Burslem, c. 1842-1851) produced his version of this body shape, that is also called "Pinched-Neck Gothic," around 1847. The body is eight-paneled with a recessed neck, a small ridge eight-sided base, and a four-petal flower finial with a center bud. The Coburg Flow Blue pattern and Foliage Mulberry patterns are found on this shape.

Full Panel Gothic — Jacob Furnival & Co.

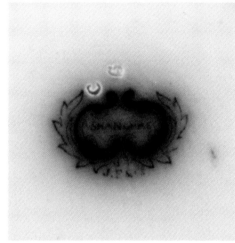

Jacob Furnival & Company's manufacturer's mark in use from c. 1845 to 1870. *Courtesy of Gail Frederick and Dan Overmeyer.*

COBURG teapot by James Edwards, *Full Panel Gothic* shape, also called "Pinchneck Gothic." 8.25" high. *Courtesy of Gail Frederick and Dan Overmeyer.* $850+

SHANGHAE tea set by Jacob Furnival & Company in *Full Panel Gothic.* 9.75" high teapot. *Courtesy of Gail Frederick and Dan Overmeyer.* $1500-1850 set.

Jacob Furnival and Company's version is also known as "Lighthouse" and was produced in c. 1850. It has an eight-paneled body, a ridged banded eight-sided base, and an eight-sided banded pyramid finial. The Flow Blue patterns on this shape are Shanghae and Chusan (on a variant of this shape); the Mulberry patterns include Castle Scenery and Strawberry Brush stroke.

Full Panel Gothic — Ralph Hall & Co.

Ralph Hall & Company's "Lighthouse" shape was produced in c. 1845 and has an eight-paneled body, a single right eight-sided base, and an eight-sided stepped low dome finial. There is no Flow Blue pattern in this shape and only the Ning Po Mulberry pattern adorns it.

Full Panel Gothic — Podmore, Walker & Co.

CHUSAN teapot by Podmore, Walker & Company in a variant of the *Full Panel Gothic* shape reminiscent of Peter Holdcroft's version featuring the Mulberry Chusan pattern. 8.5" high. *Courtesy of Tom and Valorie Hays.* $1000+

Full Panel Gothic shape MANILLA pattern teapot by Podmore, Walker & Company. 8.5" high. *Courtesy of Gail Frederick and Dan Overmeyer.* $1000+

Podmore, Walker & Company's take on this shape is also known as "Lighthouse" and was produced around 1847. It has a recessed eight-paneled body, a stepped band eight-sided base, and an eight-sided banded dome finial. The Manilla Flow Blue pattern and the Corean Mulberry pattern are found on this shape.

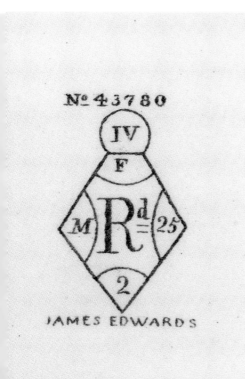

Gothic Cameo COBURG pattern covered vegetable dish by James Edwards, Dale Hall, Burslem, c. 1842-1851, with a June 25, 1847 registration mark. 8" high, 10" handle to handle. Note the cameo, the face, under the handles. *Courtesy of Gail Frederick and Dan Overmeyer.* $750-900

James Edwards produced this shape which bears a registration date of 1847. Other versions of Gothic Cameo were produced by John Alcock, Davenport, and John Wedg Wood. It has an eight-panel body, a recessed eight-sided base, and an eight-sided pagoda finial. The shape was decorated by James Edwards with the Flow Blue Coburg pattern. John Alcock applied the Mulberry Vincennes pattern to his Gothic Cameo.

Grand Loop

Mellor, Venables & Company produced this shape around 1855. It has bulbous large embossed loops on the body, a recessed rounded base, and a pomegranate finial. Mulberry patterns in this shape include Avon and Strawberry (Blackberry) Lustre.

Grape Octagon

The manufacturers producing this shape include Edward Challinor and Jacob Furnival & Company around 1847. The body shape has an eight-paneled concave embossed body, a recessed eight-sided base, and a stemmed bunch of grapes finial. Brush stroke Flow Blue and Cotton Plant, Floral, and Rose Mulberry patterns grace this shape.

Grape Octagon shape "gaudy" teapot decorated in brush stroke with polychrome overpainting, accompanied by a handleless cup and saucer. 9" high teapot, 3.5" diameter cup, 5.75" diameter saucer. *Courtesy of Tom and Valorie Hays.* $1000 teapot; $250 cup and saucer.

Inverted Diamond Primary

Thomas, John & Joseph Mayer, F. & R. Pratt (& Co., High Street, Fenton, Staffordshire, c. 1818 - present), and Thomas Walker all produced this shape around 1845. The body shape has concave upper panels over bulbous lower body panels creating a diamond (or zig-zag) effect, a pedestaled diamond (or zig-zag) embossed eight-sided base, and a diamond embossed pagoda finial. Flow Blue Arabesque, Brush stroke, Indian, and Scinde patterns adorn this shape.

"TULIP AND SPRIG" brush stroke pattern teapot in the *Inverted Diamond Primary* shape. 8.5" high. *Courtesy of Gail Frederick and Dan Overmeyer.* $850+

INDIAN teapot, sugar, and creamer in the *Inverted Diamond Primary* shape. 9" high teapot. *Courtesy of Tom and Valorie Hays.* $1500-1850 set.

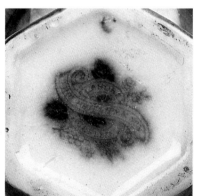

Above and left: LAHORE teapot, creamer, and sugar in the Inverted Heart Primary shape by Thomas Phillips & Son. This manufacturer's mark was in use from c. 1845 to 1846. 9.5" high teapot. *Courtesy of Tom and Valorie Hays.* $1500-1850 set

LAHORE teapot and creamer by Thomas Phillips & Sons, *Inverted Heart Primary*. 9.5" high teapot. *Courtesy of Gail Frederick and Dan Overmeyer.* $850 teapot; $450 creamer.

Thomas Phillips & Sons (Furlong Pottery, Burslem, Staffordshire, c. 1845-1846) produced this shape during their brief potting life. It has six "pseudo-heart" shaped panels, a recessed base with a six-sided footprint, and a six-sided pagoda finial. The Lahore Flow Blue pattern is found on this shape.

Long Octagon — Davenport & Co.

Long Octagon shape AMOY teapot by Davenport & Company. *Courtesy of Gail Frederick and Dan Overmeyer.* $1000++

Davenport & Company produced their version of this shape in c. 1845. The body has a cut-corner rectangular shape, the base is a recessed long octagon, and the finial is a rectangular dome. The Flow Blue Amoy pattern and Mulbery Cyprus pattern are found on this shape.

Long Octagon — T. J. & J. Mayer

Thomas, John & Joseph Mayer produced a Long Octagon shape in c. 1853. It has a cut-corner rectangular body, a recessed long octagon base, and a oval flower finial. The Arabesque Flow Blue pattern has been found on this shape.

Long Octagon — C. Meigh

Charles Meigh (Hanley, Staffordshire, 1835-1849; & Son, 1851-1861) produced this pattern around 1845. It has a cut-corner triangle body, a recessed long octagon base, and an oval flower finial. The Flow Blue Hong Kong pattern decorates this shape.

Oval

Oval TEMPLE pattern teapot by Podmore, Walker & Company. 8.5" high. *Courtesy of Gail Frederick and Dan Overmeyer.* $1000+

Podmore, Walker & Company produced this oval bulbous embossed vertical medallions body with a recessed oval base and an oval stepped dome finial in about 1849. The Temple Flow Blue and Corean Mulberry patterns appear on this shape.

Far left and left: ARABESQUE teapot by T.J. & J. Mayer in their *Long Octagon* shape. This manufacturer's mark was in use from 1843-1855. 7" high. *Courtesy of Gail Frederick and Dan Overmeyer.* $750-850

Paneled Grape

Primary — Double Line

"BLACKBERRY" brush stroke coffee pot by Jacob Furnival & Company in the *Paneled Grape* body shape. *Courtesy of Gail Frederick and Dan Overmeyer.* $2000+

Double Line Primary gaudy brush stroke decorated teapot. 8.5" high. *Courtesy of Tom and Valorie Hays.* $850+

Jacob Furnival & Company produced this shape around 1860. It has a bulbous, deeply ridged body, a recessed round base, and an embossed ring finial. The Blackberry Flow Blue pattern is found on this shape.

Pedestal Gothic

James Edwards produced this shape in c. 1845. Pedestal Gothic has a recessed eight-paneled body, a pedestaled eight-sided base, and a four-petal flower and center bud finial. Only Mulberry appears on this shape in the Foliage and Bochara patterns.

Plain Round

The potter who produced this shape with Flow Blue decoration is not currently known. This simple but elegant shape has a smooth bulbous body, a recessed round base, and a conical ring finial. The Flow Blue Snowflake pattern has been found on this shape.

"HEATH'S FLOWER" brush stroke *Double Line Primary* teapot. 9" high. *Courtesy of Tom and Valorie Hays.* $850

NANKIN large *No Line Primary* shape teapot, no manufacturer's mark. 10" high from spout to handle and 11.5" wide. *Courtesy of Tom and Valorie Hays.* $850+

John Meir & Sons (Greengates Pottery, Tunstall, Staffordshire, 1836-1897), Thomas Hughes (Waterloo Road, Burslem, c. 1860-1876 and Top Bridge Works, Longport, Burslem, Staffordshire, c. 1872-1894), and Podmore, Walker & Company produced this shape. The body is bulbous with eight-panels, the base is eight-sided recessed, and the finial is an eight-paneled pagoda. Flow Blue patterns on this shape include Brush strokes, Kirkee, Manilla, and Shapoo; the only Mulberry pattern associated with No Line Primary is Corean.

Primary — Single Line

"TULIP AND SPRIG" brush stroke pattern *Single Line Primary* shape teapot, creamer, and sugar bowl with a V shaped mark handpainted underneath, no manufacturer's mark. 9" high teapot. *Courtesy of Tom and Valorie Hays.* $1500-1850 set.

TIVOLI pattern tall, *Double Line Primary,* stretch-necked shape teapot. 10.75" high. *Courtesy of Tom and Valorie Hays.* $850+

Double Line Primary was a popular shape produced by many manufacturers including John & George Alcock, Samuel Alcock, Edward Challinor, Davenport & Company, Thomas Fell (& Company, St. Peter's Pottery, Newcastle-upon-Tyne, 1817-1890), Jacob Furnival, Joseph Heath (High Street, Tunstall, Staffordshire, 1845-1853), John Maddock (& Sons, Newcastle Street, Burslem, Staffordshire, 1842-present), Thomas, John & Joseph Mayer, Charles Meigh, Mellor, Venables & Company, John Wedg Wood (Hadderidge, Burslem & Tunstall, Staffordshire, 1841-1860), and Wood & Brownfield (Cobridge Works, Cobridge, Staffordshire, c. 1838-1850) around 1845. The shape has a recessed eight-panel bulbous embossed double-line arches body, a recessed eight-sided base, and a pagoda finial. Many Flow Blue patterns were used on this shape, including Amoy, Brush stroke, Chapoo, Excelsior, Hindustan, Homestead, Hong Kong, Scinde, Sobraon, Tivoli, Tonquin, and Whampoa. In Mulberry, only the Cypress pattern has been found on this shape.

"TULIP AND SPRIG" brush stroke pattern *Single Line Primary* shape teapot, no manufacturer's mark. 9" high. *Courtesy of Gail Frederick and Dan Overmeyer.* $850

HONG pattern *Single Line Primary* coffee pot by Anthony Shaw (& Co. or & Son, Tunstall from c. 1851-1856 and Burslem from c. 1860-c. 1900), c. 1855. 11.5" high. *Courtesy of Tom and Valorie Hays.* $2000+

Edward Challinor, Thomas, John & Joseph Mayer, F. & R. Pratt, Anthony Shaw (& Co. or & Son, Tunstall from c. 1851-1856 and Burslem from c. 1860-c. 1900), and Thomas Walker all produced this shape around 1845. The Single Line Primary shape has a recessed eight-paneled bulbous embossed single arches body, a recessed on pedestal eight-sided base, and an eight-paneled pagoda finial. Brush stroke, Hong, Indian, Oregon, Pelew, and Shell Flow Blue patterns appear on this shape. The Mulberry Scinde pattern also decorates this shape.

Primary — Straight Line

CASHMERE *Straight Line Primary* teapot by Francis Morley & Company. Note the acorn finial. 8.75" high. *Courtesy of Tom and Valorie Hays.* $1500+

Straight Line Primary, also known as "Primary, Acorn Finial," was produced by Francis Morley & Company in c. 1850. It is an eight-paneled bulbous straight line embossed body, a recessed eight-sided base, and an acorn finial. The Cashmere Flow Blue and Lady Peel Mulberry patterns appear on this shape.

Prize Bloom

Above and below: OREGON covered vegetable dish by T. J. & J. Mayer, *Prize Bloom* shape, circa 1853. 7.5" high. *Courtesy of Gail Frederick and Dan Overmeyer.* $850+

Thomas, John & Joseph Mayer registered this shape on October 22, 1853. The "Prize" in Prize Bloom, and Prize Puritan which follows, refers to this shape having won a prize at an international exhibition. This shape has a twelve-paneled embossed body, a recessed base with a six-sided footprint, and a tilted open flower or "bloom" finial. The patterns appearing on this shape include Oregon and Snowflake Flow Blue and Flower Vase Mulberry.

Prize Puritan

Thomas, John & Joseph Mayer produced this pattern around 1845. Prize Puritan has an alternating ridge and groove body with no obvious rim, a pedestaled rounded square base, and an eight-sided flattened pagoda finial. There are no Flow Blue patterns and only the Flower Base Mulberry pattern is found decorating this shape.

Ridged Square

Charle Meigh produced Ridged Square, also called "Melon," in c. 1845. It has an alternating ridge and groove body without an apparent rim, a pedestaled rounded square base, and an eight-sided flattened pagoda finial. This shape is decorated with Athens, Diamond Leaf Cross, and Hong Kong Flow Blue patterns and the Athens Mulberry pattern.

Rococo

Above and left: "BLEEDING HEART" flowing blue brush stroke pattern semi-porcelain teapot in the *Rococo* shape. This teapot has an old staple repair to the finial — these early staple repairs are now collectible. The teapot has a registration mark dating to June 14, 1843 and gold gilt decoration. It was produced by Samuel Alcock & Company. 7.5" high. *Courtesy of Tom and Valorie Hays.* $850

Rococo shape (early style) coffee pot with gold gilt, no manufacturer's mark, possibly in the "CHEAU" pattern. 11" high. *Courtesy of Tom and Valorie Hays.* $2000+

Above two and below: *Rococo* shape semi-porcelain creamer, sugar bowl, and teapot with gold gilt and old staple repairs. 8.5" high. The manufacturer's mark and pattern name are only partially legible — the flowing blue pattern name is CHIAN SPRIGS. The manufacturer is Hilditch & Hopwood (1835-59). The registrations mark dates this set to April 11, 1844. *Courtesy of Tom and Valorie Hays.* NP

This shape was produced by both Samuel Alcock and Mellor, Venables & Company around 1844. This shape has a rococo body, a four-footed pedestal base (in most cases), and a ring finial. Flow Blue patterns found on Rococo include Cheau, Gaudy Ironstone, Oriental, and Whampoa.

Six-Sided Gothic

"HEATH'S FLOWER" pedestaled brush stroke teapot by Joseph Heath, *Six-Sided Gothic* body shape. 10.75" high. *Courtesy of Gail Frederick and Dan Overmeyer.* $850

Also known as "Lantern," this shape was manufactured by Edward Challinor, Joseph Clementson, Joseph Heath, Podmore, Walker & Company, and Thomas Walker. Six-Sided Gothic has a six-paneled body, a recessed base with a six-sided footprint, and a six-sided dome finial. The Flow Blue patterns found on this shape include Brush stroke, Chusan, Manilla, Pelew, Scinde, Shell, and Tonquin. Mulberry patterns on Six-Sided Gothic include Corea, Corean, and Pelew.

Six-Sided Primary

COBURG *Six-Sided Primary* teapot by James Edwards. 8" high. *Courtesy of Gail Frederick and Dan Overmeyer.* $850

This shape was produced by James Edwards around 1847. It has an elongated six-sided body, a pedestaled base, and a six-sided finial. The Flow Blue Coburg and Flensburg patterns are found on this shape.

Sixteen-Sided Full Panel Gothic

CHAPOO *Sixteen-Sided Full Panel Gothic* teapot by John Wedg Wood. 8.5" high. *Courtesy of Tom and Valorie Hays.* $1500+

John Wedg Wood produced this sixteen-paneled eight-sided rim body shape with its small ridge sixteen-sided base and small pyramid finial around 1849. Chapoo and Peruvian Flow Blue patterns and the Peruvian Mulberry pattern decorate this shape.

Francis Morley & Company produced this shape in c. 1845. It has an eight-sided sixteen paneled bulbous body, a recessed eight-sided base, and a six-sided ridged dome finial. The Flow Blue Cashmere pattern adorns Split Panel Primary.

Split Panel Primary

Ten-Panel Fluted

INDIA coffee and teapots by Villeroy and Boch. The left hand coffee pot is in the *Ten-Panel Fluted* body shape. However, in this small size, this long neck may be associated with chocolate pot instead of a coffee pot. 8.5" high and 4.25" high respectively. *Courtesy of Gail Frederick and Dan Overmeyer.* $2000+ large pot; $750-900 for the small *London* shape teapot.

CASHMERE *Split Panel Primary* teapot by Francis Morley & Company. 11.25" high. *Courtesy of Gail Frederick and Dan Overmeyer.* $1500+

CASHMERE *Split Panel Primary* teapots by Francis Morley & Company. 11.25" high and 9.5" high. *Courtesy of Gail Frederick and Dan Overmeyer.* $800-1000 sugar.

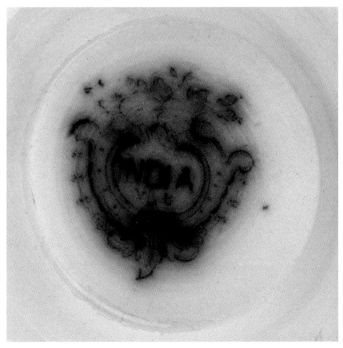

Villeroy & Boch, Mettlach, Germany, printed "V & B" manufacturer's mark including the INDIA pattern name, dating from c. 1860. *Courtesy of Gail Frederick and Dan Overmeyer.*

Villeroy & Boch, 1836-present (Mettlach, Germany, c. 1860-1900), produced this pattern around the middle of the nineteenth century. Ten-Panel Fluted has a long-necked bulbous body, a pedestaled fluted round base, and a fancy embossed ring finial. The India Flow Blue pattern appears on this shape.

Ten-Panel Gothic

TONQUIN *Ten-Panel Gothic* teapot by Joseph Heath. 9.5" high. *Courtesy of Dan Overmeyer.* $850-1000

Joseph Heath and Anthony Shaw (Tunstall, 1851-c. 1856, and Burslem c. 1858-1882) produced this shape around 1850. Ten-Panel Gothic has concave upper panels over convex lower panels forming a ridged body, a recessed ten-sided base, and a five-petal flower with a center bud. Flow Blue patterns on this shape include Brush stroke and Tonquin. The Mulberry "Birds" pattern also appears on this shape.

Ten-Panel Pumpkin —J. Furnival

SHANGHAE *Ten Panel Pumpkin* teapot by Jacob Furnival. 8.5" high teapot. *Courtesy of Gail Frederick and Dan Overmeyer.* $850+

Jacob Furnival produced this shape around 1860 with a ten-paneled body, a pedestaled ten-sided base, and a ten-sided domed finial. It is also known simply as "Pumpkin." The Shanghae Flow Blue pattern decorates its surface.

Ten-Panel Pumpkin — T. J. & J. Mayer

OREGON *Ten-Panel Pumpkin* teapot by Thomas, John & Joseph Mayer. *Courtesy of Gail Frederick and Dan Overmeyer.* $1000+

Thomas, John, & Joseph Mayer produced this shape in c. 1853. It has a ten-paneled body, a recessed ten-sided base, and a ten-paneled domed finial. The Flow Blue Oregon and Mulberry Rhone Scenery patterns appear on this shape.

Twelve-Panel Fluted

MANILLA teapot, sugar, and creamer in the *Twelve-Panel Fluted* body shape. *Courtesy of Gail Frederick and Dan Overmeyer.* $3500+ set.

Charles Meigh produced this shape around 1840. It has a twelve-paneled fluted high shoulder small base body, a pedestaled twelve-scalloped round base, and an embossed ring finial. It is decorated in Flow Blue Hong Kong, Manilla, and Warwick patterns.

Twelve-Panel Ridged

RHONE *Twelve-Panel Ridged* shape pattern teapot. 9" high. *Courtesy of Tom and Valorie Hays.* $800

Left: WARWICK *Twelve-Panel Fluted* shape teapot. 8" high. *Courtesy of Tom and Valorie Hays.* $1000+ rare.

Thomas Fell and Thomas Furnival both produced this shape around 1850. It has twelve concave body panels over twelve convex panels with a scalloped waist, a pedestaled round base, and a twelve-panel pagoda finial. Flow Blue patterns in this shape include Excelsior, Indian Jar, Japan, and Rhone. Only the Mulberry Wreath pattern is found on Twelve-Panel Ridged.

Vertical Panel Gothic — C. Meigh

Chales Meigh produced Vertical Panel Gothic in c. 1845. It has an eight vertical paneled recessed neck body, a recessed eight-sided base, and an eight-sided low banded pagoda finial. It was decorated in Athens, Hong Kong, and Troy Flow Blue and Athens, Susa, and Tivoli Mulberry patterns.

Vertical Panel Gothic — Mellor, Venables & Company

"BLEEDING HEART" *Vertical Panel Gothic* brush stroke teapot, no manufacturer's mark. The shape is attributed to Mellor, Venables & Company. 10.5" high. *Courtesy of Gail Frederick and Dan Overmeyer.* $850+

Mellor, Venables & Company offered their take on this shape around 1849. It also has an eight vertical paneled neck body and a recessed eight-sided base. In addition, however, it has an eight-sided domed stepped pyramid finial. Only Flow Blue brush stroke patterns adorn its surface, although Mulberry Aster & Grapeshot, Brunswick, and Whampoa patterns can be found there.

Above and right: TROY *Vertical Panel Gothic* pattern teapot. The pattern name is shown in the printed mark, no manufacturer's name is shown. 8.5" high. *Courtesy of Tom and Valorie Hays.* $850+

Vertical Panel Gothic teapot decorated with brush stroke and overpaint—referred to as Gaudy Ironstone, no manufacturer's mark. *Courtesy of Gail Frederick and Dan Overmeyer.* $1000-1200

Children's Tea Sets and Dinner Sets in Flow Blue

Assorted Flow Blue, Mulberry, and Gaudy children's teapots. *Courtesy of Gail Frederick and Dan Overmeyer.* NP

A variety of child's creamers. *Courtesy of Gail Frederick and Dan Overmeyer.* NP

Child's brush stroke milk pitcher with copper luster and embossed vine and grape detail, no manufacturer's mark. 3" high. *Courtesy of Tom and Valorie Hays.* $350-500

A full-sized and child-sized soup tureen in the SCINDE pattern. *Courtesy of Gail Frederick and Dan Overmeyer.* $1000+ child-sized.

The children's tea and dinner sets discussed here are the tiny wares children used for the pretend tea and dinner parties attended exclusively by their best friends and favorite stuffed animals. These tiny sets should not be confused with the larger (but less than full-sized) wares designed to serve Victorian children in their nurseries while their parents ate and entertained in the dining room. The pieces presented here are always too small to be put to actual use in serving anything but imaginary tea and meals. (Carter 1995, 65)

Today's collectors are particularly fond of these diminutive children's tea and dinner sets which may be found from time-to-time in both Flow Blue and Mulberry. The fact that these are rare items adds to the appeal. While some propose that these small items were used as salesmens' samples, the common agreement is that they were for intended for children. Some patterns and body shapes appear exclusively on these children's wares, suggesting that they were indeed for play rather than for use as samples. The fact that they were used for child's play is confirmed by the chipping, wear, and missing lids all too common among these pieces. (Frederick, et al. 1993, 3)

AMOY child's teapot and creamer by Davenport. Teapot 4.5" high *Courtesy of Dan Overmeyer.* $750 teapot; creamer $350.

Davenport manufacturer's mark. *Courtesy of Dan Overmeyer.*

AMOY child's tea set. *Courtesy of Gail Frederick and Dan Overmeyer.* $5000-7000 set.

"ASIATIC BIRDS" child's partial dinner set, unknown maker, Tureen 5.25" high 6.5" handle to handle. *Courtesy of Margot Frederick.* $3000+

BASKET PATTERN NO. 204 child's partial tea set. Notice the unusual handles on the cups. Teapot 4.75" high; plate 5" diameter *Courtesy of Dan Overmeyer.* $2500-2800

Brush stroke pattern child's teapot. 3.75" high. *Courtesy of Gail Frederick and Dan Overmeyer.* $500-650

Brush stroke child's-sized pitcher with copper luster dating to the 1840s. *Courtesy of Tom and Valorie Hays.* $350-500

CHEN SI child's teapot, creamer, and sugar bowl. *Courtesy of Tom and Valorie Hays.* $1500+ set.

CHEN SI child's partial tea set with cups and saucers. 4.5" high pot. *Courtesy of Tom and Valorie Hays.* $2200-2500

CHINESE SPORTS child's coffee pot, probably by Jacob Furnival, circa 1850. Rare. 5" high. *Courtesy of Gail Frederick and Dan Overmeyer.* $1500+

"FORGET-ME-NOT" child's partial dinner set. *Courtesy of Gail Frederick and Dan Overmeyer.* $3000-5000 set.

Gaudy brush stroke child's teapot. *Courtesy of Gail Frederick and Dan Overmeyer.* $1000-1200

JUVENILE child's tea set, Podmore Walker & Co. Teapot 4.25", plate 4 1/8" *Courtesy of Dan Overmeyer.* $2500-3000 set.

Podmore Walker & Co. manufacturer's mark. *Courtesy of Dan Overmeyer.*

LAHORE partial child's tea set, Thomas Philips & Son, double line primary, circa 1840. Teapot 5.5" high base to finial. *Courtesy of Dan Overmeyer.* $2500+

MARBLE partialchild's tea set, manufacturer unknown. 4.25" high teapot. *Courtesy of Gail Frederick and Dan Overmeyer.* $2000+

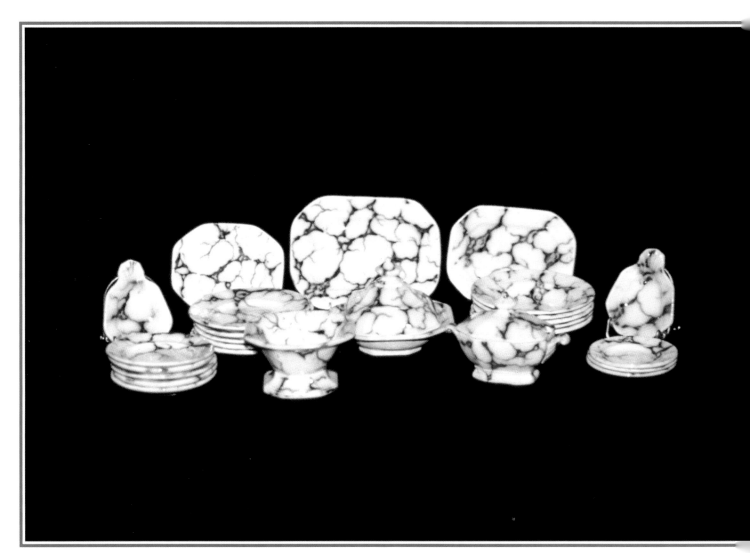

A MARBLE partial child's dinner set including tiny platters, tab handled plates, plates, covered vegetable dish, pedestalled bowl, and covered sauce tureen. *Courtesy of Gail Frederick and Dan Overmeyer.* NP

SCINDE partial child's tea set, stamped Alcock, 1840. Teapot 4" high. *Courtesy of Gail Frederick and Dan Overmeyer.* $5000+ for teapot, creamer and sugar; cups $200 each.

Below: SCINDE partial child's dinner set, 1840. 6" wide platter, 4" high sauce tureen. *Courtesy of Margot Frederick.* $5000-6000

Below: "SCOTT'S BAR" partial brush stroke child's set, circa 1830. Note the handled cups. 4" high teapot. *Courtesy of Gail Frederick and Dan Overmeyer.* $1500+

79

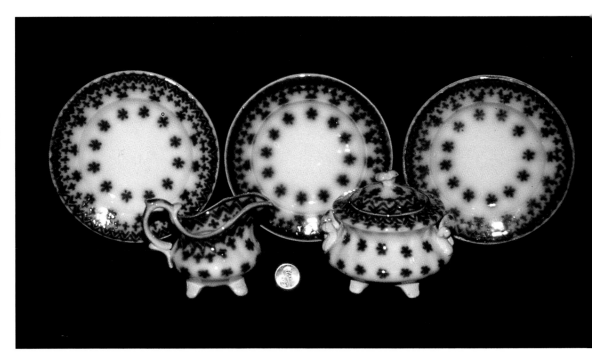

"SNOWFLAKE" partial child's set with three plates, a diminutive creamer, and a tiny sugar bowl. *Courtesy of Gail Frederick and Dan Overmeyer.* $1000-1200

Unidentified pattern child's teapot. 4.25" high. *Courtesy of Gail Frederick and Dan Overmeyer.* $750+

Unidentified pattern child's teapot, creamer, and sugar bowl. 4.25" high. *Courtesy of Tom and Valorie Hays.* $1000+

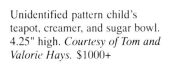

Flow Blue Patterns

"Victorian design reflects a perfect horror of undecorated space."

—James Norwood Pratt, 1982

The following is a survey of Flow Blue patterns organized into the Early, Middle, and Late Victorian periods. Among these patterns you will find both the rare and the best-loved Flow Blue, predominantly from the Early Victorian period.

Early Victorian Period

Davenport printed manufacturer's mark, dated 1848. *Courtesy of Gail Frederick and Dan Overmeyer.*

Above and left: AMOY fruit bowl/comport by Davenport. 5" high x 9.75" in diameter. *Courtesy of Gail Frederick and Dan Overmeyer.* $2000-2500

AMOY reticulated comport by Davenport. *Courtesy of Gail Frederick and Dan Overmeyer.* $2000+

ARABESQUE fruit dish by T.J. & J.
Mayer. 2.5" high x 12.5" handle to
handle. *Courtesy of Gail Frederick and
Dan Overmeyer.* $1500

ARABESQUE covered casserole by T.J. & J. Mayer, c. 1845. 4" high, 11.5" handle to handle. *Courtesy of Gail Frederick and Dan Overmeyer.* $1500

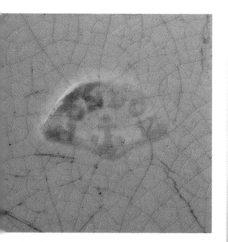

The whey bowl is impressed LONDON with an anchor mark. *Courtesy of Tom and Valorie Hays.*

"ASTOR AND GRAPE SHOT" whey bowl. 16.5" diameter. *Courtesy of Tom and Valorie Hays.* $650

83

ATHENS teapot by Charles Meigh (Hanley, Staffordshire, 1835-1849; & Son, 1851-1861). 6.75" high. *Courtesy of Gail Frederick and Dan Overmeyer.* $650-750

Right and below: BAMBOO pedestaled comport by Samuel Alcock & Company, featuring green ground and gold trim. 7" high x 11.5" in diameter. *Courtesy of Gail Frederick and Dan Overmeyer.* $1500-2000

Samuel Alcock & Company, Cobridge and Burslem, Staffordshire, printed manufacturer's initials mark used from c. 1830 to 1859, with pattern name. *Courtesy of Gail Frederick and Dan Overmeyer.*

"BLACKBERRY" brush stroke pitcher with overpaint, no manufacturer's mark. Brush stroke patterns are starting to gain a lot of attention in the collecting community. 11" high to the spout. *Courtesy of Tom and Valorie Hays.* $850

Above and below left: "BLUE BELL" pedestaled comport by William Ridgway & Company, 1834-54. *Courtesy of Tom and Valorie Hays.* $1200+

William Ridgway & Compamy, Bell Works, Shelton and Church Works, Hanley, Staffordshire, impressed "Opaque Granite China" body type and "W. R. & Co." manufacturer's marks, 1834-54. *Courtesy of Tom and Valorie Hays.*

"BLUE BELL" pitchers — all three examples originally had pewter lids. While these three pitchers had no manufacturer's marks, they are very similar to a syrup attributed to Dillwyn of Swansea, Wales, dating to 1840. These three pitchers range from 9.5" high to 6" high. *Courtesy of Tom and Valorie Hays.* $950 large; $750 medium; $650 small.

Above and right: "BLUEBELL AND GRAPES WITH CHERRY BORDER" brush stroke platter with a "STONE CHINA" impress on back. 11" wide. *Courtesy of Tom and Valorie Hays.* $350

Left: "BLUE BELL" temple jar featuring dolphins on the finial and dragons on the handles, no manufacturer's mark. 19.5" high. *Courtesy of Tom and Valorie Hays.* NP

Above and below: BYRONIA teapot on the right and INDIA teapot on the left. Both were produced by Villeroy & Boch (1836-present, Mettlach, Germany, c. 1860-1900), c. 1845. Both have the printed "V & B" manufacturer's marks. 7" & 6.25" high teapots. *Courtesy of Tom and Valorie Hays.* $750 left; $650 right.

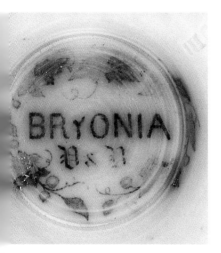

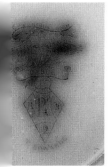

Left and right: CABUL plate by James Edwards (& Company, King Street, Fenton, Staffordshire, 1847-1900) with an 1847 registration mark. 10" in diameter. *Courtesy of Tom and Valorie Hays.* $125+

Above and right: CABUL reticulated comport by Edward Challinor, circa 1847. 6.5 " high, 9.5" diameter. *Courtesy of Gail Frederick and Dan Overmeyer.* $2000+

Above and left:
CANDIA
punchbowl by
John Ridgeway
& Co, Cauldon
Place Works,
Shelton, Hanley,
Staffordshire, c.
1841-1855. 7.5"
high x 17.75" in
diameter.
*Courtesy of Gail
Frederick and
Dan Overmeyer.*
$1200-1500

CANTON VINE creamer, maker unknown, c. 1845. 4.75" high. *Courtesy of Tom and Valorie Hays.* $500+

Above and below: CASHMERE platter by Ridgway & Morley, Broad Street, Shelton, Hanley, Staffordshire, 1842-1844. 17.25" wide. *Courtesy of Tom and Valorie Hays.* $1500+

CASHMERE chocolate/teapot by Ridgway & Morley, c. 1842. This piece does not have the customary strainer common to teapots. 12" high. *Courtesy of Gail Frederick and Dan Overmeyer.* NP

CASHMERE syrup with pewter lid by Ridgway & Morley, c. 1842. 6.25" high. *Courtesy of Gail Frederick and Dan Overmeyer.* NP

Ridgway and Morley "R. & M." printed manufacturer's mark in use from 1842 to 1844. *Courtesy of Gail Frederick and Dan Overmeyer.*

CASHMERE sixteen panel creamer by Ridgway & Morley, c. 1842. *Courtesy of Tom and Valorie Hays.* $850+

Two small CASHMERE pitchers by Ridgway & Morley, c. 1842: the example on the left is in mint condition, is rare, and has a pewter lid. Left: 5.25" high; right: 4" high. *Courtesy of Tom and Valorie Hays.* $2000 left; $850 right.

A beautiful CASHMERE waste jar (a.k.a. slop jar — part of a bathroom set) by Ridgway & Morley, c. 1842. *Courtesy of Gail Frederick and Dan Overmeyer.* $2200-2500

CARLTON broth bowl by Samuel Alcock & Company, c. 1850. 5.25" high x 6.75" handle to handle. *Courtesy of Gail Frederick and Dan Overmeyer.* $350-500

Above and left: CHAPOO platter by J. Wedg Wood (Hadderidge, Burslem & Tunstall, Staffordshire, 1841-1857; the pottery was continued by his younger brother Edward T. Wood to 1875-76), with a printed manufacturer's mark. 16" wide. *Courtesy of Tom and Valorie Hays.* $450-550

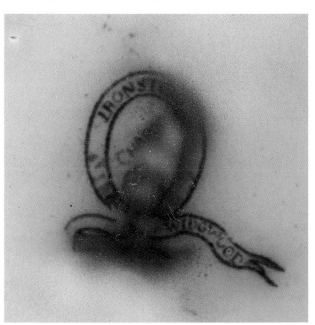

Left and below: CHAPOO teapot by John Wedg Wood. 10" high. *Courtesy of Tom and Valorie Hays.* $900-1100

CHAPOO pitcher and basin by J. Wedg Wood. 13.5" diameter bowl; 11" high to lip pitcher. *Courtesy of Tom and Valorie Hays.* $2000+

CHAPOO teapot by John Wedg Wood. 11.5" high teapot. *Courtesy of Gail Frederick and Dan Overmeyer.* $1200-1500

CHAPOO soup tureen and undertray by John Wedg Wood. *Courtesy of Gail Frederick and Dan Overmeyer.* $3500-4500

Far left and left: CHINESE vase by Thomas Dimmock & Company, Shelton, Staffordshire, c. 1828 to 1859, with pale green ground and gold. 8.75" high x 5" in diameter. *Courtesy of Gail Frederick and Dan Overmeyer.* $850-1000

CHINESE covered potpourri jar by
Thomas Dimmock, c. 1845, gold and
polychrome painting. 19.5" high.
*Courtesy of Gail Frederick and Dan
Overmeyer.* $3000

Above right and right: CHINESE
covered jar by Thomas Dimmock. This
would have been the centerpiece with
two potpourri jars, one on either side.
17.5" high. *Courtesy of Gail Frederick
and Dan Overmeyer.* $1200+

Above: Joseph Clementson, Shelton, Hanley, Staffordshire, printed "J. Clementson" and Phoenix bird mark used from 1840 onward. *Courtesy of Tom and Valorie Hays.*

Left: CHUSAN plate by Joseph Clementson, c. 1840. 10.25" in diameter. *Courtesy of Tom and Valorie Hays.* $125-175

Below: CHUSAN hexagonal soup tureen by Joseph Clemenson, c. 1840. 13" high, 15.5" handle to handle. *Courtesy of Gail Frederick and Dan Overmeyer.* $3500+

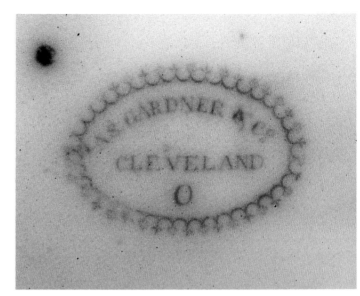

The sauce tureen undertray has an "A.S. Gardner & Co. Cleveland O." distributor's mark. *Courtesy of Tom and Valorie Hays.*

Above: CHUSAN teapot by Podmore, Walker & Company (Tunstall, Staffordshire, 1834-1859). 8.5" high. *Courtesy of Tom and Valorie Hays.* $1000+

CHUSAN sauce tureen and undertray, no manufacturer's mark. 9" wide undertray, 6" high sauce tureen. *Courtesy of Tom and Valorie Hays.* $2000+

CHUSAN soup & sauce tureen undertrays, no manufacturer's mark. 16.5" wide soup tureen. *Courtesy of Tom and Valorie Hays.* $1500+ soup; $350+ sauce.

Above: CHUSAN graduated pitchers, no manufacturer's marks. There is another pitcher that is bigger still. The heights range from 9" high to the lip down to 5" high to the lip. *Courtesy of Tom and Valorie Hays.* $450+ creamer; 550+; 650+; 750+; 850+.

Right: CHUSAN covered vegetable dishes, no manufacturer's marks. 12" and 11" wide. *Courtesy of Tom and Valorie Hays.* $650-850.

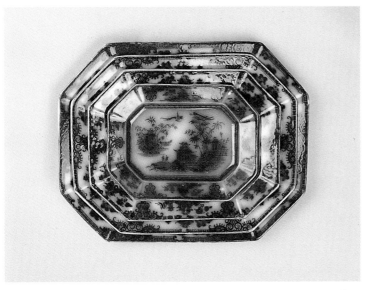

Nested CHUSAN platters ranging from 10.5-13" wide. *Courtesy of Tom and Valorie Hays.* $300-550 by size.

Nested CHUSAN open vegetable bowls. 7.25" - 10.5" wide. *Courtesy of Tom and Valorie Hays.* $450-650 by size.

Above: COBURG reticulated fruit basket and underplate by James Edwards. The basket measures 5" high and 13" handle to handle; the underplate measures 2" high x 11.25" handle to handle. *Courtesy of Gail Frederick and Dan Overmeyer.* $2500-2800

Right: Printed James Edwards, King Street, Fenton, Staffordshire, "J.E." mark and pattern name in use from 1847 to 1873. *Courtesy of Gail Frederick and Dan Overmeyer.*

COBURG reticulated fruit comport by James Edwards, c. 1847. 13.5" long, 4.5" high. *Courtesy of Tom and Valorie Hays.* $1500-1800

Above and left: COBURG teapot, creamer, and sugar bowl by James Edwards, marked J.E. 8.25" high. *Courtesy of Tom and Valorie Hays.* $1500-1850 set.

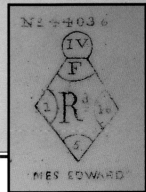

COBURG creamer by James Edwards. The registration mark dates to
July 16, 1847. 5.25" high. *Courtesy of Tom and Valorie Hays.* $450+

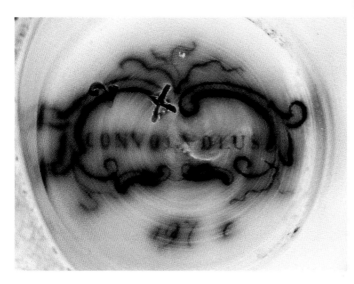

CONVULVULUS creamer. The pattern name is printed on the base. 3.5" high to lip. *Courtesy of Tom and Valorie Hays.* $350-450

EUPHRATES oriental pattern teapot with no manufacturer's mark. This is printed in a lighter blue. 8" high. *Courtesy of Tom and Valorie Hays.* $650-750

EXCELSIOR pitcher by Thomas Fell & Company (St. Peter's Pottery, Newcastle-upon-Tyne, 1817-1890), c. 1850. 9" high to lip. *Courtesy of Tom and Valorie Hays.* $850

"TULIP AND FERN" brush stroke sauce tureen and ladle, no manufacturer's mark. 12.5" high, 12" handle to handle. *Courtesy of Margot Frederick.* $1500+

FORMOSA pedestaled fruit comport by Thomas, John and Joseph Mayer. 5.75" high x 10.5" handle to handle. *Courtesy of Gail Frederick and Dan Overmeyer.* $1500+

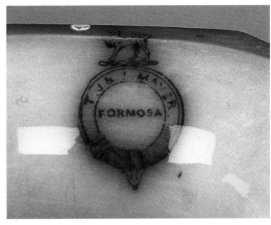

T. J. & J. Mayer printed manufacturer's mark (Furlong Works and Dale Hall Pottery, Burslem, 1843-1855) with Formosa pattern name. *Courtesy of Gail Frederick and Dan Overmeyer.*

FORMOSA pedestaled comport by William Ridgway, c. 1834. *Courtesy of Gail Frederick and Dan Overmeyer.* $1700+

Above: FORMOSA soup tureen and undertray by T. J. & J. Mayer, c. 1850. 10 " high, 12.5" handle to handle. *Courtesy of Gail Frederick and Dan Overmeyer.* $4000-5000

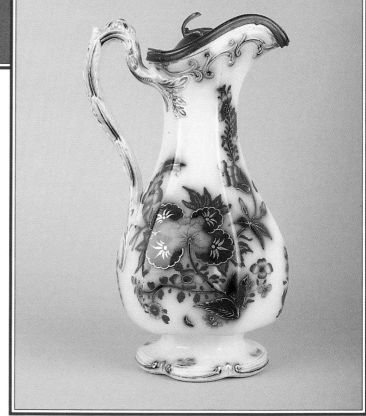

Right: "GRASSHOPPER AND FLOWERS" tall pitcher with a pewter lid and polychrome overglaze floral polychrome decoration, no manufacturer's mark. This pattern is attributed to Charles Meigh, dating from the early 1840s. 11.5" high to the lip. *Courtesy of Tom and Valorie Hays.* $850-1000

"HEATH'S FLOWER" gaudy brush stroke pattern on a vegetable plate by Joseph Heath. 7.5" high, 12" handle to handle. *Courtesy of Gail Frederick and Dan Overmeyer.* $850-1000

Below: HONG KONG reticulated fruit bowl and underplate by Charles Meigh, c. 1845. The bowl measures 6" high x 10" wide; the underplate measures 1.5" high x 11" wide. *Courtesy of Gail Frederick and Dan Overmeyer.* $2500-3000

A very rare "HEATH'S FLOWER" lidded pitcher by Joseph Heath. 5.5" high. *Courtesy of Tom and Valorie Hays.* $1000+

Left: HONG KONG teapot and creamer by Charles Meigh. 9" high teapot. *Courtesy of Gail Frederick and Dan Overmeyer.* $1000 teapot; $550-650 creamer.

Below: HONG KONG water pitcher with basin by Charles Meigh. The pitcher measures 12 " high; the basin measures 4.5" high, 12.75" in diameter. *Courtesy of Gail Frederick and Dan Overmeyer.* $1500+

Left: INDIAN JAR reticulated underplate (to a pedestaled fruit comport) by Jacob & Thomas Furnival. 1.75" x 12". *Courtesy of Gail Frederick and Dan Overmeyer.* $750-1000

Above: Jacob & Thomas Furnival, Miles Bank, Shelton, Hanley, Staffordshire, printed manufacturer's mark in use c. 1843. *Courtesy of Gail Frederick and Dan Overmeyer.*

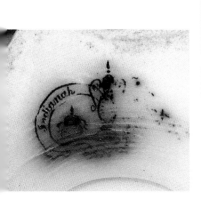

Above: Indianah printed back mark. *Courtesy of Gail Frederick and Dan Overmeyer.*

Right: INDIANAH teapot, maker unknown, c. 1850, rare. 10.5" high. *Courtesy of Gail Frederick and Dan Overmeyer.* $1000+

IVY reticulated relish dish (part of a dessert service) by Davenport, 1844. 1.5" high x 6" in diameter. *Courtesy of Margot Frederick.* $350-450

Davenport printed manufacturer's mark and impressed anchor mark. The numbers 44 that appear on either side of the anchor indicate the last two digits of the year 1844, the date the mold was produced ... not the date the pattern was affixed to it. *Courtesy of Gail Frederick and Dan Overmeyer.*

IVY lidded pitcher with a cameo under spout by Davenport. Marked. 8.5" high. *Courtesy of Gail Frederick and Dan Overmeyer.* $850+

Left: KIN-SHAN plate by Edward Challinor & Co., c. 1855. 10.5" in diameter. *Courtesy of Tom and Valorie Hays.* $125-175

Above: Edward Challinor & Company, Fenton, Staffordshire, printed E.C. & Co. mark in use from 1853-60. *Courtesy of Tom and Valorie Hays.*

Below: LAHORE pedestaled fruit comport, no manufacturer's mark. 5.75" high x 9.75" diameter. *Courtesy of Gail Frederick and Dan Overmeyer.* $1200

Right: MANILLA four part sauce tureen & undertray by Podmore, Walker & Company, c. 1845. The tureen measures 6.25" high and the undertray measures 7.75" wide. *Courtesy of Tom and Valorie*

Left: MANILLA large covered casserole by Podmore, Walker & Company, c. 1845. 8" high and 10.25" in diameter. *Courtesy of Gail Frederick and Dan Overmeyer.* $2200-2500

MANILLA sugar bowl, no manufacturer's mark. 8" high, 5" in diameter. *Courtesy of Tom and Valorie Hays.* $650-750

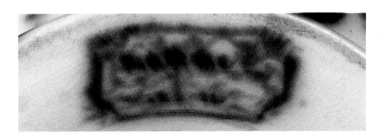

Above and below: MARBLE teapot with a pewter lid. 7.5" high. *Courtesy of Gail Frederick and Dan Overmeyer.* $1000++ for this rare shape.

"MARBLE" egg stand, no manufacturer's mark. *Courtesy of Gail Frederick and Dan Overmeyer.* $350-550

Above and right: "MORNING GLORY" brush stroke pattern teapot, lidded sugar bowl, and creamer with gold gilt, no manufacturer's mark. Note that the gold is only on to be found on one side. 8.5" high teapot. *Courtesy of Tom and Valorie Hays.* $1500+ set.

"MORNING GLORY" brush stroke pattern teapot, no manufacturer's mark. *Courtesy of Gail Frederick and Dan Overmeyer.* $850+

NING PO creamer without a back mark, c. 1845. 4.25" high. *Courtesy of Tom and Valorie Hays.* $450-550

OREGON four part sauce tureen, underplate, and ladle by T.J. & J. Mayer, with ram's horn handles. 6.5 " high, 8" handle to handle. *Courtesy of Gail Frederick and Dan Overmeyer.* $2200-2500

OREGON rosebud finial sauce tureen and ladle. 6" high x 8" handle to handle. *Courtesy of Gail Frederick and Dan Overmeyer.* $2500-3000

OREGON sauce tureen and undertray by T.J. & J. Mayer. 8" wide undertray, 6" high tureen. *Courtesy of Tom and Valorie Hays.* $2500-3000

OREGON teapot and sugar by T.J. & J. Mayer. 8" high teapot. *Courtesy of Gail Frederick and Dan Overmeyer.* $850-1000 teapot; $450-550 sugar.

OREGON teapot in a Gothic Bud variant body shape by T.J. & J. Mayer. *Courtesy of Gail Frederick and Dan Overmeyer.* $1000+

OREGON teapot decorating the eight-paneled *Bulbous Octagon* body shape manufactured by T.J. & J. Mayer. 9.5" high. *Courtesy of Tom and Valorie Hays.* $850+

ORIENTAL writing/desk set with a green ground color and gold gilt by Samuel Alcock & Company, c. 1840. *Courtesy of Gail Frederick and Dan Overmeyer.* $3000-4000

Samuel Alcock & Company created chinoiserie patterns of different character. Compare the ORIENTAL pattern on page 118 to this CHINESE pattern vase. c. 1840. 10.5" high, 5.5" in diameter. *Courtesy of Tom and Valorie Hays.* $750-1000

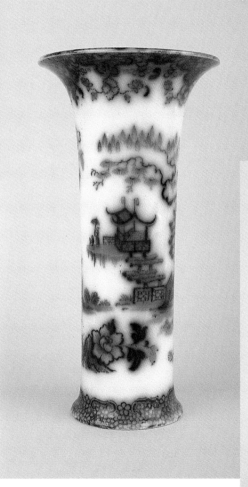

William Ridgway (& Co.), Bell Works, Shelton, and Church Works, Hanley, Staffordshire, c. 1830-54, printed W.R. manufacturer's mark and pattern name. *Courtesy of Tom and Valorie Hays.*

PENANG plate by William Ridgway, c. 1840. 9.5" in diameter. *Courtesy of Tom and Valorie Hays.* $85-100

Below: PEKING matching soup and sauce tureens with undertray, no manufacturer's mark, circa 1845. 12" high. and 8" high. *Courtesy of Gail Frederick and Dan Overmeyer.* $1500+ soup; $650-750 sauce tureen with undertray.

Above: PEKING soup tureen with undertray, no manufacturer's mark. The registration mark bears the date 1845. 12.5" high. *Courtesy of Gail Frederick and Dan Overmeyer.* $2000+

Left: PELEW high based dish by Edward Challinor. 1.25" high, 13" wide. Marked on bottom. *Courtesy of Gail Frederick and Dan Overmeyer.* NP

Above: E. Challinor, Pinnocks Works and Unicorn Pottery, Tunstall, Staffordshire, 1842-1867, manufacturer's mark. *Courtesy of Gail Frederick and Dan Overmeyer.*

RHONE reticulated fruit comport by Thomas Furnival & Company, c. 1845. Be aware that Thomas Furnival was known to vary his pattern from piece to piece. 4" high x 12" handle to handle. *Courtesy of Gail Frederick and Dan Overmeyer.* $1500+

SCINDE reticulated fruit basket and undertray by John & George Alcock, c. 1840. Fruit basket 4" high x 13" handle to handle; underplate 1.5" high x 11" handle to handle. *Courtesy of Gail Frederick and Dan Overmeyer.* $3500+

SCINDE three part butter dish with plate insert by J. & G. Alcock, c. 1840. 4.75" high. *Courtesy of Gail Frederick and Dan Overmeyer.* $1500+

John & George Alcock (Cobridge, Stafford-shire), 1839-1846 "J. & G. Alcock" impressed manufacturer's mark with an impressed "Oriental Stone" name indicating the body material of the ware. *Courtesy of Gail Frederick and Dan Overmeyer.*

Above: SCINDE soup tureen with a rosebud finial by J. & G. Alcock with underplate and ladle. *Courtesy of Gail Frederick and Dan Overmeyer.* $8500-10,000

Left: SCINDE covered vegetable dish by J. & G. Alcock. Note the rosebud finial. 7" high x 13.75" handle to handle. *Courtesy of Gail Frederick and Dan Overmeyer.* $2500+

SCINDE sauce tureen, underplate, and ladle by J. & G. Alcock. 5.75" high x 8" handle to handle. *Courtesy of Gail Frederick and Dan Overmeyer.* $3000+

SCINDE rosebud finial sauce tureen and ladle. 6" high x 8" handle to handle. *Courtesy of Gail Frederick and Dan Overmeyer.* $2500

SCINDE sauce and soup tureen with undertray and a rosebud finial by J. & G. Alcock. The soup tureen measures 12" high, 14.4" handle to handle; the sauce tureen measures 6.25" x 8.5". *Courtesy of Gail Frederick and Dan Overmeyer.* $7000-7500 soup tureen with undertray; sauce tureen: $700-1000

A massive SCINDE soup tureen with ladle and a SCINDE sauce tureen with ladle, both by J. & G. Alcock. *Courtesy of Gail Frederick and Dan Overmeyer.* Unique large soup tureen: $10,000 with ladle; sauce tureen and ladle: $2700+

Left: SCINDE comport by John and Samuel Alcock, Jr. (Cobridge, Staffordshire). 6" high x 12" handle to handle. *Courtesy of Gail Frederick and Dan Overmeyer.* $2000

Below: SCINDE comport by J. & G. Alcock. 7.5" high, 12" handle to handle. *Courtesy of Gail Frederick and Dan Overmeyer.* $2000. Note the difference in base style between these two Alcock comports.

SCINDE child and adult sized comport, no manufacturer's mark. Only border design is used on child's piece. Full sized comport: 7" high x 14" handle to handle; child's sized comport: 2" x 3.75" handle to handle. *Courtesy of Gail Frederick and Dan Overmeyer.* NP

"SCOTT'S BAR" brush stroke decorated teapot, no manufacturer's mark. This teapot has an unusual shape. 7" high. *Courtesy of Tom and Valorie Hays.* $750-850

Above: SCROLL plate by Francis Morley, c. 1845. 10.5" in diameter. *Courtesy of Tom and Valorie Hays.* $125
Left: Francis Morley (& Co.), Broad Street, Shelton, Hanley, Staffordshire, 1845-58. *Courtesy of Tom and Valorie Hays.*

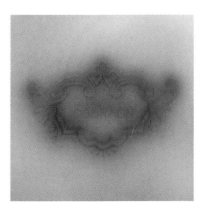

Left and above: SOBRAON platter, unidentified manufacturer, c. 1850. 16" wide. *Courtesy of Tom and Valorie Hays.* $450

Below: SOBRAON covered vegetable dish, manufacturer unidentified, c. 1850. *Courtesy of Gail Frederick and Dan Overmeyer.* $850-1000

"STRAWBERRY" brush stroke pattern teapot, no manufacturer's mark. 9.5" high. *Courtesy of Tom and Valorie Hays.* $850+

"STRAWBERRY" gaudy brush stroke teapot, creamer, and sugar bowl with polychrome overpaint, no manufacturer's mark. 9.75" high. *Courtesy of Tom and Valorie Hays.* $1750+

TONQUIN teapot, creamer, and sugar bowl by Joseph Heath (High Street, Tunstall, Staffordshire, 1845-1853). 10" high teapot (large). *Courtesy of Tom and Valorie Hays.* $2000 set.

Left: TONQUIN coffee pot by Joseph Heath. *Courtesy of Gail Frederick and Dan Overmeyer.* $3500-4000

Bottom left and below: TONQUIN pedestaled fruit comport by Joseph Heath, 6" high x 12" handle to handle, 1845 to 1853. Note that different boats are found on different pieces of Tonquin. *Courtesy of Gail Frederick and Dan Overmeyer.* $1500-1850

Below: TONQUIN sauce tureen and undertray with ladle by Joseph Heath. 6.5" high, 7.5" wide undertray. *Courtesy of Tom and Valorie Hays.* $2200+

William Adams & Sons printed manufacturer's mark in use from 1819 to 1864. *Courtesy of Gail Frederick and Dan Overmeyer.*

Above and right: TONQUIN pedestaled comport by William Adams & Sons, c. 1845. 6" high x 11.5" handle to handle. *Courtesy of Gail Frederick and Dan Overmeyer.* $1750+

"TULIP AND FERN" covered vegetable dish, no manufacturer's mark. *Courtesy of Gail Frederick and Dan Overmeyer.* $850-1000

"TULIP AND SPRIG" brush stroke charger. 13.5" in diameter. *Courtesy of Gail Frederick and Dan Overmeyer.* $650-750

WARWICK sauce tureen, undertray, and ladle by Podmore, Walker, & Company. 6" high tureen, 9" wide undertray. *Courtesy of Tom and Valorie Hays.* $2000+

Impressed Podmore, Walker & Company manufacturer's mark in use from 1834-59. *Courtesy of Tom and Valorie Hays.*

WARWICK teapot, no manufacturer's mark. 8.25" high. *Courtesy of Gail Frederick and Dan Overmeyer.* $1000+

Above and right: WHAMPOA punch bowl by Mellor, Venables & Company, c. 1845. 5.5"high x 11.5" in diameter. *Courtesy of Gail Frederick and Dan Overmeyer.* $1500-1800

134

Above: Two butter dishes: the left hand dish is decorated in the WHAMPOA pattern by Mellor, Venables & Company, c. 1845. It is possible that a stick ran through holes in the flanges at either side of the lid to keep the lid on tight or this may have been the attachment points for a wicker bail handle. 3" high, 5" in diameter. The right hand example is in an unidentified pattern and has an attached undertray. 4" high, 7.5" in diameter. *Courtesy of Dan Overmeyer.* Left: $1200+; right: with undertray $2000-2500

Left: YELLOW RIVER plate by Charles James Mason. 10.25" in diameter. *Courtesy of Tom and Valorie Hays.* $125-175

Below: Charles James Mason, Fenton Works, Lane Delph, Staffordshire, c. 1845-48, printed manufacturer's and distributor's marks, partially flown. *Courtesy of Tom and Valorie Hays.*

Left: CLAREMONT GROUPS covered jar with yellow/lemon ground, possibly by Sampson Hancock, c. 1860. Note the stylized Victorian dolphins on the finial. 19.5" high. *Courtesy of Gail Frederick and Dan Overmeyer.* $2000+

Below: As yet unidentified S & H printed manufacturer's mark and pattern name. This mark does not quite jibe with the Sampson Hancock mark. *Courtesy of Gail Frederick and Dan Overmeyer.*

Above: Thomas Fell and Company, Newcastle upon Tyne, Northumberland, printed "T.F. & Co." manufacturer's mark in use from c. 1830 to 1890 with Japan pattern name. *Courtesy of Gail Frederick and Dan Overmeyer.*

Left: JAPAN pattern plate by Thomas Fell and Company, c. 1860. 10" diameter. *Courtesy of Gail Frederick and Dan Overmeyer.* $100-150

Below: JAPAN soup tureen and underplate. 11.25" high x 14.5" handle to handle. *Courtesy of Gail Frederick and Dan Overmeyer.* $2500-3500

Left: JAPANESE NO. ___ teapot by Wood & Baggaley. 7.5" high. *Courtesy of Gail Frederick and Dan Overmeyer.* $850+

Below: Wood & Baggaley, Hill Works, Burslem, Staffordshire 1870-1880, "W. & B." manufacturer's mark and the un-numbered JAPANESE pattern name. *Courtesy of Gail Frederick and Dan Overmeyer.*

Above: John Meir & Son, Tunstall, Staffordshire, printed "J. Meir & Son" garter and crown mark. Marks of this sort were used for a long period by the company, from 1840 (when garter marks first appear) to 1897. *Courtesy of Tom and Valorie Hays.*

KIRKEE plate by John Meir & Son, c. 1861. 10.5" in diameter. *Courtesy of Tom and Valorie Hays.* $125-175

Above and left: PERSIANA cheese dome and underplate, possibly by G.L. Ashworth, c. 1862, or Wood & Baggeley, c. 1870-80. The dome measures 11.25" high; the underplate measures 2.75" high and 11.75" in diameter. *Courtesy of Gail Frederick and Dan Overmeyer.* $1500-2000

Persiana printed back mark. *Courtesy of Gail Frederick and Dan Overmeyer.*

CHINESE LANDSCAPE dinner plate by G.L Ashworth & Bros. (Ltd.), Broad Street, Hanley, c. 1880. This pattern was also produced by the company bearing a c. 1862 manufacturer's mark. This was an enduring pattern. 10.25" diameter. *Courtesy of Tom and Valorie Hays.* $125

This Ashworth Bros. printed manufacturer's mark was used from 1880 onward.

SHELL creamer by Edward Challinor (1842-1867), c. 1860. 5" high. *Courtesy of Gail Frederick and Dan Overmeyer.* $450+

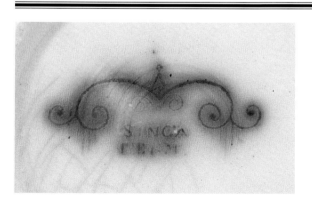

SINGA Middle Victorian period small two handled cup by Cork, Edge & Malkin, Newport Pottery, Burslem, Staffordshire, 1860-1871, with printed "C.E. & M." mark. 3" high and 3" in diameter. *Courtesy of Tom and Valorie Hays.* NP

DELPH reticulated fruit bowl by Minton, questionable as Flow Blue. 3" high, 11" wide. *Courtesy of Gail Frederick and Dan Overmeyer.* NP

GIRONDE platter, soup tureen, covered vegetable dish, pitcher, covered butter dish, covered sugar bowl, creamer, cup and saucer, gravy boat, small tray or dish, and a butter pat by W.H. Grindley (New Field Pottery, Tunstall, Stafford-shire, established in c. 1880), c. 1891. *Courtesy of Gail Frederick and Dan Overmeyer.* $450-550 soup tureen.

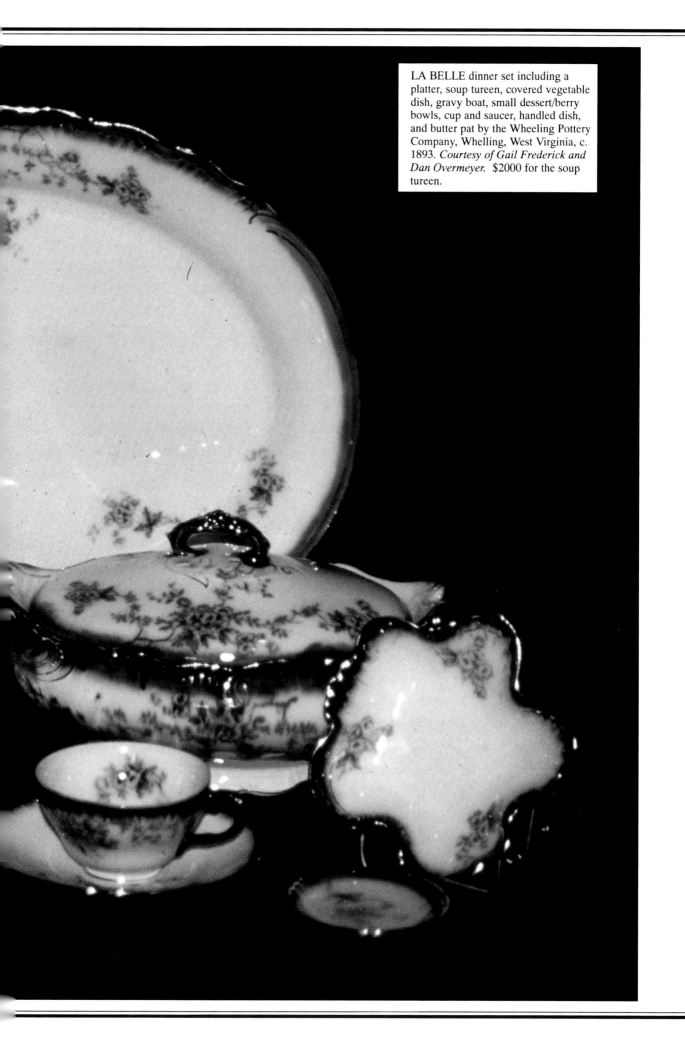

LA BELLE dinner set including a platter, soup tureen, covered vegetable dish, gravy boat, small dessert/berry bowls, cup and saucer, handled dish, and butter pat by the Wheeling Pottery Company, Whelling, West Virginia, c. 1893. *Courtesy of Gail Frederick and Dan Overmeyer.* $2000 for the soup tureen.

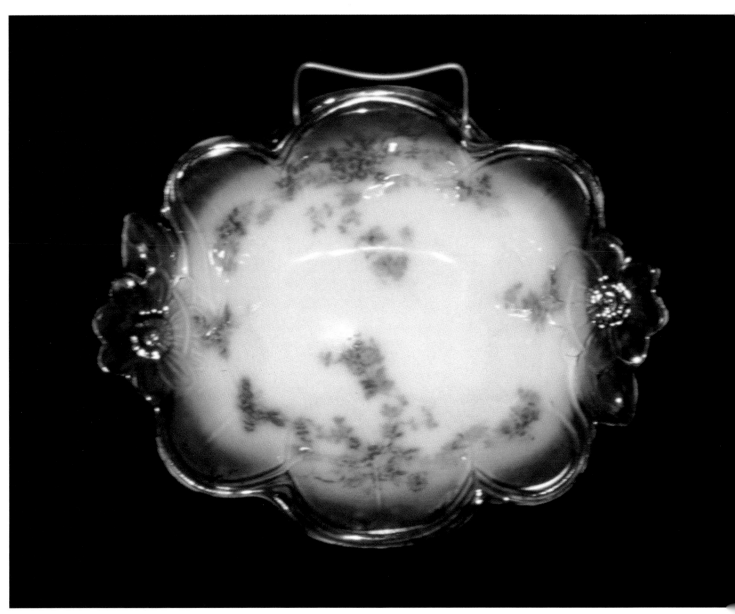

LA BELLE platter by the Wheeling Pottery Company, c. 1893.
Courtesy of Gail Frederick and Dan Overmeyer. NP

LA BELLE dinner plate by the Wheeling Pottery Company, c.
1893. 10.25" in diameter. *Courtesy of Gail Frederick and Dan
Overmeyer.* $125+

Left and below: LA BELLE portrait chop plate by the Wheeling Pottery Company, c. 1893. The center has been left blank, the portrait was never applied. 13" diameter. Compare this to the unidentified non-flowing portrait plates with the centers filled in to get an idea of the finished look. *Courtesy of Gail Frederick and Dan Overmeyer.* $500+ for LA BELLE chop plate.

Two LA BELLE fancy plates with gold gilt by the Wheeling Pottery Company, c. 1893. *Courtesy of Gail Frederick and Dan Overmeyer.* $125 each.

Above: Three LA BELLE sugar bowls by the Wheeling Pottery Company, c. 1893. The lid of the center bowl is missing. *Courtesy of Gail Frederick and Dan Overmeyer.* $350+ for complete bowls with lid.

Right: Rarely does one run across signed pieces. The back of this LA BELLE pattern piece is signed and dated "Laura Beisweinger. March 16th, 1898." *Courtesy of Gail Frederick and Dan Overmeyer.*

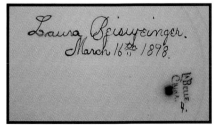

Three LA BELLE teapots in different body shapes by the Wheeling Pottery Company, c. 1893. *Courtesy of Gail Frederick and Dan Overmeyer.* $1500 left; $1200 center; $1000 right based upon scarcity of styles.

Above and right: Three LA BELLE creamers by the Wheeling Pottery Company, c. 1893. *Courtesy of Gail Frederick and Dan Overmeyer.* $250-350

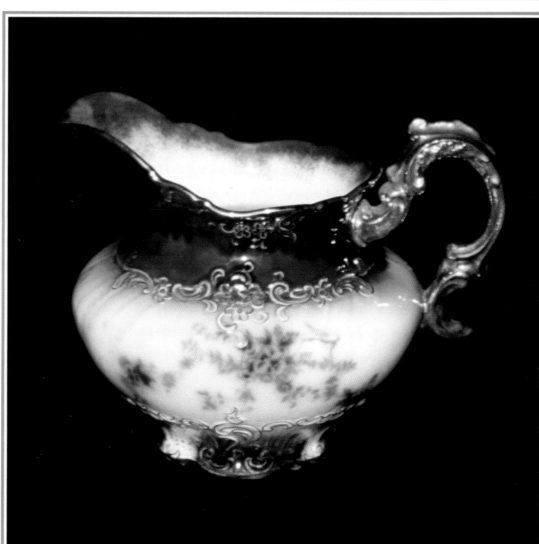

LA BELLE handless punch cups and an urn featuring a bone/ivory handled spigot. This set is marked "Wheeling Pottery Co." 15" high urn, 3.5" high and 3" diameter cups. *Courtesy of Margot Frederick. See earlier prices.*

Above: LA BELLE chocolate pot, cup and saucer by the Wheeling Pottery Company, c. 1893. The pot measures 7.5" high to the spout. *Courtesy of Gail Frederick and Dan Overmeyer.* $350-500 cup and saucer; $1200-1500 chocolate pot.

Right: LA BELLE ice pitcher by the Wheeling Pottery Company, c. 1893. *Courtesy of Gail Frederick and Dan Overmeyer.* $2000-2500

Above: LA BELLE wash set by the Wheeling Pottery Company, c. 1893. *Courtesy of Gail Frederick and Dan Overmeyer.* $3000-5000 set.

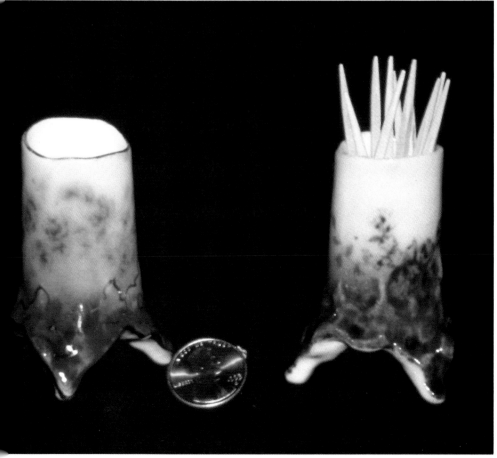

Left: Two LA BELLE toothpick holders or spill vases. *Courtesy of Gail Frederick and Dan Overmeyer.* $650-850 each.

Above: MONGOLIA bowl, platter, gravy boat, waste bowl, cup, and sugar bowl by Johnson Bros., c. 1900. *Courtesy of Gail Frederick and Dan Overmeyer.* NP

Right: NORMANDY platter by Johnson Bros., c. 1900. 18" wide. *Courtesy of Tom and Valorie Hays.* $350-450

Below: Johnson Brothers, Ltd., Hanley and Tunstall, Staffordshire, printed manufacturer's mark in use from c. 1900. *Courtesy of Tom and Valorie Hays.*

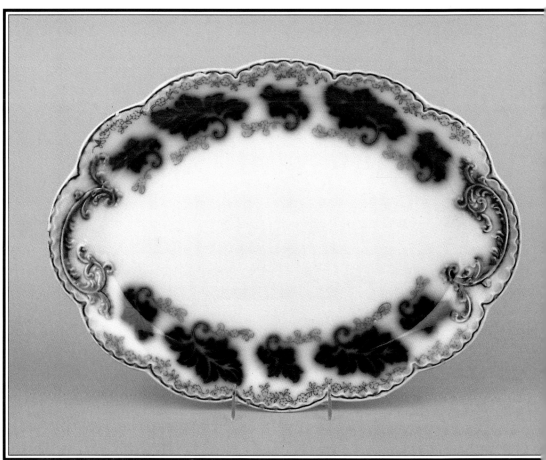

NORMANDY teapot by Johnson Bros., c. 1900. *Courtesy of Gail Frederick and Dan Overmeyer.* $2000+

NORMANDY small sauce boat and small covered condiment dish by Johnson Bros., c. 1900. *Courtesy of Gail Frederick and Dan Overmeyer.* $225-275 sauce boat; $650-850 condiment dish.

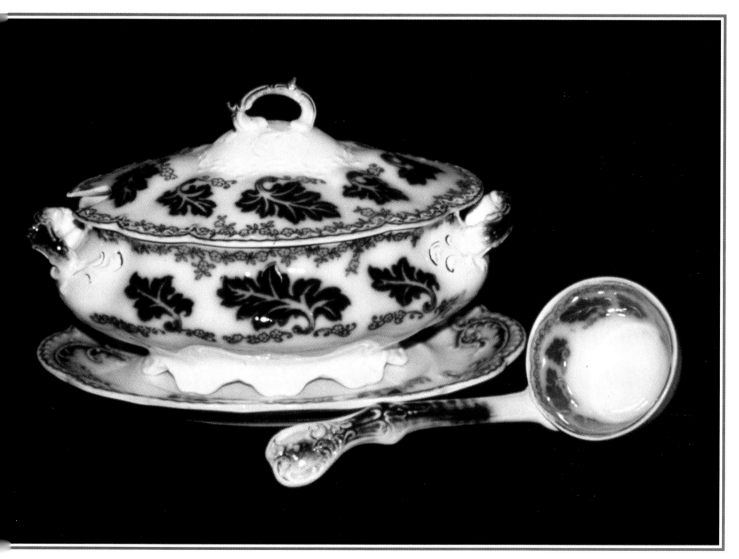

NORMANDY four piece sauce tureen, complete with underplate and ladle by Johnson Bros., c. 1900. *Courtesy of Gail Frederick and Dan Overmeyer.* $2000+

Above:
NORMANDY gravy boat and undertray and attached undertray fish sauce boat by Johnson Bros., c. 1900. *Courtesy of Gail Frederick and Dan Overmeyer.* $350 gravy with undertray; $750-800 fish sauce.

Right:
NORMANDY creamer and milk pitcher by Johnson Bros., c. 1900. *Courtesy of Gail Frederick and Dan Overmeyer.* $350 creamer; $550+ pitcher.

54

Left: An extraordinary PERSIAN SPRAY vase by Doulton and Company, 1882-1902. *Courtesy of Gail Frederick and Dan Overmeyer.* $1500+

Below: TOURAINE platter, plate, pitchers in three sizes, teapot, covered sugar bowl, waste bowl, covered vegetable dish, egg cup, covered butter dish, cup and saucer, gravy boat, butter pats, and bone dish. The Touraine pattern was produced by both Henry Alcock & Co. (c. 1898) and Stanley Pottery Co. (1903-1931). *Courtesy of Gail Frederick and Dan Overmeyer.* $3500-4000 soup tureen alone.

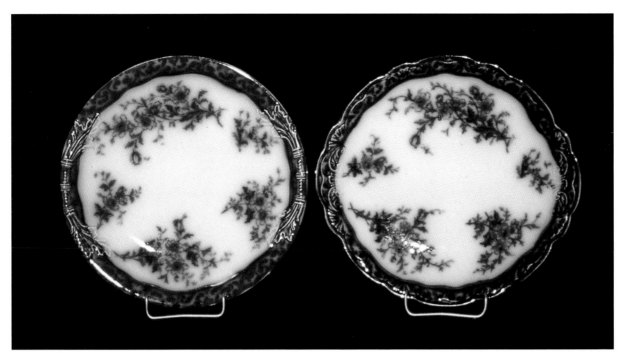

TOURAINE tab handled cake plates. *Courtesy of Gail Frederick and Dan Overmeyer.* $175-250

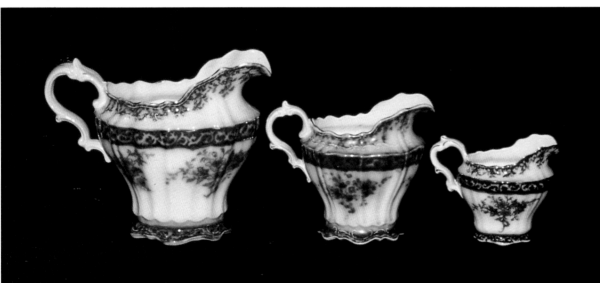

TOURAINE pitchers in three graduated sizes. *Courtesy of Gail Frederick and Dan Overmeyer.* $250 creamer. Pitchers move upward in price by size from $350 for the smallest size, $450 for the next size up and so on.

TOURAINE cups and saucers in three graduated sizes. *Courtesy of Gail Frederick and Dan Overmeyer.* $85+ tea cups and saucers; $125 coffee cup.

An unidentified pattern Flow Blue egg basket from the Late Victorian period, manufacturer unknown. Eggs not included. Egg cups are missing. *Courtesy of Gail Frederick and Dan Overmeyer.* $350; if complete $750-1000.

WALDORF dinner plates, platter, creamer, covered sugar bowl, soup tureen, covered vegetable dish, gravy boat, berry bowl, cup and saucer, cup plate, butter pat, bone dish, and waste bowl by New Wharf Pottery, c. 1892. *Courtesy of Gail Frederick and Dan Overmeyer.* $2500+ soup tureen with ladle.

WALDORF covered sugar bowl and creamer by New Wharf Pottery, c. 1892. *Courtesy of Gail Frederick and Dan Overmeyer.* $350+ covered sugar; creamer 275+

References Cited

Carter, Tina M. *Teapots. The Collector's Guide to Selecting, Identifying, and Displaying New and Vintage Teapots.* Philadelphia, Pennsylvania: Running Press, 1995.

Copeland, Robert. *Spode's Willow Pattern and Other Designs after the Chinese.* New York: Rizzoli International Publications in association with Christie's, 1980.

Coysh, A.W. and R.K. Henrywood. *The Dictionary of Blue and White Printed Pottery 1780-1880.* 2 vols. Woodbridge, Suffolk, England: Antique Collectors' Club, Ltd., 1982.

Frederick, Gale, Valorie and Tom Hays, Ellen Hill, Lou Nelson, and Dan Overmeyer. *Flow Blue and Mulberry Teapot Body Styles.* The Flow Blue International Collectors' Club, Inc., 1993.

Godden, Geoffrey A. *Encyclopaedia of British Pottery and Porcelain Marks.* New York: Bonanza Books, 1974.

_____. *The Concise Guide to British Pottery and Porcelain.* London: Barrie & Jenkins, 1990.

Hill, Ellen R. *Mulberry Ironstone. Flow Blue's Best Kept Little Secret.* Privately Published, 1993.

King, Ellen G. "Beauty and Intrigue: Flow Blue China." *Antiques & Auction News* 28(8), February 21, 1997.

Kowalsky, Arnold and Dorothy. "To Flow or Not to Flow, That is the Question." *Blue Berry Notes,* 1997.

Larkin, Jack. *The Reshaping of Everyday Life. 1790-1840.* New York: Harper & Row, Publishers, 1988.

Perkins, Fredda. "The Next Big Thing. 20 ways to find tomorrow's hottest collectibles today." *American Country Collectibles.* Spring 1997.

Pool, Daniel. *What Jane Austen Ate and Charles Dickens Knew. From Fox Hunting to Whist —the Facts of Daily Life in 19th-Century England.* New York: Simon & Schuster, 1993.

Pratt, James Norwood. *Tea Lover's Treasury.* Santa Rosa, California: Cole Group, Inc., 1982.

Savage, George and Harold Newman. *An Illustrated Dictionary of Ceramics.* London: Thames and Hudson, Ltd., 1985.

Snyder, Jeffrey B. *Flow Blue. A Collector's Guide to Patterns, History, and Values.* West Chester, Pennsylvania: Schiffer Publishing, Ltd., 1992 (revised & expanded 1996).

_____. *Historic Flow Blue.* Atglen, Pennsylvania: Schiffer Publishing, Ltd., 1994.

_____. *A Pocket Guide to Flow Blue.* Atglen, Pennsylvania: Schiffer Publishing, Ltd., 1995.

Stoltzfus, Dawn and Jeffrey Snyder. *White Ironstone. A Survey of its Many Forms.* Atglen, Pennsylvania: Schiffer Publishing, Ltd., 1997.

Strong Museum. "Flow Blue ..." *Blue Berry Notes* 9(1), January-February 1995.

Tippett, Paul. *Christie's Collectibles. Teapots. The Connoisseur's Guide.* Boston, Massachusetts: Little, Brown and Company, 1996.

Wetherbee, Jean. *White Ironstone: A Collector's Guide.* Dubuque, Iowa, Antique Trader Books, 1996.

Index

*Index of Patterns

The following is an index of patterns found in my other three books: Flow Blue (1992, revised 1996), Historic Flow Blue (1994), and A Pocket Guide to Flow Blue (1995). This should provide a useful cross-reference when you are searching for one special pattern or the value to a particular piece.

Appendix

Index of Patterns with Page Numbers*